P. MARKS.

HELYG
DIAMOND JUBILEE
1925 - 1985

GEOFF MILBURN

Helyg Cottage painted by David Hewitt.

1985
THE CLIMBERS' CLUB

First published in Great Britain 1985
    by Geoff Milburn and the Climbers' Club.

© Geoff Milburn and The Climbers' Club

ISBN 0 901601 37 3 (Limited Edition)

ISBN 0 901601 38 1 (Public Edition)

All modern photographs by Ian Smith.

Dust-cover drawing and design by P.B. Marks.

Produced by The Ernest Press, Glasgow G44 5QD

CONTENTS

FOREWORD

Saturday June 8th, 1985 was a day of great historic importance for the Climbers' Club when we celebrated the 60th anniversary of the establishment of our first Club Hut, Helyg. Many of our elderly and most distinguished members came together on this unique and nostalgic occasion to re-meet old friends, walk and climb on the hills of their youth, and reflect on the importance of Helyg. For Helyg was of vital importance to the development of Welsh climbing in that 'Golden Era' between 1925 — 1939. We were especially priviledged to have with us Herbert Carr, who had found the Cottage in 1925 and had persuaded the Committee to buy it, and what a marvellous, inspired idea that was.

This book commemorates the Diamond Jubliee and tells the story of Helyg from its founding in 1925 to the celebrations in 1985. It contains enthralling stories of the climbs and exploits of our members, and of the great characters who stayed in the cottage and helped shape the Club (particularly in that pre-war era).

We are indebted to Geoff Milburn for producing this book. Geoff has worked tirelessly on behalf of the Club for the last seven years as Journal Editor, and it is his sense of history, his enthusiasm and his dedication that have made this publication possible.

Derek Walker, President of the Climbers' Club, July 1985.

INTRODUCTION

When the Climbers' Club went through a very bad phase just after the end of the First World War, and membership sank to a mere 152, morale was low and the very existence of the club was in the balance. It was a time when a new generation of climbers was about to emerge, not only from the major Universities such as Liverpool, Oxford, Cambridge and Manchester, but also from some of the big northern cities. During this period eyes turned on the still unconquered Everest and several expeditions were to include members of our club. The death of Siegfried Herford during the First World War was a shock, but the loss of Mallory and Irvine on Everest when so close to success proved to be a traumatic experience, not only for the emerging mountaineering fraternity, but also for the British public in general. The thought-provoking enquiry, 'Why do people climb?' has always stirred the imagination and that early tragic incident near the summit of the highest mountain on earth caused widespread comment and strong feelings akin to those at the time of the Matterhorn disaster years before.

In the next decade rock-climbing in Wales was to reach new heights hitherto beyond the comprehension of a free-and-easy-going generation. Previously the ascent of Central Buttress on Scafell in the Lake District had been the major breakthrough which was to set a new standard of difficulty for British climbing, but the breach of the East and West Buttresses of Clogwyn du'r Arddu was to start a whole series of bold and committing climbs between the wars. Perhaps it was the extreme degree of commitment and the self-preservation doctrine that 'the leader must not fall' which makes that era so fascinating and unique to the modern-day climber. But certainly it was an era when many able climbers arrived on the scene and the names that linger today are legion: Pigott, Linnell, Morley Wood, Longland, Hargreaves, Waller, Kirkus, Edwards.....There were real characters such as French, Mathews, Grosvenor, McKenna.....but also another smaller group of people, the likes of Stuart Chantrell, Herbert Carr, Maurice Guinness, Raymond Greene — people who had a deep feeling for the club and were prepared to work tirelessly for the benefit of others. As a result of their efforts to revitalise the club in several distinct ways such as with publications, attracting new members and club meets, there was also one brilliant inspiration that was to play a most profound part in the future of the club.....HELYG. Although not the first climbers' hut to be opened in Wales it was certainly to be the most significant owing to its central position beside a main road in the heart of Snowdonia. The acquisition and development of the Cottage became a key factor in the whole future of Welsh climbing as for over twenty years it was to be the central hub of a highly active and

5

tightly-knit group of climbers.

This book — a compilation of material from early Bulletins and Journals — to commemorate the Diamond Jubilee of Helyg is important historically for the club as it gives a fairly complete picture rather than a merely fragmented story which is to be found in several early publications. There is however a rather more moving aspect — one which certainly ought to stir the emotions of even the hardest heart. Some time ago when watching the Remembrance Day parade a song-writer penned the following lines:

'And year by year these old men disappear;
Soon no-one will march there at all.'

And so it is for the Climbers' Club but in a different context, in that over the last few years we have lost the likes of George Sansom, Fred Pigott, I.A. Richards, C.H.S.R. Palmer, Stuart Chantrell, Raymond Greene, C.H. French and many others.

For the Diamond Jubilee, surviving members from the 1920s and 1930s have risen to the occasion and gathered together from near and far, as a unique group — not only to meet close and old friends for a last major club celebration, but also to recall those early halcyon days of 60 years ago.....to relive the great moments on our crags in rain and wind and shine, and to remember the friends who are no longer with us. To those who went before us and paved the way, this book is affectionately dedicated.

ACKNOWLEDGMENTS

My thanks must go primarily to the many C.C. members who have supported my attempts to make the C.C.J. a lively publication, but those who have written to me regularly, supported me, and given me their friendship will always remain firmly in my mind — Kevin FitzGerald, Herbert Carr, A.B. Hargreaves (who also donated his journals to be used for this volume, tried to walk me off my feet and still got me to the pub by lunchtime!), Bob Moulton, Ken Wilson, Peter Harding, Ivan Waller, Ian Smith, Derek Walker, Jim Perrin, Bill Stallybrass, Robin Hodgkin, Rennie Bere, Tony Husbands, T.A.H. Peacock, Alex Jones, Ken Milburn (for proof-reading), Dave Gregory and Jim Moran (the latter two my ropemates over a 20-year period) and lastly to one of the 'mandarins' of the club who 'stiffened his sinews and summoned up the blood' to back this venture in a tangible way so that the story of the 'jewel in the crown' could be documented for posterity.

Geoff Milburn
(Hon. C.C.J. Editor)

Helyg by C.F. Kirkus.

GEORGE MALLORY
President 1923-4

The Bulletin was already in the Press when the news of the death on Everest of Irvine and the President reached this country.

'The issue will shortly be decided', Mallory had written.

'The third time we walk up East Rongbuk Glacier will be the last, for better or worse.....We expect no mercy from Everest.'

Odell wrote: 'At 12.50... there was a sudden clearing of the atmosphere, and the entire summit ridge and final peak of Everest were unveiled. My eyes became fixed on one tiny black spot silhouetted on a small snowcrest beneath a rock-step in the ridge, and the black spot moved. Another black spot became apparent and moved up the snow to join the other on the crest. The first then approached the great rock-step and shortly emerged at the top; the second did likewise. Then the whole fascinating vision vanished, enveloped in cloud once more.

'There was but one explanation. It was Mallory and his companion moving, as I could see even at that great distance, with considerable alacrity.....'

'.....has Everest been climbed?.....It will ever be a mystery. Considering all the circumstances and the position they had reached on the mountain, I personally am of the opinion that Mallory and Irvine must have reached the summit.'

August 1924, C.C. Bulletin.

Left: George Mallory, President, 1923-24.
Right: Charles Marshall, first Helyg Custodian.

HEADQUARTERS AT BEDDGELERT

The Committee has established a Club Centre for Southern Snowdonia at Beddgelert.

It is thought that an official headquarters in this area may encourage members to visit and explore mountains which at present, are undeservedly neglected. Mr. DAVID HEWITT of THE FIRS, who is permanently resident in the village, has kindly consented to place his house at the service of the Club, and he is ready to accommodate members, or, in the event of his being unable to take them in himself, to arrange accomodation for them in the village. A log book and a small collection of books will be kept at The Firs for the use of members, and ropes, axes, and old clothes will be available for all who require the loan of such articles.

Mr. Hewitt has lived in the district for many years and members who are not familiar with the locality will find his intimate knowledge of the neighbouring mountains and climbs very valuable. As a keen mountaineer he naturally understands the wants of his visitors, and Mrs. Hewitt seems able lavishly to answer their demands at the most irregular hours with the greatest efficiency and good humour.

As a mountaineering centre, Beddgelert will receive due attention in the Guide Book to Snowdon, now being prepared, but in the meantime, the following facts may be of use.

The best route to Beddgelert for those who travel light is to detrain at Roman Bridge Station (L.M.& S., Ffestiniog Branch) and walk over the moors via Bwlch Ehediad to Llyn Gwynant, and so down the valley. 9 miles: 3 to 3½ hours.

With baggage, a 'bus from Carnarvon (3 or 4 daily, except Sundays) is most satisfactory.

The village is an excellent base for the car-owner-climber, who can get to any group of mountains in Snowdonia in three-quarters of an hour. A bicycle is also a useful adjunct, but even without the degenerate aid of modern inventions, much good climbing may be reached by walks which vary from one and a half to three hours in length, and the most puritanical walkers need not scorn the daily 'bus to Rhyd-ddu.

The Committee feel assured that the comfort and convenience of this centre will be appreciated by all members who wish to extend their knowledge of Southern

Snowdonia; the charming situation of the house is indicated in the accompanying photograph.

The terms will be 9/– a day.

There is a Post and Telegraph Office and a Telephone Office in the village. Garage accommodation can be arranged.

'The Firs' is situated by Pont Allen, a bridge over the Colwyn, 500 yards up the Carnarvon Road. There is good bathing in the stream above and below the bridge.

July 1925 C.C. Bulletin, Edited by Raymond Greene.

THE FIRS AND THE AFON COLWYN.
The Club Headquarters at Beddgelert.

HELYG — 'THE WILLOWS'

The first reference to Helyg appears to be in George Borrow's 'Wild Wales', published in 1862. He was walking from Capel Curig to Bangor.

'An hour's walking from Capel Curig brought me to a bleak moor, extending for a long way amidst wild sterile hills. The first of a chain on the left was a huge lumpy hill with a precipice towards the road, probably three hundred feet high. When I had come nearly parallel with this precipice, I saw on the left-hand side of the road two children looking over a low wall behind which at a little distance stood a wretched hovel. On coming up, I stopped and looked at them: they were a boy and a girl; the first about twelve, the latter a year or two younger; both wretchedly dressed and looking very sickly.

"Have you any English?" said I, addressing the boy in Welsh.

"Dim gair," said the boy, "not a word; there is no Saesneg near here."

"What is the name of this place?"

"The name of our house is Helyg."

"And what is the name of that hill?" said I pointing to the hill of the precipice.

"Allt y Gog — the high place of the cuckoo."

"Have you a father and mother?"

"We have."

"Are they in the house?"

"They are gone to Capel Curig."

"And they left you alone?"

"They did. With the cat and the trin-wire."

"Do your father and mother make wire work?"

"They do. They live by making it."

"What is the wire work for?"

"It is for hedges to fence the fields with."

"Do you help your father and mother?"

"We do; as far as we can."

"You both look unwell."

"We have lately had the cryd" (ague).

"Is there much cryd about here?"

"Plenty."

"Do you live well?"

"When we have bread we live well."

12

"If I give you a penny will you bring me some water?"

"We will; whether you give us the penny or not. Come sister, let us go and fetch the gentleman water."

They ran into the house and presently returned, the girl bearing a pan of water. After I had drunk I gave each of the children a penny, and received in return from each a diolch or thanks.

"Can either of you read?"

"Neither one nor the other."

"Can your father or mother read?"

"My father cannot, my mother can a little."

"Are there books in the house?"

"There are not."

"No Bible?"

"There is no book at all."

"Do you go to church?"

"We do not."

"To chapel?"

"In fine weather."

"Are you happy?"

"When there is bread in the house and no cryd we are all happy."

"Farewell to you children."

"Farewell to you, gentlemen!" exclaimed both.

"I have learnt something," said I, "of Welsh cottage life and feeling from that poor sickly child."

———————————

Before Helyg was obtained by the Climbers' Club in 1925 it had originally been a road-mender's hovel, occupied by a Mr. Jones. It consisted of the present kitchen, divided by a partition into two rooms, and a loft. The loft was accessible by means of a ladder from the inner room. There was a skylight in the loft and a window in the inner room. The front door occupied the position of the present south window.

According to Mr. Williams of Gwern-y-Gof Isaf, Mr. Jones brought up six children in this hovel and they all survived and his father, from whom he inherited Helyg, brought up fifteen and they also all survived. So much for modern ideas on light and air! Now which Mr. Jones was the sickly-looking boy who spoke to George Borrow? If it was Mr. Jones the younger, then he must have been nearly eighty in 1925. I incline to the view that the boy was Mr. Jones senior.

At a later date it is most likely that the cottage was substantially improved prior to the club purchasing the property.

                                                                    T.A.H. Peacock

Clogwyn-y-Ddisgl.

THE START
OF THE GAMBIT CLIMB.
Photo by B.L. Bathurst.

FINDING A SUITABLE PROPERTY

RAYMOND GREENE

The desirability of building or acquiring some form of Club headquarters in the heart of the Snowdon district has for some time past received the attention of the Committee. A fortunate opportunity occurred in May for opening negotiations with the Penrhyn Estate and the suggestion was made by Mr. Trench, the agent for Lord Penrhyn that a cottage named 'Helyg' might be found suited to the purposes of the Club. The cottage is situated on the South side of the main road, about 400 yards from Gwern-y-gof-isaf Farm and is 2¼ miles from Capel Curig Post Office.

The position was judged sufficiently suitable to merit the careful consideration of the Sub-Committee, and that body decided to investigate the matter forthwith, with all its customary energy and élan. A week-end raid on Wales was organised for the 16th to 18th of May, and the journey to Snowdon and back was successfully carried out by road between 11.30 a.m. on the Saturday and 4 a.m. on the Monday. Carr acted as chauffeur throughout. He picked up the Vice-President at Chipstead and drove with him to Oxford, where the Acting Hon. Sec. and the Hon. Editor were gathered in, folded up and neatly compressed into the hinder-parts of the vehicle (a Morris-Cowley). The journey was continued *via* Stratford-on-Avon, Bridgnorth, Shrewsbury and Llangollen to Bettys-y-coed where, of course, it came on to rain, though a sub-tropical heat had been encountered throughout the 'steamy, stuffy Midlands.'

The new Club headquarters at Beddgelert were reached soon after midnight, and a few hours of well-earned repose were enjoyed. However, time was precious and well before 8 a.m. the Vice-President was roaming about in search of breakfast, and the Hon. Chauffeur was in the Colwyn. The drive round to Ogwen on a calm, grey morning was a fitting reward for toil, and the Vale of Gwynant in the spring is indeed a sight for road-weary eyes. Not a ripple broke the mirror-like surface of the lake.

At Capel Curig an attempt was made to get the key of the cottage, but Capel Curig was observing the Sabbaoth to a man and there was no one to answer to the knocking of the Sabbaoth-breakers. But the absence of a key is a matter of small moment to such men as the Vice-President, and the admirably accomplished technique with which he removed the window-pane with a pen-knife left the rest of the party wondering how many cribs he had cracked before. In a few minutes the window was open, and the Sub-Committee solemnly entered one by one.

15

The walls proved to be some eighteen inches thick and generally the place seemed equally well adapted to resist the elements or stand a siege. It is dry, appears clean and well found. The interior proved to consist of one large room about 15ft. by 20ft. partitioned into two and provided with a 'guide quarters' in the roof, the latter approached by a serviceable ladder. There is a good grate and a separately heated oven, capable between them of providing hot water in plenty and cooking a dozen chops or a joint.

Such are the plain quarters offered, and properly laid out they should provide a primitive sort of comfort. There is a garden, walled properly, but the latter defences are somewhat out of repair. They need the services of a working party — on one of those warm wet 'off-days' the stalwarts among the hutters will perhaps lend a hand....

The place is somewhat hidden from the road, a seclusion that will be appreciated. Water would probably have to be fetched from nearby and the sanitary arrangements improved. A rough shed would, when repaired, form an admirable coal store or wine cellar. One could sleep a dozen men in comfort, but the door should please be left open.

When their inspection had been completed, the Sub-Committee turned from work to play. It drove round to the Pass of Llanberis and made a very gallant attempt to make the first ascent of the Nose of Dinas Mot. If this was unsuccessful, the existence of a feasible (though very severe) route was ascertained with considerable certitude. The vapourings of the old critics ought not to keep modern experts any longer from a splendid stretch of rock. After nearly four hours' climbing, during the latter part of which it came on to rain, the party adjourned to Pen-y-Gwryd to prepare for the return journey.

This was begun shortly before 4 p.m. Coventry was reached soon after 9 p.m. and an excellent meal was provided at Lister's hospitable abode. The last stage was begun at 10.30 p.m., without the Hon. Editor who remained at Coventry, and London was reached without incident in the small hours. The Hon. Chauffeur reached his bed at Reigate as the east paled before dawn, and what his pupils thought of his temper throughout the ensuing day it were wiser not to record.

*   *   *   *   *   *

NOTE BY THE SECRETARY.

At the time of writing the negotiations for taking the place on a long lease have just been concluded.

The advantages which the possession of this cottage should bring to members of the Club are manifold and obvious. All too many of us are hard up for cash in these

Maurice Guinness on Gimmer.

M. W. G.
ON GIMMER.

days, and the possibility of securing accommodation that costs nothing beyond the price of one's food may often make the difference between a holiday in Wales or in seaside lodgings. This applies of course with especial force to such seasons as Easter and Whitsuntide when the expense of putting up at a hotel or farmhouse, over and above the rather costly journey, has often been just enough to prohibit an excursion to the hills.

Then again it is a common experience to find all accommodation in Wales booked in advance when circumstances have prevented a decision to attend a Club Meet until the eleventh hour. On three occasions in the last three years the writer has been compelled to abandon a projected expedition to Snowdonia owing to the impossibility of finding an unoccupied bed at any of the ordinary centres. If the cottage is secured members will be able to set out at the last moment, at the most popular holiday seasons, with the certainty that they can sleep under a roof.

Another valuable purpose that the cottage will serve will be to provide an official Club Centre for Northern Snowdonia and to give members better opportunities than they have hitherto enjoyed for making each other's acquaintance. The primary object of a Club Meet is to enable individual members to get into touch and to learn something of each other's climbing capabilities, with a view to making future expeditions in company. The value of such opportunities to the young climber on the threshold of his climbing career can scarcely be realised by those who have been fortunate enough to receive their first introduction to the sport through a party of experienced friends. The writer of these notes first discovered the joys of mountaineering, not through climbers to whom they were already familiar, but owing to a chance perusal of Whymper's 'Scrambles' which had the effect of awakening all his innate instincts. For four years he had to rely for companionship on the hills upon the few non-climbing friends whom he could induce to accompany him, the results being not always too happy. It needs a great deal of hardihood to force oneself upon a party of total strangers; besides which, nearly all authorities condemn the practice of climbing with 'chance companions' about whose abilities one has no means of obtaining information. It was not until he joined the Climbers' Club that he could ever be sure of finding anyone to go with him to the hills and accompany him on roped expeditions. Almost all the friendships he has since formed with mountaineers have come about through meetings arranged by the club and by another mountaineering club of which he is a member.

That the Climbing Meets of the Club in North Wales have hitherto scarcely fulfilled their most important function has been due chiefly to the number of 'centres' in the district and the wide distances by which they are separated. Save for those who have chosen Pen-y-Gwryd or Pen-y-pass for their headquarters, members have had little chance of establishing contact with each other during the Meets, and more than one young climber has gone expectantly to North Wales at Easter and come away again without making the acquaintance of a single fellow member.

When the cottage is in working order not only will all who stay in it be brought into close contact — in all probability, extremely close contact — with their fellow members, but those who put up at outlying hotels and farmhouses will be able to visit the place, when their climbing day is over, with the assurance that they will find there something they may have never before encountered — a Club gathering. The value of having such a centre was amply demonstrated at Whitsuntide when full use was made of the new headquarters at Beddgelert.

The experiment of establishing a Club Hut in North Wales was tried some years ago by the Rucksack Club, which secured the use of a cottage in Cwm Eigiau. It is understood that the experiment was dropped partly owing to the war, partly because the hut was several times pillaged by labourers working in the vicinity, and partly owing to its remote situation which rendered the transport of supplies difficult and made it unsuitable as a centre for any climbs save those on the Carnedds.

Profiting by the experience of the Rucksack Club, it will be a simple matter to render 'Helyg' immune from the attacks of chance marauders.

As regards accessibility, the situation of the cottage is ideal. The East face of Tryfaen and probably the Llanberis Pass can be reached more easily than from Ogwen, while the latter place itself is only forty minutes distant for the pedestrian. Twenty minutes should suffice for the walk to the Milestone, and 'Helyg' is situated at the one point on the main road from which Craig yr Ysfa can be attained with the greatest facility.

It is proposed to run the cottage on the lines of an Alpine Hut. Bunks to the number of a dozen or so will be installed and these will probably be equipped with spring mattresses. Additional camp beds or hammocks will be available, permitting the sleeping accommodation to be expanded considerably during Meets and other popular seasons. Inmates will provide their own food and cook it themselves in utensils supplied by the Club.

Some structural alterations will have to be made before the cottage is habitable, and these will be put in hand as soon as the lease is signed. In the interests of economy it is highly desirable that paid labour should be employed only for such work as really demands the skill of a professional mason, and it is hoped that public spirited members staying in the cottage or vicinity during the summer and autumn will be willing to help with whitewashing, clearing the garden and performing similar tasks of a light and agreeable description. It is too much to hope that there will be no rainy days this year, and when the elements are unkind the knowledge that there is useful work to be done beneath a roof will be a pleasant sop to the conscience.

Similarly it is hoped that the generosity of individual members will enable the cottage to be equipped with a minimum of expense to the Club. There must be many amongst us who have such articles as blankets, kitchen utensils, old chairs, lamps, etc., which could be dispensed with without great sacrifice.

C.C. Bulletin, July 1925.

'S.A. Marples told me when I met him at Bosigran some years ago that he was Chairman of the C.C. Committee Meeting in London at which they discussed whether to acquire Helyg OR buy premises in London where they could "read the morning papers"! The Committee was evenly divided so he, Marples, gave the casting vote in favour of Helyg.'

Dave Thomas, 1985.

Above: Standing - Herbert Carr, Graham Wilson, G.R. Speaker, Lawson Cook.
Sitting - W.G. Pape, Brenda Ritchie, Evelyn Carr, Edmund Hodge, Raymond Shaw.
Photo: Douglas Milner.
Below: A group at the Col des Montets.
Back row: H.G. Balfour, C.H.S.R. Palmer, H.R.C. Carr, W. McNaught, R. Acland, C. Garnett, E. Downes.
Seated: G.A. Lister, R.C.C. Carr, J. Poole, G.L. Reid.
Front: F.M. Coventry, H. Poole.

THE TWILIGHT IN THE 1920's

H.R.C. CARR

The Editor has asked me to write about the early 'twenties for this number of the *Journal,* a very flattering request because my active association with the affairs of the Club only lasted a few years, from 1924 to 1927. That was due to misfortunes; first a fall in Cwm Glas in September, 1925, then matrimony on the income of a 'poor beggarly usher,' combined to prevent further co-operation in the climbing 'life force,' that Nully Kretschmer has described so ably in his chapter on the period between the wars in this year's edition of *The Mountains of Snowdonia.*

Compared with the brilliant climbing period which was ushered in by the conquest of the main cliffs of du'r Arddu, the early 'twenties were certainly a time of twilight. The war of 1914-18 left terrible gaps in the small climbing world of those days. My own discovery of the hills happened in the early months of that war, and with so many in like condition both then and since, I had my vision of the mountain Grail across the valley of the shadow of death; what heaven it was to find oneself in 1919, alive, more or less whole, and with Oxford's glorious vacations to be devoted to the hills which had been waiting so long. The members of the Club who survived the war were mostly in positions of responsibility which allowed them scanty leisure; some, of course, were honoured — almost canonised — members of the Old Guard. It was some years before youngsters began to stir the embers into new flames (I refer to exertions other than post-prandial eloquence, which was always of the highest order and often had big results — like the Helyg garage, whose inspiration was due to Myles Mathews' customary brilliance at a Northern Dinner).'

In 1923 and 1924 I was often in North Wales at work with George Lister on the scheme of our book (we are delighted that the long delayed 'revised and enlarged' — and cheaper! — edition should come out in the year of the Club's first Jubilee), and we had little time for climbing, for our editorial labours involved many strange excursions and curious interviews. We always stayed with David Hewitt, the artist, at his charming little home at Beddgelert, and the many happy days we spent there set me thinking of a cottage of my own where climbing friends could meet at holiday periods. I began to take an interest in derelict buildings on convenient sites; for instance, Helyg. I paid a visit to the agent at Bangor, but put off a decision. Then Maurice Guinness interested me in the Climbers' Club and soon, between us, the idea of Helyg as a Club Hut in Ogwen took shape. The place was previously a mere hovel, but the current condition was ideal. The Rucksack Club's Cwm Eigiau

22

Hut in the pre-war days had failed; it was too remote, too far from the best climbing. The subject had long been contemplated by members of the Club, so our idea found ready support. One week-end in May 1925, Maurice, Raymond Greene, Marples and I made an 'official' visit to the property. For some reason we could not get the key that Sunday and had to break into the place. Helyg's devotees of antiquarian tastes may care to look up the illustrations in the Club's Bulletin of that year: you behold the infenestration of a very good physician, the first Club member to set foot within the doom-burdened precincts: there is also a group showing the opening ceremony in October that year, at which I was delighted to be able to be present, though in a very battered condition. Maurice and I (both crocks) stayed there in the early spring of 1926, when we worked hard while a Mr. Roberts put in a moderately comfortable and even sanitary 'closèt.' There was a jolly party at Easter the following year, when we entertained distinguished members of the G.H.M.

May I recall one memory of C.W. Marshall, the first custodian? Marshall was, indeed, a man; Helyg's old walls almost burst asunder at his energy, and well he knew how, when roused by the carelessness or apathy of some unhappy young member, to call a spade something more than a so-and-so shovel. One week-end he and I had the job of buying the site for the garage on the other side of the road. I think the land there was worth about £5 an acre; it had quite recently been sold by the Penrhyn Estate to the local farmer. Of course we only needed a few square yards. The farmer (120% Welshman facing the ancient Saxon foe) saw the strength of his position: his price, he said, was £25 an acre: we couldn't bring him down. At last Marshall said: "Well, you must have £25 an acre?" "Yes," "Right. We only want quarter of an acre. We'll give you £10." "£25 is my price for a quarter of an acre, whatever." For nearly five minutes Marshall surpassed himself; the farmer changed colour...but would not change his price, and in the end we had to pay.

In 1925 I undertook the publication of a Snowdon guidebook to complete the Club's series. Work for it had to be sandwiched in between other Club business, Helyg and the first Alpine Meet. I hope I do not err in saying "first": elder statesmen usually recall earlier events — and ascents. So I did not dare to say that any climb was new: what did it matter? We had some splendid days on rock 'as good as new.' Some are good climbs (or so I still think!) and quite hard; over others I was wrong in my estimates. As for Clogwyn du'r Arddu, if you care to look up the *Journal* of the Rucksack Club, Vol. 4, No. 2 (1920), you will find that I predicted the conquest of the main buttresses; the unfortunate phrases I used in the Guide were based on the reports of very strong parties which had begun the attack and gave lurid accounts of their gardening operations.

Others have found, as I did, so much to do; so little time in which to do it. I fear this was the root cause of the accident in Cwm Glas — Van Noorden and I were both rather tired after a longish day exploring first on Clogwyn du'r Arddu and then on Clogwyn y Ddisgl, trying to fill in gaps. We dashed down to look at the cliffs in lower Cwm Glas for an hour before trekking to Pen-y-Gwryd to catch an evening bus back to Beddgelert. The climb we were trying was a hard one: too hard to be taken so late in the day.

I suppose the provision of guidance for walkers as well as climbers was not a success: the idea was to widen the appeal.

A final word about the Alpine Meets. The 'collective' in the Alps had long been familiar to continental climbers — but I believe I am right in saying that the British Clubs had not attempted much in this line: there was not really a great need in the small mountaineering world of the pre-war days, when access was so easy — and so cheap. We tried Alpine Meets first with the O.U.M.C. and then with the Club in 1925, 1926 and 1927. I look back upon those Meets with great pleasure, and I hope others can do so too. I feel they carried some slight inheritance in the Pen-y-Pass tradition. Club Meets are now of vital importance to the future of British mountaineering. I hope I may again help with them, if only they may be held in the only month possible for a schoolmaster!

In those days the sands of time ran all too swiftly through the glass. Good fellowship, mountains in plenty and accessible both at home and abroad, lovely grub, beer which had had some acquaintance with hops. A time of twilight? Perhaps — but in memory a twilight for the Gods.

HISTORICAL FOOTNOTE

The author of the foregoing article has touched only lightly on the period of depression through which the Climbers' Club passed after the first World War, and the activities which led to its revival. This is understandable, as Herbert Carr was himself the prime mover in these activities, and modesty would preclude him from enlarging on the theme. At the risk of making his ears burn I am adding this footnote. It seems wrong that half the story should remain untold, in case future historians should delve for material in this Jubilee Number of the *Journal*.

There can be few today who realise how low the Club had sunk in the early 'twenties. The war had dealt it a hard blow. Numbers had dwindled to a disturbingly low figure. Active members were resigning right and left, and no new candidates were coming up for election. Each year a smaller Connaught room had to be found for the Annual Dinner. Councils of despair were freely uttered in the Committee, and from one most influential quarter it was even suggested that the

Helyg

Marples leads

Greene hesitates

Guinness follows

Club's period of usefulness had passed, and that it should be wound up forthwith.

When Mallory learnt these depressing facts, on becoming President in 1923, he refused to accept defeat, and appointed a special sub-committee to study measures for putting the Club on its feet again. This body — which became known amongst its members as the "De-moribundisation Sub-Committee" — consisted of S. A. Marples, Raymond Greene and the present writer. We met, deliberated, dined, consulted and, finally, produced a Report. Its recommendations sounded very well on paper — a Club Hut for North Wales, Club Premises in London, regular production of Bulletins and Journals, new Guide Books, revival of Club activities, etc. etc. But how to get action on all this? The members of the sub-committee eyed each other despondently. Clearly what the situation called for was not Measures but a Man.

I think it was Raymond who had the inspiration of co-opting Herbert Carr — who at that time was not even a member of the Club.

From that moment onwards the sub-committee was swept along like the tail of a peculiarly active comet. Within a few months Helyg was found, inspected and approved, rail-roaded through the main Committee, negotiated for, repaired and equipped. Alpine Meets were organised. New Club headquarters were established at Beddgelert. A guide-book to the Snowdon climbs was put into production. Journals were brought out with something approaching regularity. Fresh climbing grounds were explored, and neglected old ones were reopened to traffic. New members, individually sought out and canvassed, were inducted in such numbers as to effect a real transfusion of fresh blood. (When one recalls how much bullying and cajolery were needed in those days to win a new recruit for the Club, it is interesting to learn now that it has been decided to *limit* membership in future!)

In all this activity Marples lent staunch and invaluable support, but it was Herbert who supplied the motive power, and much of the work was done by him single-handed.

By mid-1925 the danger that the Club might die of inanition had faded, but the membership figures were still distressingly low, and financial insolvency was not far off. It was not enough that a new spirit was abroad; the world at large had to be made aware of it if the spontaneous flow of new candidates was to be stimulated. A little advertising seemed to be indicated, and to provide a suitable medium for it the defunct Club Bulletin was revived. Then began a period of intensive literary activity, with Herbert as Chief Scribe, and Raymond Greene performing prodigies of editorship from the academic groves of Oxford. Articles, climbing notes, reports of Club events, and features of all kinds began to fill the pages of the Bulletins. These 'contributions' were sometimes based on the flimsiest material, and appeared for the most part over *noms-de-plume* or phony initials in the hope of creating the

'The Sub-Committee entered solemnly, one by one...'   *Photos: Raymond Greene*

impression that the entire Club was seething with activity. Our journalistic consciences during this period were necessarily somewhat elastic. In writing, for example, the account of a Club Meet at which only one member had turned up, it needed a certain amount of *suppressio veri* and *suggestio falsi* to convey the notion that the affair had been a howling success!

Participation in these somewhat dubious literary activities nearly cost me the friendship of that pleasant writer and good mountain companion, Claude Benson. The Hon. Editor (Raymond) had commanded that a controversy should be started in the Bulletin. Obediently I concocted, as the first move in the game, a provocative letter on the classification of climbs, or some such topic. This appeared over the pseudonym 'Moderate Climber.' Nobody rose to the bait, so the lot again fell upon Matthias. The next number of the Bulletin featured an abusive answer such as no man of spirit could endure. This was signed 'Mountaineer.' Benson, who happened to know that I was the author of the first letter, wrote to me commiseratingly and begged me to let him take up the matter with the Committee, with a view to getting 'Mountaineer' identified and ejected from the Club. There was nothing for it but to tell him the truth. He was not amused.

It was while his labours for the Club were at their height that Herbert met with his accident in Cwm Glas. His injuries were severe, but there was no loss of enthusiasm or slackening of effort. From a hospital bed he continued to direct and inspire, and as soon as he was allowed up he was off to Wales to superintend the alterations to Helyg. These were finished just in time for the formal opening in October, 1925. A photograph of the ceremony published in one of the Bulletins shows Herbert swathed in bandages and surrounded by what for those days was quite a respectable Club gathering.

The opening of Helyg probably marked the real turning point in the fortunes of the Club. We knew that the issue was no longer in doubt. Since then there has been no looking back, and the Club has progressed from strength to strength. Its vigour and prosperity today far exceed the most optimistic hopes we entertained in that dim and distant era.

M.W. GUINNESS.

ON THE TERRACE WALL.
Showing the quartz traverse, with the Belle Vue
Terrace above.

THE OPENING OF HELYG

RAYMOND GREENE

DESPITE the inclemency of the weather and the shortness of the notice which it was unavoidably necessary to give of the event, the Autumn Meet in Wales attracted a good attendance, and the formal opening of Helyg on October 31st took place with considerable *éclat*. The first arrivals on the scene were Zimmerman and Lowin, conveying the Acting Secretary together with an immense pile of furniture and miscellaneous luggage. They found Mr. David Williams, the contractor who was carrying out alterations and repairs to Helyg, just completing his task. The work was well done and the cottage presented a very different appearance from when it had last been seen a month earlier. Nine efficient bunks had been installed in the outer room, while matchboarding in this and in the inner room brightened the walls and imparted an aspect of clean snugness to the whole interior. Shelves and other conveniences adorned the walls. A stronger door and the addition of two bars to the window by which the Sub-Committee had effected a burglarious entry on their visit of inspection, fortified the place against invasion by passing tramps or natives possessing the propensities ascribed by tradition to their race.

A busy afternoon was spent in Bethesda purchasing items remaining on the preliminary equipment list. The need for a woman's advice was sorely felt by the harassed Secretary when required to weigh up the respective merits of such objects as brooms, glass cloths and sausages, but the judgement of his two companions proved of great value in solving the many domestic problems which arose. At five he was left at Helyg amid a shower of good wishes and surrounded by a heterogeneous collection of parcels and gear of all kinds. Several hours of hard work were required before the place was shipshape, and it was not until midnight that he could put to a practical test the comfort and soporific properties of the gas-pipe-and-canvas bunks.

At 3 a.m. he was awaked from a deep sleep by the irruption of four cold and weary travellers — the Junior Vice-President, the Hon. Editor, Hewson and G.L. Reid, all of whom had driven straight through from London. The fire was relit, soup was brewed and consumed, and much talk took place before the party finally retired to rest.

Next morning all were unanimous in extolling the comfort of the bunks, but more than one confessed to have been troubled by a cold wind which entered Helyg without invitation sometime before dawn. This called early attention to the importance of being as warmly protected below as above, and suggested the

Above: 'The Vice-President (Marples) inserted a key...'   Helyg Opening-Ceremony.
Below: L.R. Wager, Jack Longland and Bobby Chew at the Promontoire Hut, La Meije, 1928
Photo: Jack Longland.

desirability of equipping the bunks with mattresses stuffed with straw or some similar non-conducting material.

Four out of the five huttites (or should they be described as 'cottagers'?) started Saturday well by plunging into a frigid pool which the Afon Llugwy had conveniently formed within a hundred yards of the cottage. (We refrain from mentioning the name of the fifth member. The censorship of the Hon. Editor would almost certainly be exercised if we did so. We will only say that, if rumour be correct, the member in question has taken an oath to abstain from cold water in any form, whether for external or internal application.)

The opening ceremony was due to take place at 11.30 on Saturday morning, but the P.y.g. and Beddgelert contingents were slow in arriving and it was not till 12.30 that the meeting had swollen to seventeen and it could be announced that a quorum had assembled. The following members and friends had now assembled: — Messers. Carlisle, Carr, R.C.C. Carr (non-member), Greene, Guinness, Hewson, Hewitt, Lister, Lockwood, Lowin, Marples, W.H. Marples (non-member), Mc Naught, O'Malley, H. Poole, G.L. Reid and Zimmerman.

The first rite to be performed was the consumption of a case of beer very generously provided by Lockwood; a distinctly hilarious note was observable in all the subsequent proceedings. The photographers next demanded an innings, and much posing had to be gone through before the business of the day could be commenced. Finally, at 1 o'clock, the Vice President addressed the company with a few appropriate words, inserted a key in the new door (carefully locked in advance) and — completely failed to turn the lock! It was then discovered that the key should be inserted upside-down a fact which future visitors would do well to note. The error having been repaired, the door at last swung back and Helyg was officially open for the use and enjoyment of the Climbers' Club.

Saturday afternoon was virtuously spent by the majority of the members present on the East Face of Tryfaen. Four parties were formed and each attacked a separate buttress. The Heather Terrace was not reached until 3 p.m., and doubts were expressed whether some, if not all, would be benighted on their climbs. In the event all completed their work with time in hand and reached the summit early enough to witness an unusual and striking sunset effect.

After tea a motoring expedition was made to Beddgelert under the leadership of the long-suffering Vice-President who, throughout the week-end, was denied that repose and leisure to which his office should have entitled him. Various misadventures were enjoyed en route. The automobile hired by the Vice-President began to show preliminary symptoms of a vicious disposition. Its gears refused to engage. It ran out of petrol — fortunately within pushing distance of Capel. It withdrew all light from its headlamps just as the most dangerous section of the Gwynant Road was being reached, and, frustrated in this attempt to destroy the party, it sulkily endeavoured to escape notice in leaking away all its petrol outside Pen-y-Gwryd. The iron nerve and skill of the Vice-President triumphed over all these vicissitudes, but it was not till 10 p.m. that the cottage party, now numbering seven with the addition of Poole and Marples junior, could sit down to its first dinner at Helyg. (Needless to say, it was the Vice-President who did the cooking; equally it is unnecessary to remark that in this, as in driving cars, climbing rocks or cracking cribs, he betrayed an accomplished technique which was the envy of all beholders.)

The first London party had to be under weigh for home by two o'clock next day at the latest, and an early start for the rocks was therefore decreed for the following morning. Accordingly, under the stern eye of the Vice-President, the Hon. Acting Secretary set his alarm watch for 7 o'clock and the party went to rest. It may be mentioned that with seven occupants the cottage gave no feeling of being overcrowded, although no use was made of the attic apartment. When the latter is equipped with camp bedsteads it is reasonably certain that it will be possible comfortably to accommodate a dozen climbers, or even so many as fifteen at a pinch, without acute overcrowding.

At 7 o'clock to the tick the alarm delivered its strident message to the sleeping bunk-room. Straightway the heavy breathing which had proceeded from six out of the seven bunks was exchanged for an uneasy stir followed by a silence pregnant with apprehension. But it was alright. The occupant of the seventh bunk slumbered on. The summons of the alarm had failed to interrupt the Vice-Presidential dreams. As soon as the situation was realised, a series of subdued chuckles went round the room as six relieved climbers turned over happily to renew their intercourse with Morpheus.

In the end it was not until 10.30 that a start was made for the rocks, the objective this time being the Idwal Slabs. The conditions were excellent and some very enjoyable climbing was obtained. 'Hope' and 'Charity' were each selected by a party, while the Vice-President and his son, apparently having no need for the sole remaining virtue, ascended by what appeared to be a new route. This started near the base of the Staircase Gully and led diagonally to the left, keeping throughout below the formidable wall which constitutes the right hand boundary of the Slabs. It was an interesting route and presented some difficult pitches. In general standard it was comparable to Hope.

Unfortunately time was too pressing to permit the re-united parties to continue together up the Holly Tree Wall as had been intended. They therefore slid down the easy way and returned to Ogwen, where it was discovered that the Vice-President's auto had once more shown its teeth. A violent wind was blowing down Nant Ffrancon and the ill-conditioned hireling had allowed its hood to escape from its fastenings and rise up vertically into the air. In this position it acted as a powerful sail, and the car was blown backwards to the confines of Mr. Jones' yard. Luckily the woodwork of the hood gave way just in time to save a ton or so of expensive metal from crashing into the Idwal stream.

By now it had started to rain, and a violent storm raged throughout the remainder of the week-end. But the cottagers are far from wishing to grumble at the behaviour of the weather. On the contrary, they wish to render it a cordial vote of thanks. A fortnight of almost uninterrupted rain had preceded the Meet, but on Saturday morning, at precisely the moment when parties were starting out to climb, the clouds rolled off over the Carnedds, the sun came out, and the rocks were left dry and warm. At all other times, when the party was snug within the walls of Helyg, a violent storm of wind and rain was made to rage, as if for the special purpose of impressing upon us the weatherproof properties and emphasising its cosy comfort by contrast with the disagreeable conditions outside. The fury of that storm was something to be remembered. Probably none of us were surprised to read, two days later, of the bursting of the Eigiau Dam. (Incidentally we would like to take this opportunity of officially denying the persistent rumour that the Climbers' Club were responsible for breaking down the dam, whether as an exuberant *geste* to celebrate Helyg or by accidentally dropping stones on it from Craig yr Ysfa. A complete alibi can be proved for all members present at the Meet.)

After a hearty lunch at the Cottage the Vice-President's London party took the road for home at 2.30, confidently expecting to be in by midnight. Alas! they had not reckoned on the vengeful character and bitter determination of their conveyance. This truly diabolical machine had still one shot left in its locker. Selecting a moment when a corner was being rounded at the vigorous pace characteristic of the Vice-President's driving, it relaxed some essential part of its steering mechanism, spun round through an angle of 540 degrees and crashed violently into a wall. Happily none were hurt, but the party finished their journey by train.

The four remaining cottagers spend a quiet afternoon at home and had the pleasure of entertaining to tea Messrs. Waller and Longland of the C.U.M.C. These enterprising gentlemen had on the preceding day made what is believed to be the first ascent of the Idwal Slabs direct from Cambridge — an 8 h.p. Rover being an important item of their mountaineering equipment — and were now returning, again direct to Cambridge, after an extremely cold and wet day on Tryfaen. Fortunately there is no Climbers' Trade Union to prohibit the 48 hour mountaineering day.

The last night seemed to be the most comfortable of the three spent at Helyg, and it was with feelings of very real regret that the last of the cottagers packed up their rücksacks for departure on Monday morning. Helyg had done more than merely justify its acquisition; it had won a warm place in the hearts of all who enjoyed its hospitality, and endeared itself to them as a very snug and friendly little 'home from home.'

December 1925, C.C. Bulletin.

Christmas Dinner in the Club Cottage, 1925. (F.M.C., P.W.H., F.S.K., P.H., C.J.N., G.R.).
Photo: Maurice Guinness.

CHRISTMAS AT HELYG 1925

A party of members enjoyed a memorable sojourn at the Club Cottage during the Christmas Holidays. The journey to Wales was carried out by road in spite of the snowy conditions, so traditional and yet so rare at this season. The first day, the beauty of which will not easily be forgotten by all present, was devoted to winter sports, but the break in the severely cold spell of weather enabled a fair number of rock-climbs to be undertaken. The evenings were spent in an appropriately hilarious manner, and no one appeared to suffer from the elaborate and copious meals which were prepared in the cottage 'kitchen', much to the credit of the cooks. A noticeable addition was made to the heap of empty bottles in the corner of the garden. A night ascent of the Milestone Buttress was made as an after-dinner digestive exercise. This need not be regarded as a precedent. Arctic conditions did not quell the enthusiasm of the company for open-air baths.

There were present: F.M. Coventry, M.W. Guinness, P.W. Harris, T.S. Knowles, W. McNaught, C.J. Norton, G. Reid and Peter Hughes (guest).

July 1926 C.C. Bulletin.

Note: What has not been known except to a very small select group is that one of the party at Helyg, Christmas 1925, was in fact a WOMAN - 'Peter' Hughes. Later Maurice Guinness proposed to the Committee that women should be admitted to the hut as guests. However, Myles Mathews stamped on the idea so hard that the younger generation shrivelled in their seats. Maurice in fact did admit that the Christmas party of 1925 had included one woman - but it wasn't against the rules as the rules had not then been drawn up!

Geoff Milburn, 1985.

FROM THE HELYG LOG BOOK

C.H.S.R. Palmer was at the Cottage from January 4th to 11th, and was joined on the 8th and 9th by J.L. Longland and W.S. Dyson. The last-named gentleman seems to have found some difficulty in discovering the Cottage in the dark and spent most of his first night in his side-car two miles up the road.

The Committee wish to take this opportunity of expressing their sincere thanks to the considerable number of members who generously responded to the appeal for help in the equipment of the Cottage. Welcome monetary donations have been received from Messrs. Nettleton, Marler and Brant. For gifts in kind the Committee are indebted to Messrs. Cyriax, Hewson, Hewitt, and especially to Mr. Lockwood who, besides contributing a really princely offering of crockery, cooking utensils and equipment of every kind, has throughout lent the project his sympathetic support and practical assistance. The Committee wish also to thank those numerous members who gave valuable help in preparing the Cottage for habitation and in transporting furniture and other supplies.

December 1925 C.C. Bulletin.

'We hear that during the Easter Vacation a member of the Cambridge Club entered Helyg by picking the lock. We must warn these gentlemen that the ideal rock-climber is not necessarily an expert cracksman. A Yale lock will be fitted to the door.'

July 1926 C.C. Bulletin.

EASTER MEET 1926

The Club was, as usual, very strongly represented in Wales during the Easter Holidays. Groups of Members gathered at Pen-y-pass, Pen-y-Gwryd, the Royal Hotel, Capel Curig, and at the Firs, Beddgelert. There were also those who camped in Cwm Dyli.

The Club Cottage was well-filled and the following account has been received from one of its occupants.

The Easter Meet at Helyg, under the care and cuisinerie of the most excellent of Vice-Presidents, and blessed with ideal weather, was equally enjoyed by Messrs. E.N. Bowman, J. Donkin, O.V. Heath, T.S. Knowles, W.M. Marples, I.M. Waller and Mr. S.A. Marples himself.

By midnight on Thursday, all seven were peacefully slumbering, surrounded on all sides by butter, of which everybody seemed to have brought a more than ample supply. A bathe in the stream and early breakfast were followed by a general exodus to Tryfan, where Guinness and his party from the Royal were encountered, and practically everything was done by someone.

On Saturday, all except the Marples went to Lliwedd; Knowles, with Donkin and Heath, experienced great difficulty, and spent a perilous day looking for

Route II on the West Peak, while Bowman and Waller, together with King, who was staying at Capel, ascended the Slanting Gully, but being seized with a sudden inward nervousness at the foot of the slab, traversed off, and finished up the Wall.

The following day the Vice-President led Waller and Bowman up the Great Gully on Craig yr Ysfa, while Knowles returned with his party and successfully accomplished Route II. In the evening the numbers were increased to eight by the arrival of Poole, who had unfortunately been delayed by the wedding of his brother John.

On Bank Holiday Knowles took his party to Craig yr Ysfa to do the Great Gully, Poole spend a solitary day on Tryfan, Waller took Bowman up Hope and Charity, while Marples and Son went a tour of the Glyders, climbing whatsoever they encountered. Poole and Waller departed that evening, and the rest the following day, leaving the Afanc to resume his interrupted inhabitation of the hut, for he has now naturally forsaken his draughty cave in favour of the supreme comforts of Helyg.

July 1926 C.C. Bulletin.

The Teyrn Slab.

REPORT ON THE CLUB COTTAGE

HERBERT CARR

The question of building or acquiring some form of Club headquarters in the Snowdon district had for some time received the attention of the Committee. An opportunity occurred in May, 1925, for opening negotiations with the Penrhyn Estate and, at the suggestion of Mr. Trench, the agent for Lord Penrhyn, a cottage named 'Helyg,' situated close to the main road about half-way between Capel Curig and Ogwen Lake, was inspected and, finally, taken over by the Club.

The cottage had been well-built, but it was, after some years of neglect, in a state of considerable disrepair. Mr. Williams of Nant Gwynant was employed to do the work required, under the direction of Mr. S.A. Marples and Mr. M.W. Guinness. A sum of £80 was spent on repairs and equipment. Mr. A Lockwood kindly helped by presenting a quantity of crockery and a number of utensils. The work was carried out in September and October and the ceremonial opening took place at the beginning of November. Over a dozen members were present and the week-end was memorable in that its stormy weather contributed to the weakening of the Eigiau dam which caused the terrible disaster at Dolgarrog on the following Monday night.

In the twelve months which have elapsed since the official opening, between thirty and forty members have stayed at the Cottage, some upon several occasions and for periods varying from one night to two weeks. More than twenty non-members have been entertained as guests. The Cambridge Club held a meet at the Cottage last March.

The taxes at present in force are sixpence a night for members and two shillings a night for non-members. Non-members cannot use the Cottage unless they reside there with the member who introduces them.

It is interesting to note that the income for the first twelve months will be in the neighbourhood of £16. This will more than cover running expenses, which comprise rent (£5 per annum), fuel, cleaning, repairs and renewals.

In September last the Hon. Secretary's attention was drawn to the fact that Mr. Ellis Evans, at Tal-y-braich Farm (situated about 500 yards from the Cottage on the north side of the road), was anxious to dispose of a house which was standing untenanted upon his land. Accompanied by Mr. C.W. Marshall, the Hon. Secretary inspected the house and afterwards brought Mr. Williams from Nant Gwynant to give an estimate for the repairs which would be required. It was estimated that a sum of about £200 would have to be put into it in order that the house should be made habitable and fitted out as a Club House offering a degree of comfort somewhat superior to that of the Cottage. The scheme was an attractive one, in that it might have enabled the Club to provide accommodation for its members and the members of kindred societies on a widely extended scale. There is every reason to believe that, if such accommodation were made available, there would be no lack of appreciative visitors, while the prospect of a steady increase in the membership may make the very limited accommodation at the Cottage a serious problem in the not remote future.

However, after going into the scheme very thoroughly, the Committee decided against it. Various considerations urged them not to make such a heavy addition to the commitments of the Club in the Ogwen Valley at the present time. It was thought, moreover, that the upkeep of larger premises would make too exacting a demand on the time of responsible officials. The success of a scheme such as this depends almost wholly on careful management and constant supervision, and the Committee felt that they could not guarantee, without a permanent and paid staff, the adequate maintenance of the house over a period of years. It was also evident that the experience of a single year could not be too freely relied on in estimating for a much larger plan.

As far as the Cottage is concerned, however, the figures are undoubtedly encouraging. The Club is obviously supplying a want in the north Snowdon district — a climbers' headquarters easily reached and close to the best climbing. The Cottage affords an excellent centre for Club meets. It throws members together and helps to build up the sense of association and the desire for fellowship in life as it should be lived among the mountains. For at the Cottage, especially in winter, we can live apart from the world of men; there the hills can gather round us and make us feel, as perhaps we have never felt before, that we are indeed heirs of a very goodly heritage.

The accommodation afforded is simple, but, even in the depth of winter, a high level of comfort can be easily maintained. There are two rooms and an attic. On the ground floor are the kitchen and the bunk-room. The bunks, ingeniously contrived by Mr. S.A. Marples, are much more luxuriant than anything we have come across in Alpine huts and they might succeed in comfortably bedding nine climbers in a space which might gravely disturb the equanimity of an Inspector from the Ministry of Health. In the attic are three camp beds. The kitchen provides all the implements for cookery and the necessary accessories for preserving, preparing and consuming food. There are also a drying rack for wet clothes, a pair of ski and a small library. Outside the cottage there is a small enclosure adorned with trees, and in the summer the *ensemble* has a very attractive appearance.

It would be easy to suggest improvements which could be made by additional expenditure of capital. The chief need at the moment would appear to be a garage.

Whether the Club can afford to build one and to undertake the necessary construction of a suitable approach may come up for consideration in the near future. Another improvement would be a proper fencing in of our property, so as to exclude vagrant cattle and sheep — which often penetrate the weak spots in the existing defences.

1928 C.C.J.

'The following articles would form useful additions to the equipment of the Cottage. Members who can assist in providing any of them are invited to communicate with the Hon. Secretary:

    An alarm clock.
    A waterproof motor cover.
    Deck chairs.
    Books. Such as old journals etc.
    Table cloths.
    A water filter.

We have to thank the Staines Kitchen Equipment Co., 94 Victoria Street, S.W.1, for the gift to the Cottage of one of their "Quickfri" cookers. A member of the Committee thrown for a fortnight entirely upon his own culinary resources, found it a fool – proof apparatus and a boon to the ignorant amateur. The basin is filled with frying oil and anything which has to be cooked is put in the wire strainer. The oil having been brought to the boil the strainer is lowered into it, and anything from a small joint to an apple is cooked in record time. The great advantage of the "Quickfri" is that the same oil can be used over and over again for a variety of goods. You can cook fish, meat, and anything else in it without any bitter memories.

July 1926 C.C. Bulletin.

For some time every visit was a working party — apart from the first Easter, when we were hosts to our French friends of the Groupe de Haute Montagne (Henri de Segogne, Jacques and Tom de Lépiney) and for two nights the hut echoed to our songs. My own part I should like to forget. I had gone round on my cycle to Beddgelert and returned with my handlebar adorned with a large pot or 'vase de nuit', as our guests had our only small upper room and we thought it would be a good idea to save them nocturnal exits. Alas! too late it was found that the article was not watertight, and the man below was not amused.

Herbert Carr, 1985.

Gashed Crag, Tryfan.   *Photo: J.P. Walker.*

WEEKEND MEET, N. WALES. SEPTEMBER 11th-12th, 1926.

The Club Cottage was the centre of a goodly gathering of members and their friends. The following were present: Ackerley, Bathurst, Bowman, Carr, Downes, Gotch, Greenwood, Grosvenor, Hewitt, Lister, Longland, McMillan, Marshall, Pain, H. Poole, G. Reid, Sinker, G. Williams. The following non-members were present: Agnew, Bloor and Fairbairn.

The Cottage accommodated ten, while the remainder stayed at Gwern-y-gof-Isaf, Pen-y-pass, and the Club Headquarters at Beddgelert. The weather showed a distinct inclination to be wet, but this did not prevent people from visiting many well-known climbs. On the Sunday it is worthy of record that the intrepid party which went to the Great Gully of Craig yr Ysfa got wet, while the no less intrepid 'rope' which made the ascent of Lockwood's Chimney and of one or two other climbs in the neighbourhood of Pen-y-pass, did not; and whatever rude persons may say about rain and Silin, the Hon. Secretary is a cunning fellow at avoiding the showers. Of course, if people like the late Editor must go out when the whole district is obviously the centre of a severe climatic depression, he must expect to get a trifle damp about the knees.

The world's workers arrived on Friday night and Saturday morning, and left on Sunday evening, but a few were left to enjoy a glorious morning on the Monday, when Bathurst and McMillan executed a new route on the Bochlwyd Buttress.

The Hon. Secretary was only visible at intervals during the week-end. He was sometimes to be seen in one of the many 'Baby' Austins which were parked in the 'garage' outside the Cottage.

October 1926 C.C. Bulletin.

In 1926 Maurice Guinness, after a great deal of hard work for the Club was transferred overseas to the West Indies to work for the Asiatic Petroleum Co.

'Why we cannot have petrol to pump into our Rolls-Fords on the way to Wales without our Mr. Guinness being despatched to that unimportant hemisphere beyond the Atlantic whence the oil comes, we are at a loss to understand...... In his absence, we must derive what comfort we can from the anticipation of his promised freedom in 1930. With rubbers ready, rope on shoulder, sack on back, we will await the vessel of his return. And, when again we have his quiet smile to welcome us as we arrive panting at the top of the difficult pitches, and feel again the inspiration of his friendly presence beside the evening fire, the earth will once more seem very good to us and we may recapture something of the happiness of former days.

H.R.C. Carr. October 1926 C.C. Bulletin.

HELYG NOTES

Between October 30th, 1925, when it was officially opened and September 12th, 1926, the Club Cottage has been used by 31 members. Twenty guests have also been accommodated there during this period. The Hon. Treasurer will have a sum of £12 3s to collect; of this amount £6 18s is demanded for the guests, who are charged at the rate of 2s a night. It follows that the guests have been entertained on 69 nights, and that members have used the cottage on 210 nights; a total of 279. These figures are very encouraging. They prove that the Club is providing something that is really needed in the Snowdon district - cheap accommodation in a position close to the best climbs. The periods of residence vary from one night to fifteen and the cottage has been occupied in every month, even through the winter. There can be little doubt that more spacious quarters would be adequately filled. An enterprise of this kind may be relied on to pay for itself once it is properly started and if it be efficiently maintained.

The following extracts from the Log Book are of interest:

Motorists will find it easier to get into the 'garage' when it is fine, than to get out when it is wet. — (J.W. Booth, March 14th.)

During the Cambridge Club Meet which was held from March 16th to 23rd, the following were among the climbs visited: Craig yr Ysfa, Vanishing Gully and Arch Gully. Clogwyn Du Gully, left-hand branch. Gribin Facet, Angular Chimney, Monolith and Zig Zag Climbs. Ysgolion Duon, Central Gully. Pinnacle Crag, Cwm Cywion. Creigiau Gleision South Arete. Elidir Fawr, West Gully and Rift, Craig Crwgl. Tryfan Castle Rocks. Milestone Buttress, Canopy Climb and Sylvan Traverse.

Bochlwyd Buttress. A very entertaining climb. The first chockstone is very difficult to use as a thread for the rope until it has been surmounted. Threading is purely precautionary. — (C.H.S.R. Palmer, 26th March.)

Messrs. Raymond Greene, Denis Forster, and Mr. M.G. Pearson (23rd - 26th March) did not consider their exploits, hair-raising though they were, of sufficient general interest for permanent record. They suggest that the ration of pillows be raised to one per bunk and that 'bus and railway time tables be provided.

Tryfan, Central Buttress. The big block below the overhang in the Curved Crack at the top of this climb is distinctly loose and should be avoided as far as possible. — (O.V.S. Heath, 2nd April.)

Messrs. Knowles and King. — (22nd - 24th May.) Grooved Arete; Bochlwyd Buttress; Oblique Buttress, Glyder Fach; Progressive Cracks, Far South Buttress,

Tryfan. Lliwedd, East Peak. An uninteresting route in heavy rain and thick mist, thought to include Horned Crag, Stack Shelf, and Black Arete.

J.L. Longland (June 13th — 15th) left Cambridge 7.45 p.m. and arrived at Helyg 3.45 a.m. Climbs: East Gully, Lliwedd, (in rain); Hope and Holly Tree Wall (also in rain).

S.A. and W.K. Marples, with C.B. Jerram (14th — 16th August) record the rescue of three sheep on the Milestone Buttress.

F.C. Mayo and W.S. Dyson, during a stay at the cottage in August took a camp round to Cwm Glas for a night. Crib Goch Buttress, Reade's Route. Failed after two hour's search to find Abraham's route.

C.W. Marshall's notes (August 28th — September 12th). On the 31st attended seance at Royal Hotel: became member of A.O.F.B. September 2nd. Super-direct route, Milestone Buttress. 4th. Route II, Lliwedd, via Solomon. This variation up to the Quartz Babe makes Route II a much harder climb. 8th. Tennis Shoe Climb, Idwal Slabs went quite well in the rain. Did it in stockings, but feel sure it would go in boots. Charity: first 80 feet are much more difficult than any pitch on Hope. 10th. Yellow Slab Route, Lliwedd: found 2nd pitch very hard to start.

Many ascents of the more familiar routes are also recorded. An attempt has been made to extract notes of climbs which are rarely visited. The Log Book is a most interesting guide to the relative popularity of crags and the courses upon them. Members are requested to continue the good work. — Ed.

October 1926 C.C. Bulletin.

Helyg Accounts

Some members do not seem to understand that a small charge is made for the use of the Club cottage. The Hon. Treasurer informs us that he has received a very inadequate response to his requests for payment of cottage charges. Will the members who have not yet paid for their visits to Helyg during the past twelve months kindly send their payments to the Hon. Treasurer, Mr. Walter Marler, 14, Charles Street, Hatton Garden, E.C.1?

It may be mentioned that the repeated issue of requests for settlement of these accounts gives Mr. Marler a great deal of trouble and the Club an expense it can ill afford. The Hon. Editor (who has paid HIS account) was in favour of publishing a black list in the bulletin, but the Hon. Treasurer preferred to deal leniently with the offenders. So the Hon. Editor contents himself with saying as forcibly as the conventional politeness of print permits - PAY UP!

November 1927 C.C. Bulletin.

'A night club has been founded by two of our members. Though its constitution and character are shrouded in profound secrecy, it is rumoured that the Club has been named the Montmeenay, a name which may or may not possess an obscure connection with Montmartre. The Club motto is: "We don't get home till morning".'

'There is no truth in the rumour that the committee has altered the wording of the title, "Custodian of the Club Cottage" to "Lord Marshall of Helyg".'

November 1927 C.C. Bulletin.

Improvements

Bunks are now laced at both ends, obviating loss of pillows and cold feet.

Fixture of galvanised iron is now fitted on chest of drawers instead of old wooden top, which was in an insanitary condition.

A gate is being fixed at entrance opposite kitchen window and the pathway made up from that point to the doorway. A gate is also being fixed at exit from garden to river. A protest is expected from the cattle and sheep!

November 1927 C.C. Bulletin.

HELYG GARAGE

The following note was written by a member of the garage Committee and should be of great interest to all those rich members of the Club who have become poor from the purchase of cars, and to all those poor members of the Club who sit on the edges of the poor-rich people's cars, for all these will be for ever grateful to Mr. W.E. Corlett.

When the late Charles W. Marshall was elected Hon. Custodian of Helyg, in 1926, the Club was in urgent need of a garage. The nearest shelter was half a mile away at Gwern-y-gof-Isaf with room for one medium-sized car.

Marshall, with his usual energy, set to work to remedy this defect. No ordinary shed, however, would satisfy him, and Club funds being low he was on the point of suggesting to our Hon. Treasurer that he should borrow the necessary capital from the members.

Holly Tree Wall, Glyder Fawr.   *Photo: Eric Byrom.*

Fortunately for all of us, the Liverpool dinner was held in January, 1927. The Custodian there met Mr. W.E. Corlett, one of our original members, and casually mentioned to him that our only pressing worry was the absence of a garage at Helyg. After a few moments reflection, W.E.C. said: "Do you really want a garage? If so, you can go ahead at my expense. I do not want to hear any more about it until it is finished".

Marshall was delighted with this generous and unexpected offer, which was made after due consideration and in cold blood before dinner.

Soon after, a small local committee was formed who submitted their ideas to the architect, Mr. Stewart McLauchlan.

The problem was to design a building that would not be too prominent a landmark and would fit in intimately with its surroundings.

With this object in view the cottage was visited many times, and eventually one quarter of an acre of land was purchased from Mr. Ellis Evans, of Tal-y-Braich farm, on the opposite side of the road to Helyg and about seventy yards nearer Capel Curig. After various delays and disappointments building was started.

There were several reasons for choosing this site. Apart from the fact that we could not purchase Helyg from the Penrhyn Estate, a garage erected on the south-west or Helyg side of the road, however perfect in design and material, would detract from the wilderness of the surroundings. The ground slopes steeply downwards and much filling in would be necessary.

On the north-east the land slopes gently upwards, and our site was already partly excavated, thanks to road repairers.

Messrs. J. and G. Gregory completed the building in November, 1927, and most people will agree that the architect has designed a very suitable garage which, owing to its low setting, local stone, and Capel Curig slates, snuggles down to the moorland like a native.

All users of Helyg must realise our great debt to Mr. Corlett, who insisted on presenting us with a much larger garage than we expected (there is at least room for two big cars and several baby cars), and also paid for the land. Generations of climbers will, we hope, benefit by his gift.

Perhaps many of our younger members do not know that Mr. Corlett was one of the committee, and one of the pioneers of Welsh climbing. He was a frequent visitor to Pen-y-gwryd at all seasons, long before our club was even thought of, and has done much climbing in the Alps and other parts of the world.

1928 C.C.J. Edited by Malcolm Pearson.

DISASTER AND TRAGEDY

THOMAS FIRBANK

(The following account is taken from 'I Bought a Mountain' by Thomas Firbank, and is reproduced with the kind permission of Harrap Ltd. It is included not to cause pain to those who may still remember what took place 58 years ago — rather it serves as a reminder to us all of what can so easily go wrong when one is amongst the hills. Ed.)

On a rough November day in 1927 four men set out to climb the Great Gully of Craig-yr-Ysfa. The Great Gully is one of the longest climbs in the British Isles. It is difficult when dry, and extremely difficult when wet, as it was on that day. The leader of the party was a very fine climber named Giveen. He chose to take with him on this severe ascent in such bad weather three novices, Stott, Taylor and Tayleur. The party were staying at the Climbers' Hut at Helyg, and were no doubt quite fatigued, wet, and cold before they reached the foot of the climb, which lay two hours walk away over the Carnedds. The rain and wind so delayed the three inexperienced men on the actual ascent that it was seven o'clock when Giveen led them to the top by lantern-light. All four were soaked to the skin, half frozen with cold, tired out, and faint with hunger. They began to scramble down off the Carnedds on their long walk back to the Hut for shelter, food and warmth. And then Tayleur dropped the compass! They could not find it, and struggled painfully on. Almost at once the lantern gave out, and in the darkness Stott and Taylor blundered into a lake. Stott managed to scramble out of the icy water, but he heard Taylor still struggling, and dived back to pull him out. Both men collapsed on the shore.

Previous to this disaster Tayleur had been the most distressed man of the party, for he was not physically so strong as the others. Giveen decided that Tayleur too would collapse unless hurried to shelter. He dragged Stott and Taylor behind a windbreak, where they would be to some extent out of the wind and rain, and then assisted the failing Tayleur towards the Hut. It was another four hours before they reached it. They stayed there only long enough to snatch a bit of food, before getting out a car and driving to a hotel some five miles away which was, and still is, kept by a climbing man, who has considerable experience of rescue work. A party was organised at once, but the croaking of ravens led the searchers to the frozen bodies of Taylor and Stott.

That was the story which Giveen told later at the inquest. Everybody was sympathetic except young Stott's father. He insisted that it was madness to take three novices up so severe a climb in such weather. And soon his criticisms became more pointed. Probably instinct told him that there was something amiss. He persuaded friends to visit the scene of the disaster, and to calm him they went. But they returned in a very different frame of mind, for on the trampled lake shore, stopped by immersion, lay Taylor's watch. The hands said 6.40. Through the Press old Stott challenged Giveen to explain what he had done during the twelve hours which had evidently elapsed between the accident and his arrival by car at the hotel to demand help. Ugly rumours became current locally. Tayleur, the other survivor, when questioned, began to admit that he had not been particularly exhausted that night, and that there had been no need for Giveen's solicitude. Finally he said that Giveen's statement was "a damned lie."

The rescuers then began to recall the finding of the bodies. The dead men had been lying face down in a bog, just as they must have collapsed. Their equipment was still on their backs. Taylor was smothered by the peaty mud. It began to be clear that Giveen, anxious for his own safety, had persuaded the weaker-willed Tayleur to hurry off with him, and had left the bodies where they had fallen. Stott's father now had stages of the route timed. Under the most adverse conditions the Hut was only a two-hour journey from the top of the climb. It was apparent that Giveen and his companion had reached shelter at about 9.0 p.m., and after a meal had slept through till morning. There are farms within ten minutes or so of the Climbers' Hut. Giveen's inhumanity was so callous as to be insane. Even when he had at last gone to the hotel to report the accident he had ordered breakfast, and had conveyed no impression of urgency.

Many members of the Climbers' Club threatened resignation unless Giveen were expelled. The club held an inquiry, but before they could reach a verdict the defendant himself marched in and resigned. He alternately laughed at the members and cursed them before he left the building. So universally was the man condemned that later he was turned out of the house by the poor landlord of a remote mountain inn, who refused to serve him or to take his money. But there had probably been more than a glimmer of insanity in Giveen's mind that night. Not long afterwards he was a patient in a mental home, and on his release he met his death by suicide.

Of course, it is easy to be wise after the event. If Tayleur had really been physically distressed Giveen might have been justified in hurrying him off in order to save at least some one from the disaster. But even so he should have spared some of their clothes for the other two, and should have found help for them without the delay of a second. If one man of a party of two meets with an accident the sound man is in a difficult position. He must decide whether to leave his companion and seek help, or whether to stay with him and trust that they will be missed and searched for.....

THE COTTAGE 1929

Helyg continues as popular as ever. Though there was no September Meet either of our own or of the Cambridge Club, ninety-four members and guests made use of the cottage — as many as in any previous year and more than in most years. Since the last Bulletin there have been many alterations and improvements and further work is now contemplated.

First, as to what has been done. The Cottage has been painted within and without, worn-out gear has been replaced and two new camp-beds installed. Crockery, cutlery, a 'Famous' incandescent paraffin lamp and several 'Primuses' (total is now six) have been added to the household stuff. The front door path has been cemented and members need no longer bring gum-boots. The garden wall has been strengthened and gates have been added at both ends, while the cows, which in wet weather made of the garage porch a byre, are now kept away by a stout fence.

Secondly, as to what is being done. The 1925 blankets are being allowed to march out with the honours of war and a new garrison is every day expected. At the same time a chemical apparatus will replace the present antediluvian sanitary arrangements.

Lastly, the future hopes. There are ambitious schemes afoot. First, the old ruined out-house can, with patched walls, slated roof, a door and skylight, be turned into an excellent storehouse for coal, oil etc, with possibly one end of it as a drying-room. Next, the great idea, a water supply. From a small cistern at the present source a pipe can be led to a tap inside the cottage. A new kitchen range with oven and boiler will soon be installed and then - plenty of HOT WATER.

All this for £20? No. For once more the Club has found in Liverpool a Fairy Godmother with an anonymous gift of £50. Mere words are hopelessly inadequate. But there is no other medium through which to convey our gratitude.

The Committee has decided in future to make a charge of sixpence a night for the use of the garage, starting March 1. This will help to defray the cost of painting and minor repairs.

1930 C.C. Bulletin. E.S. Chantrell.

THE 1929 EASTER MEET

Nearly a year having elapsed since the last Easter Meet at Helyg, all that is left in our mind is a blur, and this short note, in consequence, is of the 'penny-a-line' variety.

The whole affair seems to hinge around Grosvenor's luncheon basket. This was without doubt THE feature. Never before have the walls of Helyg beheld such fare. Looking back it seems as though a dozen empty faces were fed exclusively from this one source. Maskelyne himself must have packed it. Pate de foie gras, chicken, lobster — ye gods — what a spread! The basket was escorted by twelve pint bottles of beer, and, as they were guests we couldn't exactly leave them outside, so we did our duty and took them in. But — lest it should be suggested that we went down to guzzle and not to climb — we have raided the Log and elicited the following bare facts.

Climbs done over the weekend included: Hawk's Nest Buttress, Direct (including Gibson's Chimney), Oblique Buttress, Milestone Buttress, Canopy, Pinnacle Rib, Gashed Crag, Holly Tree Wall, Rectory Chimneys, Gambit, Crib Goch Buttress, Great Gully and Amphitheatre Buttress, Route II and the Helyg Boulder.

PRESENT: J.E. Grosvenor, A.B. Hargreaves, G.S. Halliwell, E.S. Chantrell, C.F. Kirkus, A.H. Goodger, G.F. Peaker, R.P. Verschoyle, G.M. King, J.R. Clarkson, T.R.W. Deakin.

Reference must be made to the sundry visitors who looked in upon us. A bottle of whisky accompanied by the Honorary Treasurer, various members of Tal-y-Braich, The Marples, Malcolm Slater and Fowler, two lady members of the M.A.M., who showed us how to climb on the Sunday, and a native from Penmaenmawr who joined us each day in wondrous garb, and in return was permitted to wash the dishes. It must be noted also that this visitor was the only one who showed the proper respect due to age and called Grosvenor "Mr. Grosvenor - Sir" and he didn't eat foie gras, so it must have been respect.

In the 1929 C.C.J. the New Climbs section, written by A.B. Hargreaves, included a description of West Buttress Climb (Longland's) and J.D. Hills, the Editor, felt compelled to write the following note.

The following accounts of new climbs in North Wales are more detailed than any previously published in the Journal. It may be urged against them that 'they leave little to the imagination of the climber' and, moreover, that they suggest a change of policy and a deserting of old traditions. But these 'rock gymnastics' are in no way comparable with the old routes on Tryfan and Lliwedd. There the fuller joys of mountaineering, with all its attendant route-finding, are still to be appreciated by those who seek them. But on the Idwal Slabs and the Holly Tree Wall most, if not all, the climbs are pretty artificial. If then accounts are to be published — and the Ogwen Guide has already the Tennis Shoe and Terrace Wall climbs, both of the rubber-shoe severity — it is essential that they should not be misleading. To send a party up with a vague 'severe; sixty feet of rope' may be to court disaster. Those who read these carefully worded descriptions, verified as they have been by subsequent climbers, will know the exact nature of their problem.

As far as possible the old standards of difficulty and severity have been maintained. The Editor feels that many of them deserve the 'Insurance Policy' warning that Mr. Bower gives to 'Eliminate B' on Doe Crag — or, at least, 'Not to be attempted by those who have reached years of discretion'.

For the rest, it was rumoured that Hargreaves, in the course of his wanderings, saved his worthless life when Wales tried to get some of her own back on him, by secreting himself in a finger-hold. But the Hon. Custodian's only claim to honourable mention seems to have been that he fried eighteen eggs on two mornings without breaking a yolk.

Altogether it was a mostly jolly party, and we are sure everyone enjoyed himself thoroughly. The weather was quite well-behaved for that time of year, and in consequence we could catch glimpses of the fire in the evenings. There is but one regret — only about two members of the party braved the stream in the mornings (the writer was not one of them) — "Now — in the old days....."

We are all hoping to get together again this Easter, and are looking forward to another good week-end, although we have heard that the luncheon basket will not be with us, but will be staying in the village in state — not, we are informed, because it did not enjoy itself last time, but because the owners will not let it out of their sight. We can see a repetition of the Mountain and Mahomet.

1930 C.C. Bulletin. T.R.W.D.

HELYG NOTES 1930

The twenty-seventh editorial appeal for news from Helyg, news of the Easter Meet, news of recent climbs brought in the usual crop of replies. "Give me time, old boy"... "It's all in the Helyg Book"... "Who wants to know how many times the Gashed Crag's been climbed?"... "Go to H...! (Hellyg?)" and so on.

J.D. Hills in the November 1930 C.C. Bulletin.

Above: Helyg 1930.
Below: J.R. Clarkson, E.S. Chantrell, J.C.G. Tilby, N.E.W., A.W. Slater, T.R.W. Deakin.
                                                                    Photos: J.B. Allan.

'Both in number of visits and in log-book pages, A.B. Hargreaves is an easy winner. But his seven pages include two entirely devoted to a pitch-by-pitch description of a dream (not categorised, but presumably supper-severe). So C.F. Kirkus wins. His five and a half pages are no dream-stuff, though they might induce nightmare, but readers can judge when they read his descriptions.'

November 1930 C.C. Bulletin.

HELYG NOTES MARCH 1931

Hargreaves records seven visits which include two good Lliwedd expeditions, an Avalanche — Yellow Slab — Horned Crag — and a Central Gully and East Peak — Garter — down Route II. The first was with R.O. Griffith, the second with Hicks and French as well.

The Custodian paid six visits, taking with him on two occasions, Deakin, whom he tried to drown in Lockwood's Chimney, and at another time W.R. Reade.

The most interesting entry in the Book records the first meet of a new Club, the Liverpool University Rock Climbing Club. Of their doings there is not need to speak here, except to say that those who climb the Terrace Wall Variant in boots and make possibly new climbs on the Far East Peak of Lliwedd can hardly be called young recruits. The weather, kind to them at first, wept at their departure, but their loss was our gain. For John Poole, on his way to Beddgelert two days later, 'admired the great cleanliness of the hut', so no doubt they made good use of the wet day.

It would seem that others were not always so conscientious. The Custodian calls attention to the MOP and BUCKET and adds that a little Jeyes fluid works marvels, while another member has a somewhat pathetic 'tried to clean up cottage'. But perhaps the weather was as much to blame as any party. There is an ominous entry in the midst of December's rains. 'Water slowly rising through Helyg floor'. As the initials which follow this entry do not reappear in the book, this may be the last message of two drowned clubmen.

THE NORTHERN DINNER 1931

On Saturday, March 28, the Northern Dinner was held at the Constitutional Club, Liverpool. Roderick Williams was in the Chair and some sixty members and guests welcomed General Bruce, the Guest of Honour in the Club's palatial new quarters...

But first a word as to those present. The guests included Dr. Thurston Holland and Dr. Stallybrass representing the Wayfarers' and Liverpool University Clubs, Mr. Caroe from the F. & R.C.C., and Mr. Bushell, who, as Head Master of

Birkenhead, has been mainly responsible for producing many of the most daring climbers of the north. Corlett and Solly formed with the Chairman a trio of original members and more than compensated for the absence of all Office Bearers except the Editor. The Northern Committee was present in force. W.R. Reade was where he should be, amongst the younger generation. This Peter Pan of the Devil's Kitchen had a table, whose legs must surely have been shod with rubber. Longland was there and Hargreaves and Waller and Kirkus and other desperate-looking men...

Deakin, too, held a table end where all talked at once and for the whole time, except when they all roared with laughter, which they did for most of the time.

HELYG NOTES

Marco Pallis, A.M. Uttley and C.F. Kirkus 'slept in sleeping bags... built enclosure of snow as shelter from wind... temperature at Helyg 22°F, at camp on Snowdon 14°F... very cold wind'.

May 1931 C.C. Bulletin.

HELYG NOTES - May 1932

From Helyg comes news of much activity. The cottage has been frequently crowded and at some week-ends members have had to be turned away. One, says the Log-book, found the company so uncongenial, that he left his bed and after climbing Hope, Faith and Charity solo in the dark, walked up Tryfan and spend the rest of the night on the summit asleep between Adam and Eve — most tactless.

Mysterious doings at Christmas are darkly hinted at, but not yet fully revealed by the Hon. Custodian and others who participated. All that can be discovered is that the usually immaculate Kirkus was seen hurrying in the direction of the Robertson Lamb hut with hair unbrushed and without collar and tie!

'In spite of snow and ice in March and a very wet April, the Helyg Log-book records three meets (Oxford University, our own club and Liverpool University), one ceremonial visit, one case of lunacy, and much good climbing.....

.....Not only is Helyg much more easily within the reach of the Northern Members, but their comparatively short journey enables them to face the rigours of hut life with more equanimity than can those southerners, who have made their eight-hour journey after being released from London offices at Saturday midday. Could the fleshpots of Capel Curig, Pen-y-gwryd and Pen-y-pass reveal their secrets, it would be found that the south, though living more luxuriously, is climbing no less keenly. Moreover, let the North remember that it was from the south that the Guest of Honour came who was responsible for much of the hilarity of their famous dinner.

This little apology for the south need in no way dim the bright glory of those hardy northern climbers, Longland, Kirkus, Waller, the Edwards brothers, Hargreaves, Peaker, and all those enthusiasts who continue to develop the prehensility of their extremities upon the most desperate Welsh rocks.'

J.D. Hills, May 1931 C.C. Bulletin.

Since then the Hon. Custodian has been painting, furiously painting the interior of his palace until one is forcibly reminded of Mr. Kipling's shipowners 'who hid their defeeciencies wi' paint and cheap gilding - paintin' her all over like the Hoor o' Babylon'. Let us hope that the Club Jehus (Waller, Kirkus and Co.) will not demand any 'throwing down'.

But the future is more important than the past. Helyg is to be enlarged. Schemes are afoot to buy the site, with a sufficient strip of road frontage to safeguard the water supply and to leave room for the addition of a new wing. This is to be done without alteration to the present interior which has, they say, an unaccountable attraction for many members. The new wing, to contain more bedroom accommodation, is to be added to the western end of the cottage. It is not proposed to interfere with the pretty little garden and its tasteful bottle-borders.

May 1932 C.C. Bulletin.

1928 - 1929 CLIMBING NOTES

A.B. HARGREAVES

CLOGWYN DU'R ARDDU.

THAT Clogwyn du'r Arddu is the grandest crag in Wales, few will deny who have seen all the big ones; some, indeed, consider it a finer sight than Scafell — and there is certainly nothing on Scafell to compare with the sheer walls of the East Buttress or the central slabs on the West Buttress.

Most Lake District rock climbers look upon the *Central Buttress of Scafell* as the Mecca of their ambitions, and it should not be long before the Welsh climber comes to regard the two buttresses of Clogwyn du'r Arddu in the same way. The *East Buttress* is much the hardest long climb in Wales and although the *West Buttress* is not as difficult technically, its finer quality and even greater length bring it with the other into the same class as the *Gimmer Crack* and the *Central Buttress*.

The remarkably fine season of 1929 so dried up the usually damp and greasy cliff that on an unusual number of occasions the climbs were in condition, and each of the four visits made by certain denizens of Helyg produced a first-class ascent.

Our first pilgrimage, on June 29, was suggested by the articles by Pigott and Smythe in the *Rucksack and Y.R.C. Journals* about Longland's great climb on the West Buttress. We had not heard of a second ascent, and although rumours had been going about that the climb was 'harder than C.B.' we thought, from the published accounts, that it could not be as bad as that and that we might reasonably go and have a look at it — especially as C.F.K. was in such fine form.

The weather was perfectly beautiful, and we will never forget our first near sight of the walls of the Clogwyn rising sheer from the green pool of Llyn du'r Arddu to the haze shimmering about the ridge.

After some little trouble with the wet grass fall, we were soon changing into rubbers by the bollard on the edge of the buttress. The first few pitches of the Slab went much easier than we had anticipated and we had the time and inclination to do a good deal of drastic gardening. A word should be said in praise of our trusty third — E.A.S. — who patiently bore the long waits, and the clouds of earth (not unmixed with stones) which almost continually enveloped him. In due course, we were to be seen hopping gingerly about on the tiny grass ledge below the crux thinking admiringly of Longland's 'guts' in going ahead and of Pigott's genius for selecting just the right size of chockstone for just the right place. C.F.K. was soon up and attached to the piton, after giving us his opinion that the 'Faith and Friction Slab' was 'intriguing' — his followers found it hard. The grassy upper groove was as

60

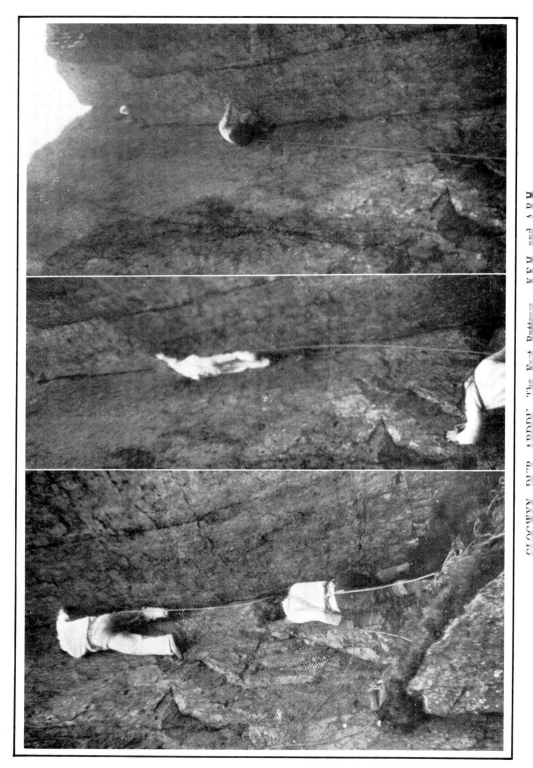

GLOSSYN DER ABBEY   The East Buttress   F.T.F. and A.D.M.

much dangerous as difficult and the opportunity was taken to drop over the edge a number of particularly wobbly spikes. One remembers best about this section a remarkably airy stance on the edge of the slab — and of C.F.K. experimenting therefrom in the science of gravity! We were soon basking on the quartz ledge below the overhang and agreeing that it was the most romantic situation that any of us had ever been in on a climb. The twin cracks hardly bothered C.F.K. at all and we were not long in reaching the top of the buttress, some four and half hours after we started, in time to enjoy the sight of the evening sun lighting up Llechog and flashing on the deep set Llyn beneath us.

This was the kind of climbing day that one never can forget.

The second raid was made on July 20, this time with F.E.H. as leader. Our objective was the *East Buttress*, which had only been done twice (the second ascent went to A.S. Pigott, Morley Wood, Eustace Thomas, and H. Summersgill — all of the Rucksack Club — on 6/8/28).

The weather had been fine for several days, but the ominous stillness of the air and the overcast sky showed that it was about to break. However, it was decided to carry on and to take the considerable risk of being caught by heavy rain, in rubbers, on a climb of such great length and difficulty, and no time was lost in roping up and getting on with the job.

The first few pitches went easily enough and the second was soon with the leader below the 'ten-foot corner.' At this point, we received the first of the series of shocks which cause this climb to stand out in our memories as perhaps the most exciting that either of us has been on. We had imagined there to be below the corner at least a good platform (we knew, of course, that there was no belay), and we were distinctly jolted to find that the base of operations was to be a sloping turf ledge about eighteen inches wide with another smaller one a little below — with practically no holds above! The 'book of words' gave only some cynically brief instructions about 'shoulders' and we began to suspect that there was probably some truth in the rumour that Pigott and Wood (both big men by the way, and well known to each other) used to practise the pushing up manoeuvre in Manchester before attempting it on the climb! However, the corner went, after a determined effort by F.E.H. and we were soon re-united in the 'Conservatory' and sniffing suspiciously at the broomstick piton!

It should be realised that the lead of this pitch was a really fine one because the twelve-stone leader could get but little help from his willing but wobbly assistant, who weighs about eight stone (and with whom, by the way, it was his first climb). Also, neither of the two belays below the fourth pitch is entirely reliable, and the stance is poor; the third man perched some thirty feet away has little or no chance of checking a fall — in fact, a slip on the part of the leader would almost certainly result in the whole party being put "on the floor in one" — a little matter of 200 feet.

As we were working quickly up the comparatively easy pitches between the 'Conservatory' and the foot of the Crack the worst happened and a drizzle set in; we began to have uneasy visions of some hectic roping down — especially from the aforesaid rotten broomstick! However, the Crack is comparatively sheltered and was fairly dry, so after the second had carried out the painful task of fitting a new loop on the much-discussed 'art' chockstone the leader set off up it.

We consider that Pigott's first lead of the Crack done 'unseen' and without certainty of being able to finish, must be one of the finest ever brought off. Lake District 'purists' (who have such quaint ideas about the standard of Welsh rock climbing) are invited to put their theories into practice on this Crack on du'r Arddu and attempt it after removing all the 'artificial aids.' We guarantee them some fun and games.

F.E.H. struggled steadily up the Crack, which was obviously very hard, and took a well-earned rest tied on to the second chockstone before going straight up to the good ledge above. The very small second man found that he had an advantage on this pitch and soon joined his superior. It was with a sigh of relief that we stood in the now steady downpour and surveyed the final pitch, thinking that it would be an easy matter to get the leader up it — in fact to save time we didn't even bother to have the third man up the Crack.

But the climb had kept its biggest 'kick' for the last. Reading in a comfortable arm-chair about 'throwing the rope over a nick on the skyline' is a very different matter to performing the feat in practice — if the nick is of minute size and lies at the top of a slightly overhanging fifteen-foot wall! After twenty minutes of futile patience-exhausting and temper-wearing would-be Indian Rope Tricks, F.E.H. was for giving up and trying the pitch without aid; number two, however, wouldn't have that and suggested just one more throw, which, as it happened, did the trick. All now appeared well, we imagined ourselves belayed, and after the second had waddled gingerly round a remarkably exposed corner to get a straight pull on the rope, the leader started off up the Wall. Now the account of the climb said that the leader would have to use the rope as a handhold near the top, in order to reach a finishing hold; so he did, but at that crucial moment the rope came clean off the nick (which is too shallow and badly shaped to hold securely a wet rope) and the leader only saved himself and the party by a superhuman grab at the one good hold above. To negotiate this pitch safely the whole party should be on the ledge, securely tied on to the *old* chockstone in the crack, and both leader and second should be held.

NORTHERN DINNER, 1931—GUEST OF HONOUR

THE CHAIRMAN

THE ADELPHI

G. A. S.

A.B.H. and E.A.S. came up the now streaming wall like sacks, and congratulated the leader on a great performance.

It may be said that the passage of the Green Gallery was by no means easy in wet rubbers and we kept the rope on until we reached the Terrace.

This was one of the very best leads of a whole season of good leads by F.E.H. and C.F.K.

The third visit was on September 13 (a Friday, the superstitious please note!), in cold but dry weather. On this occasion A.B.H. had cut loose from the rear of his over-eminent executive and gathered to his banner two non-members — Marco Pallis and R. Nicholson. The *West Buttress* went slowly (five and a half hours), but surely, and we had time on this second acquaintance really to appreciate the superb quality of the climbing and the unique situations. The overhanging crack at the top was found to be extremely hard for a short man and A.B.H. was 'full out' and still stretching on the last few feet! This crack would be a distinct snag to a really tired party and it would be as well always to have a tall man on the rope who could give an efficient shoulder. Incidentally, those of us who have been up this climb are quietly amused about Smythe's bright idea of 'swinging the leader into a nearby groove!' etc.

In September F.E.H. put in a week's intensive exploration round Ogwen, ticking off two new climbs of merit and a fine Girdle Traverse of the *Holly Tree Wall*, and by the twenty-seventh he was in good enough form for a visit to du'r Arddu. Although we had been thoughtfully provided by the 'Manager' with a lengthy typewritten guide to the *West Buttress* he succeeded in wandering off the route above the first pitch proper and making a very severe and dangerous direct route to the bollard at the top of the second pitch. The line taken in this variation follows the lower part of the groove in which the climb lies for about 110 feet, and may sometime be repeated by a conscientious party with a liking for vertical grass.

This party (F.E.H., C.V.A. Cooper, and W.E. Woosnam Jones) believe that their time for the climb was three and a half hours only, which means fast moving.

The *West Buttress* will soon be recognised as one of the finest climbs in Britain, and may even become popular; but we cannot imagine the *East Buttress* ever being done frequently.

A fine expedition would be to 'traverse' the crag, going up one buttress and down the other — this would give about 1000 feet of first-class rock climbing and is one of the biggest things yet to be done in Britain. An expert party of three might manage it in seven hours. Several people formed New Year resolutions about this!

HISTORICAL

CLOGWYN DU'R ARDDU.

East Buttress.

First ascent	1.5.27	A.S. Pigott, Morley Wood, L. Henshaw, J.F. Burton.
Second ascent	6.8.28	A.S. Pigott, Morley Wood, E. Thomas, H. Summersgill.
Third ascent	20.7.29	F.E. Hicks, A.B. Hargreaves, E.A. Stewardson.

West Buttress.

First ascent	Whit. 1928	J.L. Longland, A.S. Pigott, F.S. Smythe, W. Eversden, Morley Wood.
Second ascent	29.6.29	C.F. Kirkus, A.B. Hargreaves, E.A. Stewardson.
Third ascent	13.9.29	A.B. Hargreaves, M. Pallis, R. Nicholson.
Fourth ascent	27.9.29	F.E. Hicks, C.V.A. Cooper, W.E. Woosnam Jones.

The Helyg Rat and A.B. Hargreaves, captor and executioner.

THE HELYG RAT

March 24. 'That night saw the unexpected arrival of Brother Rat - to whom, however, we hesitate to attribute the unwashed plates, ash-filled hearth and unfolded blankets which we found on our arrival!'
'Brother Rat spent rest of night sharpening his teeth in a very ostentatious manner.'

March 25. 'Dainty sandwiches of poison tastefully set out for Brother Rat.'

March 27. 'Brother Rat, thriving on the first dose, had returned for more poison in the night. Decide to call him Mithridates (He means Nemesis, but let it be. — Hon. Ed.).'

IN his speech at the Northern Dinner, Mr. Longland referred to the Helyg Rat as 'sitting in the pub at Capel and drinking beer to the damnation of the C.C. and those who set poison for it.' This Climber has also referred to the same animal in his Log-book entry (quoted below). It was later reported that the rat had been killed on April 3 and buried in the garden. We, therefore, sent our special reporter to Helyg to discover the true story of the death of this noble beast and, if possible, to secure for the *Bulletin* a full account of the funeral. Readers will picture our surprise on learning from our representative that there is no trace of the grave in the garden and that all references to the killing have been purposely omitted from the Log-book by order of the Custodian. It is true that a blank page has been left, ostensibly to fill in details, but there is little doubt that the truth is being deliberately withheld for reasons which our readers will readily conjecture after reading the following.

On receiving the report of our representative it was first thought that the Rat had perished from lack of sustenance due to the *maigre* fare provided on Good Friday. But our suspicions being roused we sent a second representative to visit Helyg, whose report is now published for the first time.

"Acting on instructions received, visited Helyg on April 16. Owing to recent occupation by Liverpool climbers, who had left everything spotless, could find no foot or fingerprints. Slight trace of blood and hairs on tongs in fire-place. Rat probably met violent end. Examined rat-hole in skirting board. Removed skirting board. Found extensive rat run leading to fine residential quarters on east side of the fireplace. Rat had apparently led luxurious life. In one corner, pile of arsenic biscuits, dated in sequence from March 29 to April 3 — near them one pink sandwich in glass case, undated. Spiked to a nail in the wall a series of bills dating from March, 1929, all addressed to B. Rat, Esq., Dr. to A. (?) H. (middle letter is invariably obliterated by the nail, might be R. or B., probably B.). Items debited include special vegetables, cheese, biscuits, fruit; mostly 'account rendered.' Later bills contain threats of prosecution, followed by threats of violence. These suggest possible motive for murder against A.R.H. or A.B.H. — latter known to have been present in hut on April 3, alleged date of Rat's death. J.L.L. also present on that date, but previous confessions of attempted poisoning suggest innocence, if Rat met violent death. Poisoners seldom willing to use force.

"Shelf of books over bed; mostly novels. Three vols. MSS. Vol. I, 'Overheard Conversations'; all in shorthand; will require translation. Vol. II, 'Diary'; most shorthand, but following in longhand.

1930, April 18.	deekn agane spilt bere. good. bed sozled.
Various dates.	peker rived late. no food susual. lent im cheezenbiskts.
Various dates.	nuther bil. wont pay. dam im.
1930, July 6.	noisy parti. grovners spicy potd meet. good. et blak lump. pane in stumk. must not truflz in fucher.
Various dates.	chantrl bizy with mop and stink again. dam im.
Various dates.	.....left place kleen. dam em.
Various dates.	.....left place dirty. good luck to em.

Vol. III, entirely in longhand, 'Stories told by A.W.S.' This being forwarded to you. Suggest publication in *Bulletin.* * *Investigations continuing. Will report progress in due course.* "

[Note: Legend has it that Rex P. Bloor even turned up at Helyg with a service revolver to put an end to the infamous rat. Ed.]

* Not a hope — not even 'for private circulation.' Hon. Ed. J.D. HIlls. May 1931.

'No doubt you already know of the demise of the said rat, but my memory is of waking up in the night to the sound of continuous gnawing followed by "Oh stop that bloody row!" and climbing boot hurled in the direction of the noise. The following morning proved the accuracy of the aim and the lethal effect of a climbing boot. I though that Chantrell threw the boot but the wording under the photo points to Hargreaves!'

                                                                    John B. Allan

Above: Helyg, Easter 1931.   *Photo: J.B. Allan.*
Below: The climbing party - S.A. Marples, T.R.W. Deakin, E.S. Chantrell, A.B. Hargreaves, A.W. Slater,
N.E.W., G. Mitchell, J.C.G. Tilby, W.K. Marples, A.H. Goodger, J.B. Allan.   *Photo: J.B. Allan.*

LIVERPOOL UNIVERSITY ROCK CLIMBING CLUB

EASTER MEET

On April 9, Helyg once more saw the somewhat disturbing events incident upon the arrival of a Club Meet, with innumerable variations on the theme of coming and going, though not so bad as usual, since we arrived strictly one by one and the commissariat preceded all — indeed there was still almost a whole commissariat which seemed to have exceeded all.

And then about the climbing, most felt thoroughly and horribly fit, but two of us had just been badly bent at Ben Nevis and imparted a pleasantly somnambulent effect to the day's work. The beginners were, as ever, inconsistent but happy, though one of them would insist on a belay which his leader said was not there, so the leader wrought one of stones, which were later responsible for the said beginner's downfall. There were only three beginners, and there were seven others who all wanted to lead, and even to be told what to lead, all of which rendered the path of the beginners somewhat tortuous, and so harrowed the secretary that he spilt the same ten sausages four times in succession, and then forgot not to eat them. However, something was done occasionally.

On the Glyder Fach an ascent of the *Hawk's Nest* after an *East Gully* seems to have provided some of that mild excitement which, we hope, experts still sanction, and two parties report that 'the angle of the *Slab Climb* has become noticeably less.' The Upper Glyder Fawr cliff was done by the buttresses several times, and these were found rather uninteresting for the length: meanwhile the lower slabs were overworked every wet day.

The *Grooved Wall*, always in boots, went three times up and once down; a very pleasant climb in its upper part, whose small intermediate holds are getting quite a polish. About a dozen variations were tried hereabouts, but all failed. The easy ledges route *(Route 5)* was also done and is certainly far the easiest way up. The *Holly Tree Wall* went twice, followed (both leaders were of the energetic type) by that wretched 'groove above.' Before the meet, on a rather weepy day, two of us arrived below the *Holly Tree* after the inevitable *Grooved Wall*, and being too weary and unfit for the ordinary start, had to do the *Direct Start;* naturally the leader was forced to accept a shoulder on the second move, and No. 2 after complete attenuation accepted a heave on the first move. After this they found the *Piton Route* strenuous, and had to mount by a series of well-planned short rushes, interspersed by long halts — one particularly uncomfortable at the *Piton* itself,

72

where we agreed with Mr. Hicks that it most certainly should never have been put in there.

Two parties attacked the Craig yr Ysfa *Great Gully* in close order, and the leader of the following party was so overcome by the sound of the first party going up the crux that he went quite white and demanded a rope. All seemed highly satisfied, but rather mystified about that hold you should have to reach for.

A little was done on Tryfaen. *Grooved Arête* was done once, *Pinnacle Rib* in possibly record time — six hours, excluding the top chimney — and Mr. Peaker took a large party of us up the *Terrace Wall Variant.* Also two revivalists donned the unaccustomed rubber, and went up a decidedly sudoriferous *Belle Vue Bastion,* finding it difficult and very good.

Incidentally two members explored Craig Dinas on the homeward journey; they were not amused.

And then Lliwedd which came in for perhaps most of our attention. On a really bad day the *Central Chimney* was done and found to be the hardest of the old climbs, and a route of great distinction: first the double traverse, or rather swing, and then the upper slab are really good — if decently greased. The same day a party reported unclimbable rock half-way up the *Slanting Wall,* which they seem to have met direct. The next visit was on a nice day when *Solomon* went and then *Paradise.* The first is a pleasant little bit where reach is useful, but *Paradise* was found a very fine climb — long and tiring. Meanwhile a party which had gone up and down *Route II* went down and up *Solomon* in a fit of unbridled curiosity. Then came an ascent of *Purgatory,* a climb which the moralist seems to have modelled a good deal before recounting. Though 'stance' it is clear, means somewhere where standing is possible, and, undeniably, reference to a grass overhang on the one route does not disallow one on the other, also we do not doubt that the climb is harder than the *Slab Climb,* and has not a great man said that the function of prose is to persuade? The two — one was a beginner — then descended the first pitch of *Paradise* with a feeling of pleasurable ease, and started out to look for the *Elliptical Route.* After hunting hard for some hours, and seeing here and there the scratches of Mr. Hargreaves's party, they descended again, deciding that even had they jumped there was no apparent proximate receptacle. Why is not this route called *Ecliptical* as in the diagram? It seems so obviously suitable.

Last a very gallant act which I must mention — tea at Pen-y-pass from Mr. Young who seems absolutely determined to be kind to any climbing movement. Of course, this is only an outstanding individual example of a very general kindness from the Climbers' Club, which among other things made possible a very pleasant meet.

J.M. EDWARDS.

Opening of new Helyg
18 March 1933

MEMBERS PRESENT AT THE HELYG "REFORMATION" BANQUET
Pen-y-Gwryd, March 18, 1933

HELYG 1933
OPENING CEREMONY

RODERICK WILLIAMS

THE formal opening of the enlarged Helyg Cottage ought not to pass without some record: it marked the end of one stage of the devoted services of Mr. E.S. Chantrell. Only one stage; because, before the extension was undertaken, Mr. Chantrell's help was counted upon as a matter of course; and now that the Cottage is completed and has to be maintained, his help is as necessary as it ever was. The amount of time which Mr. Chantrell gives to his self-imposed task is indicated by his initials which, it may not be generally known, stand for Every Sunday.

About thirty-five guests and members of the Club gathered together at Helyg on March 18, 1933. The President with Mr. Donkin and Mr. Bartrum made a special journey by road from London, and it is said that Mr. Donkin's car passed one or two other cars on the way. It may not be out of place to say that the President had taken a lively interest in the progress of the work from the beginning and it was only fitting that he should be present to see its completion. The Rt. Hon. L.S. Amery whose interest in everything relating to mountaineering rivals his interest in political affairs, was present as a guest of the Club.

The opening ceremony was carried through in the most approved style. A silver key was presented to the President by Mr. McLauchlan: and a bottle of champagne, produced by some modest donor who withheld his name, was poured into one of the enamelled cups belonging to the Cottage — the nearest approach to a loving cup which could be found — and passed round. Several photographs were taken; and most of the results have, from motives of kindness, not been published.

After the Cottage, and tea, had been duly inspected, the assembled company adjourned to Pen-y-Gwryd where they dined in great comfort under the personal supervision of Mr. Lockwood. After dinner Mr. Amery replied to the toast of 'The Guests' in a speech which was both interesting and amusing; much less serious than the political speech which he delivered on the following Monday to an enthusiastic meeting at Stockport.

Later in the evening the President spoke of his climbing experiences in India, and gave much useful information with regard to the Gangotri district to which Mr. Marco Pallis had arranged to lead an expedition later in the year. Mr. Kirkus, who contributed in no small measure to the success of that expedition, has on more than

75

one occasion expressed his thanks for the valuable assistance given by the President.

About midnight, the more robust members of the Club returned to Helyg, and so ended an eventful and successful day.

Note: Lest the foregoing should lead one to suppose that the week-end was entirely spent in riotous living, it will be as well to mention the following display of energy:

Saturday — Milestone Buttress — Direct Route.
Central Buttress — Pinnacle Rib — Terrace Wall Variant.
Sunday — Oblique Gully — Glyder Fach. Lliwedd — several attempts on various climbs frustrated by the weather and abandoned.

A party consisting of Messrs. G.L. Bartrum, L.S. Amery, W.R. Reade, S.B. Donkin, and E.S. Chantrell walked up to the East Peak in a blizzard.

HELYG WEEK-END

J.S.T. GIBSON

THE car stopped outside Helyg at 4 a.m. It was a perfect example of a June night. Apart from the battering of the rain and the howling of the gale, silence reigned. After a pause John woke up and said: "Why have you turned off the engine?" Then Hugh woke up and said: "Good Lord, we haven't got there have we?"

We stumbled and slid down the path to Helyg with our suitcases, entered, and after much fumbling and blind manipulation of levers the light came on. We turned on all the fires we could find and went to bed.

In the morning the gale continued with unabated fury, and so did the rain. We had intended to do Route 2 on Lliwedd, but as none of us wanted to lead it in this weather, we gave up the idea. Anyway, the guide book says it is unsuitable in wet conditions and that was a good enough excuse for us. Doubtless when the new Lliwedd Guide comes out Route 2 will be 'a pleasant scramble suitable for beginners who have forgotten the rope.'

Anyway, we bundled into the car, and went down to Ogwen. When we started to put our boots on it transpired that Hugh had left his at Helyg, so we had to go straight back for them. At last we set off up the path to the Slabs. We climbed Hope and the Central Buttress of Glyder Fawr, and the rope was new, and all around was wetness unrelieved. The rope tied itself into every conceivable knot it could think of, belaying itself round every rock it was meant to run over, and unbelaying itself from every rock it was tied round on purpose. When we reached the top we compassed our way rapidly back to the car, and Helyg, where we turned on all the amps at our disposal.

All night long the tempest raged (what *is* that a quotation from?) and next morning it was just as bad. We unanimously decided to try a climb on Cader Idris, where it might be finer, and then go straight home from there: we had to be back at Oxford that evening anyway. So we packed up our things and set out for Cader. At Capel we asked the A.A. man how long the weather had been like this; he replied that he had only been there three months. We went on by Blaenau Ffestiniog, and the road had a permanent wave which made the car wheel wobble, so we stopped at a garage somewhere the other side of Blaenau Ffestiniog. There we made the amusing discovery that we had left most of our food, most of our money, and a few of our clothes at Helyg. There was nothing for it but to go back, which was infuriating, for it looked slightly finer over Cader. After collecting the left behinds, we just had time for a short climb on the Milestone Buttress before starting home.

The next day our friends at Oxford all said: "You must have had a wonderful week-end in Wales; it was so hot here that we hardly knew what to do with ourselves."

In fairness to Wales I must add that the next time we visited Helyg was in November, and the sun shone down with hardly a break, the rocks were dry, and the views extended as far as the curvature of the earth would allow.

CRAIG YR YSFA MEMORY

A.B. HARGREAVES

READING the most excellent Craig Yr Ysfa Guide published in the 1943 Journal, brought back to me a number of sudden, clear-cut memories, particularly of an old adventure, one of many experienced during the period 1927-1934 when I had the good fortune to be in at some of the major proceedings of the Welsh revival in the matter of rock climbing.

The Guide says 'Pinnacle Wall, Direct Start — C.F. Kirkus and A.B. Hargreaves — 1932' and describes this item as 'Standard VI' (which, being put back into the old nomenclature means, I understand, 'very severe'). Well, it certainly was very 'VI'.

As I was constrained to 'retire' from serious climbing a couple of years after that I think it would probably be the last time I climbed on Craig Yr Ysfa and the day dug itself into my memory, not only because this new thing was done but because of a little bit of 'fun and games' — as a happening 'not according to plan' used then to be called. I had always had fun on my occasional visits to the place because they were usually to do the Great Gully, which is hardly a small man's climb. For instance, I remember, very early on, being introduced to the place by those *maestros* of a previous generation, J.M. Davidson and W.R. Reade. I believe my language, when trying to back up the Big Pitch with one ear on one wall and my toes scratting on the other wall, was considered shocking — and there was also some little trouble over my going to ground in a hole under the Capstone and refusing to move until towed out on the rope — though I believe I got a bit of my own back on that nice little penultimate pitch. Later on, when I had acquired cunning and the habit of not taking much notice of how six-footers did things, I used to go up the right-hand crack of this Cave Pitch, most interesting, certainly 'stiff,' as per Guide! I also remember a winter ascent when our party of three got so wet and cold that we had to walk all the way back to Helyg *roped,* the knots having somehow got seized...

But this day with Colin was much 'funnier.'

The previous year he had made the Pinnacle Wall climb — solo — and he proposed that we should go there to do it *(a)* so that he could get my opinion for classification purposes, and *(b)* [*(a)* turned out to be only a blind] so that he could have a go at a little thing he had tried the day he did the climb and which he thought might go if he had a bit of moral support... I suppose I ought to have detected that there was something out of the ordinary in the lad's mind because he not only piled a lot more food than usual into the sack (that is, about a war-time week's ration of body-builders and energisers) but also a little bag which jingled, and the Helyg poker. This latter was quite a normal item of our equipment in winter because funds did not run to ice axes — but we did not usually borrow it in summer time — though the hearth brush was sometimes requisitioned then. Well, it was a nice fine day, not too hot, and we talked a lot on the way over about Clogwyn du'r Arddu (and gardening, and about Menlove and *his* gardening activities on Idwal East Wall (blast him!), and about a certain young woman who had recently changed ownership) — and about the Pinnacle Wall, of course, but no information was given me about the 'little thing' we were going to try. We began by doing the Amphitheatre Rib (very good climb) just to warm up, and from there I had pointed out to me the run of the Pinnacle Wall climb ("It's a pity one has to go right along that Bilberry Terrace to get on it instead of straight up the corner") and then my attention was drawn to the wall below the said Bilberry Terrace ("What about that crack, that would straighten it out a bit, wouldn't it?") I was cocky enough to second this proposal but I did jib at Colin trying to do the thing unseen, because it looked a perfectly horrible place, and I insisted that we commence operations by my going to the top of the crack and fetching him up it on a rope. This turned out to have been a wise move; it took about an hour, several pulls and a lot of Colin's energy to get him up. He then reported that it would probably go if thoroughly gardened (he had already removed quite a lot of stuff) so I was sent down with the poker and spent another hour preparing the pitch for the lead. Then Colin led it, having very great difficulty, especially at the start and the finish (which would have been quite impossible as it was before it was cleaned up). I remember very well the 'poor belay' near the top — and the difficult traverse out to finish; that was about the hardest bit. It was just the sort of pitch to justify Menlove's famous description — 'very annoying.' We were both pretty exhausted after this and were glad to fall to on the sardines wrapped in sliced tongue, and the jam sandwiches laced with Nestle's milk; we also opened a tin of bully which, with Carlsbad plums, was to constitute a final *bonne bouche*... But before we had got to that stage the aforesaid little bag was produced and I was surprised and rather shocked to see that it contained a little hammer and a couple of flat pitons. I say shocked because we two were generally agreed that steeplejack's ironmongery was out of place on crags, British crags at any rate, *unless* there was something that could not possibly be led safely without such aids and which, if it could be done, would result in the completion of a climb — such as on the Overhanging Wall climb on the East Buttress of Scafell, made by Linnell and my namesake. Anyway, this was the first time to my knowledge that C.F.K. had thought of using the things and the place where he thought they might be required was directly above us where we sat on the Bilberry Terrace at the top of the Direct Start crack. This was a nasty-looking V-groove of perhaps 30 feet, approximately perpendicular to start with and definitely overhanging at the top where it gave on to the Quartz Ledge of the Pinnacle Wall climb. I again proposed to go round to the top of the pitch and drop a rope so that Colin could try it that way first, but he said he had already been some way up it when he had done the Pinnacle Wall climb and he thought it would certainly go if he could get a piton fixed below the top overhang; also, time was getting on, so he decided to try it 'clean.' With some difficulty my leader got himself lodged in a sort of saint's niche about 20-25 feet up and then proceeded to fix the piton in a crack at the back. This was not so easy because he had to hold himself into the niche with one hand while hammering the piton with the other. However, he eventually got it in to his satisfaction, then he ran his rope through the ring and climbed down for a rest. We both pulled hard on the rope and the piton was O.K'd as firm. Then Colin went at the pitch. His idea was to use the rope running through the piton to hold him in (a la Leo Maduschka, *vide* British Mountaineering Journal of about that time) while he leaned back and reached upwards for the holds which he hoped existed above the overhang. He tried once — and came back into the niche — he tried again (harder) with me holding the rope taut — and then — (a loud "ping" and a "whirr") — the piton was out and Colin was in mid-air... Fortunately, although the Bilberry Terrace from which we were operating was quite broad at that point, I had a belay, though rather a small one, and was able to get some rope in during his gracefully parabolic descent, because he landed on his stomach at the very edge of the Terrace and just as the rope came tight on him he bounced over the top of the Direct Start crack... The brakes held, but only after I had been dragged several feet with the belay rope (line) stretching like elastic. I can still see his legs waving in the air... But although the leader was saved (it was a fairly soft landing) — at the usual cost in second man's hand-skin — a disaster had occurred; the bully tin had got kicked overboard during the proceedings so we had to eat the Carlsbad plums neat.

We did *not* do the Pinnacle Wall climb (ordinary way) just to preserve our nerve, according to the old prescription, although we did try dithering down the Quartz Ledge into the corner and then back, even more ditheringly — in fact, as the sun fell we crept silently up one of the Amphitheatre gulleys (roped — short run outs) and slunk, chastened, down to Helyg where nothing was said about the day's doings — in fact I don't think even the Direct Start was logged.

As I did not try the pitch myself I cannot say whether or not it seemed climbable, with or without artificial aid, but it does seem worth commending it to the attention of post-war 'tigers' because if it would 'go' the combination of it with the Direct Start and the upper and difficult part of the original Pinnacle Wall climb, would obviously form a superb route worthy to rank with the best on Clogwyn du'r Arddu.

Pinnacle Wall, Criag-yr-Ysfa.   *Photo: D.M. McKellar.*

'The Epicure' - *A.B.H. by C.H. French*

'The Little Man' - A.B. Hargreaves - one of the truly great characters of the climbing world.
Photos: Ian Smith.

At the beginning I referred briefly to the new Guide to Craig Yr Ysfa and I must say that it seems to me a very fine job of work, particularly because it must have been a most boring business combining the uninteresting sections which form the major part of the cliff. However, the authors evidently had the satisfaction not only of making several new routes but of breaking new ground where there are further possibilities. Being one of the last generation to regard the rest of Craig Yr Ysfa as useful merely to hold up the walls of the Great Gully I should certainly like to be taken on a conducted tour, secured by competent tugs fore and aft, of the Cirque and the Dancing Floor.

FRANCIS EDWARD HICKS

(Member Circa 1928/1936)

A.B. HARGREAVES

Ted first came to notice within the rock-climbing fraternity (a very small body of people all well-known to each other at that time) on May 6, 1928. On that day he and Warren, and Bere and Spence, had been climbing all over Gimmer, doing the Alphabet etc. and in the afternoon they came down to have a look at the 'gentleman's side'—for more climbing on known routes. There they observed a Fell and Rock party doing the first ascent of Gimmer Crack, led by A.B. Reynolds who had previously (as was customary in those days) explored the upper half of it on a top rope. After witnessing this they asked Reynolds and Co. if it was 'interesting' and they said, "Yes, very!" This in fact was probably the hardest climb in Langdale! (Indeed it held that reputation for several years). So Ted and his party, 'the fledglings and innocents abroad', said, "Right, we'll have a go". Now the sartorial fashion then was to wear Oxford Bags—voluminous trousers with masses of material flopping around the feet. The Fell and Rock were able to observe, with something like horror, Ted proceeding up their new climb, rather nonchalantly, from time to time lifting the folds of his Oxford Bags from under the tips of his rubbers—which was hardly the seemly sort of procedure then followed by the Fell and Rock! Anyway Ted and Co. got up The Crack, casting down on their way a chock-stone which the first party had used on their ascent, much to their annoyance as they watched events from across the gully. This hilarious story soon began to travel around.

Ted's next appearance on the climbing scene was towards the end of 1928 when he did a direct start to the Terrace Variant, Tryfan, followed by a direct start to the Holly Tree Wall in March 1929 and the first free ascent of the Piton Route in April 1929. During this period he also climbed a lot at Helsby and visited Gritstone edges such as Hen Cloud and Black Rocks.

In June 1929 Ted Hicks and Colin Kirkus met each other for the first time; this was on Tryfan's East Face, where Hicks was climbing some normal route with Warren, and they observed climbing alongside them, solo, this rather strange looking young man. So, being responsible people fearing for his safety, they commanded him to join their rope. It then transpired that he had the night before cycled down to Helyg from Liverpool! Coming near to the Terrace Wall Kirkus suggested that the party should do Belle Vue Bastion, that excellent and difficult climb done a year or two previously by Ivan Waller; and he proceeded to lead them up it (!) thus tremendously impressing Hicks and Warren.

85

Left: Menlove Edwards on the right helps with the extermination of 'the' Helyg Rat.
Right: The Helyg Rat and A.B. Hargreaves, captor and executioner.

They were not to know however, that he had just previously been climbing in the Lake District with me when we did the third ascent of Esk Buttress, Scafell (after Bower and Frankland), as well as quite early ascents of Eliminate B and Eliminate C on Dow Crag; and we had also done several of the Pinnacle Face routes. Hicks had begun this day by going up to the Heather Terrace in bare feet and bivouacing there for the night, which was something that Kirkus himself might well have done. After doing Belle Vue Bastion the party went over to Glyder Fach where Kirkus indicated Lot's Groove as a possible line and after being given a look at it on a top rope he promptly led it—with only Hicks able to follow.

This extraordinary encounter opened up a new dimension of rock-climbing to Ted, evidently encouraging him towards pioneering. He started operations on the Idwal Slabs by doing that fine climb, Ash Tree Wall, which had a very exposed and precarious crux. For the last pitch Hicks' second had no belay.

I came to Helyg to join up with Colin Kirkus with whom I had then been climbing for about a couple of years, and on June 29 we did the second ascent of Longland's on Clogwyn du'r Arddu, Colin leading, with a very good Wayfarer, E.A. Stewardson, as our number three. I came again to Helyg on July 19 and there I met Ted for the first time. We began talking about Clogwyn du'r Arddu and its wonderful opportunities. I had brought with me a crib (from the Rucksack Club log book at Tal-y-Braich) of Pigott's Climb on the East Buttress which Kirkus and I had already thought of having a go at after his second ascent of Longland's. Ted became enthused with this idea and we said, "Let's go tomorrow". This we did—walking over the Glyders and Snowdon, again with Stewardson. We found the climb difficult, and time consuming, particularly in its lower reaches, and I thought fit to thread a new sling round Morley Wood's artificial chock-stone of two years before. It was not only the first climb Ted and I had together but was very nearly the last climb for all three of us ... When Ted and I got to the grass ledge at the top of the crack it was raining and blowing. The original finish was up the steep wall of about fifteen feet at the right-hand end of the ledge, and the Pigott and Morley Wood instructions were for the second to go round the corner to the right and from there flip the leader's rope over the top of this wall, where there was a notch. Thus the party would be secured and the leader could use the rope as a handhold when getting up the holdless part of the wall at the top. The crack in the corner at the left-hand end of the ledge had not then been cleaned out and we were not to know that there was a perfectly good chock-stone belay at the foot of it; so the party was dependant, for security, on the rope manoeuvre prescribed by Pigott and Wood. After many attempts we did succeed in getting the rope over the top of the wall and it seemed to have caught securely. Ted set off up, but the moment he started pulling on the rope as a handhold the thing came off and it was only by a split second's adjustment and grab for the top that he escaped falling off. If he had done so we would all three have been at the foot of the crag within seconds. This was one of the narrowest shaves I ever remember in more than forty years of climbing with many hazardous incidents. On subsequent ascents I found the crack in the corner much easier and, of course, there is the security of that chockstone. As this was the first lead after Fred Pigott's two, I think it virtually ranks as a second ascent.

This was quite a day because, by the time we had finished, it was getting dark and we were very wet and tired so we went down to P.y.G. to consider how to get back to Helyg. There, in the bar, we had the good luck to meet with one J.E. Grosvenor, later to become a Vice-President of this club — particularly notable for coming to Helyg in a chauffer-driven car bringing hampers full of delicacies for the party. On this occasion, when he realised what he had done, he kindly offered us a lift to Helyg, thus saving us a tiresome further walk.

A word here in praise of our third man, Stewardson, who, as was the case when he had been with Colin and me on the second ascent of Longland's had been subjected to a constant bombardment ot turf mixed with stones as we gardened our way up. Present-day climbers can hardly appreciate what Cloggy was like in those early days, literally covered in turf. In the C.C. Bulletin of April 1930 anyone interested will find three photographs, taken by Stewardson, showing Hicks and me going up the long crack.

After this event Kirkus, Hicks and I teamed up and we did a lot of climbing together, mostly in the area of the Idwal Slabs where Ted began a very thorough exploration of all possibilities. He was leading strongly and confidently by now and Heather Wall was yet another poorly protected route:

'An apparently weak spot was attacked light-heartedly in boots: after about an hour's hectic work, in which the Helyg poker played its part nobly, and during which the leader changed into rubbers, a heaven sent belay was reached ... after several abortive attempts on the holdless corner above an inspired lead across a rickety traverse and up an impossible-looking bulge gave us Heather Wall.'

And then in September came the hardest of them all—Rowan Tree Slabs—which still holds its rating as V.S. even though it may now be possible to get some protection on it, which Ted did not have. The route is now considered as being an even harder proposition than Central Route on Tryfan, a Kirkus route which Hicks had failed to follow. (At that time the only route in that area that was considered to be as hard was Longland's direct finish up the flake edge at the top of Javelin Buttress.) On the same day as having done Rowan Tree Slabs, Hicks went over to the Holly Tree Wall and did the first Girdle Traverse of the cliff.

At about this time Ted also had a really good go at Suicide Wall and very nearly got up it, but he would not risk the extremely difficult moves near the top with no protection except for me hitched to a little spike above that tiny ledge 20 feet below. So I got down, ran round to the top of the Slabs (quite a run that was!) and got a top rope down to him so that he could finish it, which he did without aid. At that time we also had a good go at the West Wall Buttress of the Slabs, Homicide Wall, and he got quite a long way up it before having to retreat from where it becomes very steep and difficult, and again I had to run round to give him a top rope. Modern climbers, with their artificial aids to protect them on such places, should realise how good were such climbers as Ted Hicks who very nearly got up them climbing 'free'.

At that time the Central Buttress of Scafell was still the greatest ambition of all young climbers—the 'Eliminate'. Hicks had already had one go at this with Warren and Bere but because of unfavourable conditions they had had to retreat. On September 6, 1929, Ted, Colin and I got a lift to Langdale from another very kind man, R.O. Griffiths, a Wayfarer and a Senior Lecturer at Liverpool University, and on the following day we did C.B. Not without incident (!) as Colin slithered off the lower part of the crack, which was wet. We fielded him on the Oval! It was then Ted who led to the chock-stone, after which Colin, having recovered, did the upper part of the flake. Accurate counts of ascents of C.B. had been by then lost, but I then made this to be about the seventh or eighth and it was certainly the first ascent by an entirely C.C. party (who were also Wayfarers). On his form that day Ted was probably capable of leading the top part of the flake without aid at the chock-stone but we restrained him from trying to do so because we wanted to do the climb in the then orthodox fashion. It remained for Menlove Edwards a year or two later to be the first to perform the feat of leading the upper part without aid or even a thread at the chockstone!

HAMLET AT HELYG

II B, or not II B — that is the question:
Whether 'tis safer on the whole to risk
The bitter scorn of outclassed climbing skill,
Or else deceive the cragsman's feeble mind:
By overgrading, fool him? To grade, to brood
No more, and by this subtle means to end
The blasphemous remarks in certain logs
That I could mention — 'tis a supposition
Too frenzied to be true. To grade, to doubt; —
To doubt! perchance to think — ay, there's the rub;
For in that dubious mood what thoughts may come,
When we have classed some frightful climb as mild,
Should make us pause: this is the time
The youthful pioneer may quickly age;
For who would bear the stigma consequent
Upon such deeds, the editor's delay
In publishing the journal, and the spurns
Received from fellow-members of his club.
O, what a rogue and peasant-slave is he!
When he himself might his quietus make
By piton hammer. Who would rucksack bear,
To grunt and sweat along the Idwal path,
But that the dread of those who write our guides,
Those satirising jesters, from whose cracks
Few Lakeland climbs escape, defeats him still,
And makes him rather do his climbs in Wales,
Than fly to regions that he knows not of?
Thus criticism cows us, every one,
And thus the pallid hue of city life
Is crusted o'er with Gallt yr Ogof sludge;
And expeditions of importance great,
That nightly gull him with intelligence,
Are made to Capel Curig.

R.L. PLACKETT.

89

YOUNG CLIMBER

J.M. EDWARDS

THIS purports to be a brief account, accurate as far as it and memory goes, of some of a group of new climbs recently done in Wales.

To write of mere performance is so trying. The whole dense, overweighted figure of a man must be shoved up this fine cliff, and then, forsooth, the mind may come after. What a pulling and a pushing; and what a fat margin of safety the coward body must wrap around itself! These oversized holds, in case you get tired; these metaphorical sorbo cushions of belays that it would desire us to land upon; the active second it requires to sling this imaginative receptacle, and manoeuvre it well and truly in the plumb line beneath the seat of its apprehension. *Eheu fugaces,* says the body, alas we had better get down. And the mind must be chained to this stout old man by the rules of climbing custom. Not but what the old man gets a little much needed exercise out of it, and a few unusual tremors through him, but as for the mind the after-effect of this chaining is altogether deleterious. By what inversion of guidance may the mind be so entirely the follower? And to arrive at the particular, I, for one, do not wish to take more than the merest tracing paper outline of these new routes themselves. They are not worth it, especially if there is some day to be a guide. They are not themselves a sport, so much as the brief symptoms of some various psycho-neurotic tendency.

There has always been a good deal of odd criticism of so called "acrobatic" new climbs. But is it an acrobatics more of the body or of the mind? And if of the mind, is it worth while regarding whether rubber is being used for the feet, or whether the lines on the cliffs are getting rather close together? It would be a discussion of the physical conveniences of what, in essence, was a type of lesson of inconvenience for the mind and resulting from the mind, and it would be so very beside the point. If an influenza of the mind is perhaps assuming rather more epidemic proportion than it has usually done, why worry at the last whether it puts on nails or not, or whether those lines upon the cliffs are being pointed out in too meticulous a fashion?

All this climbing seemed so little a part of us: we were restless then, and did not sleep overwell of nights: we were thin with the great world. In years ago, perhaps, men wore their iron longer and more easily than we. A science of care and little techniques has come into the world: careful, energetic little techniques, grown up round the neck of the man, over the whole body, and the convulsions of his head wring not so true, gesticulating wildly there above the padded trunk of him. It is not often nowadays the full man, standing, body, legs, and head astride the route of his heart. We must go round about it and consider where, and why, and to what extent, and there is not so much fineness about our suffocated neck expressions as the eye swings unhappily for something new. Convulsive young neck climbers, while only the far off trunk realises the deep flux of things, the continuity of change, and can lean back upon timelessness. The eyes rove over the grey, precipitous world for new routes and good moves, and continually they regret that padded trunk of theirs, feeling the height of it, the man's broad chest of things, and the pulsing cloud and sun of it.

And to arrive again at the particular, I, for one, can see no fine sagas to write of these eye jerks of ours. And of the saga there behind the pads? Perhaps the brain has not the justice of it. Perhaps the Editor has not asked us to try.

And so to Wales — where Helyg has conceived again of her old age, and where, naturally, a fair number of new routes have been done since the last *Climbers' Club Journal.*

Of Wales in general, what strikes one most is the large number of unclimbed faces still staring down upon a pretty stiff-necked generation. What is the fascination to young climbers in the old Slabs and that still older face of Tryfan?

But to get to the routes, the Devil's Kitchen group, Clogwyn-y-Geifr, is an interesting spot, and may be dispensed with quickly, as the guide to it hopes to be coming out soon. It has every natural advantage, being steep, composed of pretty rocky sort of rock and being covered with vegetation: also parts of it have been long overdue for public exploitation. It is the sort of place where one can feel the full glory of stepping in perfect safety on somebody else's considered opinion. It is not of course the cliff for those who attack the problem tooth and nail nor yet for those who rise by seizing every opportunity, but I think it may by now be considered safe for democracy. It is years since anybody was killed there. Indeed, it is generally agreed that the greatest danger on the harder climbs is that they are best done in good weather, and it is no simple matter to push one's resolute way through the haunted lower slopes of the fantastic valley of Idwal. It is crowded with yelling couples clad in white or khaki shorts (usually both!), and they sing their community songs and dance their fine, dynamic dances, while they urge the restless courses of their loves. The youth of to-day does live dangerously. Of the climbs perhaps the Devil's Buttress and the Devil's Dive are the best and hardest. The Devil's Dump is nice: the steep bit is an interesting study in mosaics, but they did not finish it off very well. Alternatively it may be regarded as an excavation in the Dump, and you get holds on the bits sticking out: it is decidely decomposing. Herein lies its charm. The Coal Shute Exit succeeds in waking up a little the rather ageing Devil's Cellar, and I gather that Kirkus's left hand exit does the same, in a greater degree, for the Hanging Garden Gully. Little Corner and North Slabs and the Pipes are nice rock climbs. On Dump Crack it is not easy to force a way through the forest of plants.

The accounts of the first ascent notes: "A tall spike rises above the fernery on the left. It is fairly firm"; then, "Straight up into a good cave which obviously has not been wiped for years. Up its messy depths." On the South Cliff also there is much loose rock over to the left. Of the Piece by Piece Climb in Botany Bay it was said, "As it has not yet been unearthed this climb should be considered Severe."

Much of the best exploration on the Kitchen, as elsewhere, was abortive. There was a nasty incident, at a point not marked, when the leader got a little too high up in the surroundings with which he was not adequately in touch. Anon, there came a rope from above, and the doughty explorer continued jerkily upward for the next hundred feet to the sound of heavy breathing in triplicate. This, however, is considered a bad thing.

On the Idwal Slabs things are getting a trifle congested; there are so many people and so many scratches that it is very difficult to find any fresh ground whereon to eat one's sandwiches, or leave people one may not want. Balcony Cracks is quite an arresting little piece; and there is that new thing we did on the rope, but, alas, when we returned after the months to it "radical alterations in the rock structure" had occurred: we could not even get into the thing.

On the Upper Cliff the Grey group has been shown up for the fine piece of rock that it is. The Wall is very spasmodic and youthful, but you may wait indefinitely between bits of it. It is only one pitch. The Slab, on the left is longer and more staid, and on the long second pitch there is less excitement to linger. A very pleasant pitch. It was on this route that a small boy showed very notable courage in trusting himself entirely to the pull of the rope for 100 feet. His confidence in the rock is unshaken. High Pastures is a nice walk on beautifully soft, yielding grass. Then there is the new West Gully route. The old is good but the new has more of fun and games. Those who do not like grass, will probably class it at the end of the Frankly Borings or the beginning of the Definitely Unpleasants. The first pitch is a grassy groove overhanging the old route. I do not know whose fault it is but probably the stuff was badly stuck together in the first instance, and the fact remains interesting for about eighty feet. Above that the right hand branch of the gully is taken. The second was accorded shelter in the little cave below this, but he still seemed to be deriving some discomfort from falling materials, and his agitation appears to have been considerably increased by the sudden loosening of several large blocks in the roof of the cave itself. But beyond getting sympathetic the second did not seem really to mind. He never really minded anything. It is perhaps not generally realised that there are in the climbing world one or two seconds who display more courage and sagacity in the face of emergencies (e.g. the aforesaid cave) than ever has been shown by even the most reckless of leaders. I do not know precisely what these persons are made of, but circumstances (more especially when the stance is small)

Idwal - The Piton Route. *Photo: R.J. Collinson*

leave them quite unmoved. They are responsible for many of the best climbs. Their leader dare not do anything else. If, in evil pass, he says, "I think I had better come down," his second says, "Oh," and the leader has to try again. And if a little later he says, "What do you think? Had we better go on?" the second simply replies, "Yes, let's," or, "Oh, we might as well," and again what can the leader do but go on if he can and fall off if he cannot? This moral ascendancy of the second over the leader is the greatest danger in modern climbing. In point of technique, however, the menace may occasionally be observed to quicken his pace a little, as if not entirely sure of his ground. I have even seen him completely caught up by the turn of events at a moment when he simply had not got a leg to stand on. This is very gratifying to the leader. To return to the second pitch of this right-hand route — it has much less loose matter on it than it used to have.

On the Glyder Fach there have been two small developments since Lot's Wife. The Chasm Rib is the rib right of the Chasm, and some way from the foot of the cliff. There is a pleasant little gully up its centre, and the main part is on the left of this, giving the Rib climb. It is started from the left above the initial wall. It is not difficult, but — give it a name, and say we did it. The other is less simple. The final bastion of the Direct Route, with the final crack on its right, has three cracks down its face, the right-hand pair being formed by a large, split wedge. The Final Flake goes up the right of these two and can be horribly strenuous, indeed, quite unbelievable for balance climbers. It is a layback problem of nearly thirty feet, and seemed to be harder than the other problems I knew. One has even been asked to linger a little on it for the benefit of a photographer.

The only new thing I am personally acquainted with on Tryfan is the very short Direct Finish to the little Wall Climb on the Milestone. It takes the crack going up from just round on the right from the tree. It overhangs a little and is unutterably adolescent, but it quite graces Tryfan.

Alt-y-Ogof though so close to Helyg has never come in for much attention: probably because the rock tends rather to the type associated with more low-lying outcrops. On its lower and right-hand arm are three routes based on the main, large, right-angle gully. They none of them seem to have any particular distinction except that all seem to have been done after seeing the accounts of the earlier ones, but quite without realising their immediate proximity. The routes do differ slightly. Palmer's crosses both Gotch's and the guidebook climb, from left to right, and it is the most difficult. Then there is the buttress on the right of the gully, which gives a good, if rather cumbersome, sort of climb. It starts with excellent, strong heather for some distance, and above this are three large rock steps which require a little mild route finding. The first turns out easy, the second a pretty slab pitch round to the left, and the third an ideal but easy form of exit from a pillar over on the right.

You poke a cautious head round the edge and, behold, the top. It is not difficult. It is named Bee's Buttress because the first party was very puzzled by the peculiar attitude of a swarm of bees en route. They wrote that a small swarm of these animals had hovered around the leader at the top of Pitch V, though, they said, their interest seemed incompletely aroused. The reason had become clear when No. 2 had arrived, for the bees immediately turned their attention to him. Mr. Stallybrass, however had rebuked them, and they had then seemed equally content with some coils of rope with which they had been presented. They were still routing around when the party had gone; and the party had not fully understood this. It had seemed very queer. On the Upper part of the Cliff, the one with the cave, a neat little climb has come to light, and now lies spread out up there, to watch the evening sun in the long days. Tracing the foot of the cliff to the right from the cave, it descends a little to the corner before it starts ascending. At the corner it is met by the top of a rib of outcrop rising from below and immediately above the right side of this is the start of the route. The first pitch is the hardest with a very slight overhang section at its foot. The second goes round to the right, and at this point care should be taken not to drop off with fright if a large falcon swoops at you. Rumour has it that on the first ascent a stern struggle took place up there between man and beast locked in a death grip, high up among the clouds, and that there was much bloodshed and much scraping of nails before the great bird eventually had its indescribably nasty neck wrung. Above this is the large and obvious grass ledge, and the final pitch is taken either right or left. It is not Severe. As we were coming down, the shepherds had set fire to the heather on Ogof, and it was by then night. The flames made their great red scars against the dying sky, and the smell of fire, — and it gave one that queer, plucking memory of things that does catch at one now and then, aside from the highway. Fantastic life. We had had no grudge against the heather: it had borne us well. The crackling noise was a funny thing to call beautiful; and the bunches of flame made only curious shapes on the dark hill for a time. What is it in life that it is so curiously alive, and that it is so curiously dying? What is it in change that is so very still and so old? The sky was much too darkly coloured to be black.

On the other side of the valley a new climb has been done, on Creigiau Gleision the younger, above Llyn Cowlyd. It is on the first layer of cliff you come to, and the largest, clean, steep buttress on that. There is a cairn at its foot and it is interesting all through, though only short. Lovely, scrapey rock, and nasty, sticky little cracks. The finish is easy, but rather a surprise. This, too, is quite near Helyg, and suitable for those who like to appreciate the grim loneliness of man's handiwork. There is also good practice for skilled trundlers, and if you do not want to climb you can go a little further, beyond some strikingly ugly spots of rock, and get perhaps the most unpleasant walk to the top of a hill in England or Wales. In fact the whole place has much to recommend it. The lake is specially warmed up for bathing during an hour or so per day, on some sunny days in the summer. But I do not know that they could ever do anything with the place. As they were saying at the time, " 'Tis the Inchcape rock, 'tis the man of few words."

The Llanberis valley has produced a very good bit of rock in the cliff opposite Dinas Mot. It is variously called the Castle, Columnar Cliff, and some long Welsh name that I have forgotten meaning something fine and central in Welsh legendry that I cannot just place. Haskett Smith writes of this place with his usual acumen: "It is somewhere in this neighbourhood that we must look for the mysterious precipice of which Edward Llwyd wrote two hundred years ago as being strikingly columnar in structure..." It is very striking. In another publication it was quite rightly advertised as an "excellent sport for the artist, gardener, or master plasterer." These last two are in reference to the fact that much of the structure shows a regrettably low degree of cohesion, especially with regard to sticking out pieces. Also the place is full of plants: not just dank, like the Devil's Pasture: it goes in for horticulture on a larger scale. If there is a crack or anything anywhere to get roots into, it almost always keeps several large holly trees in it, and a few yews. There is nothing small about the place, not even the holds: they project in a large, officious manner, and they pull off likewise. Cenotaph Corner is the big, obvious right angle in the centre. Left of it, and half way up, is a grass and tree covered scoop. An easy climb traverses to this from the foot of the Cenotaph, and out again to the left, fairly low down. Being an easy way of going up, it was called Spiral Stairs. A harder climb goes straight up to this ledge from below its lower end. It starts in a crack up a tree, and then swings out on to the steep rib on the right and up this. It is definitely steep, but with good holds. It was called Dives because they had hoped for better things above; but, being clad in rubbers, the rain came, and they had to traverse out of Heaven low down. Left of Dives is tne Holly Buttress route. It starts up another crack a few yards to the left, with a tree half way up, then you squeeze behind some thorny bushes on the left and ascend, keeping in the corner. After a good deal of odd vegetation a large holly tree is ascended for some twenty feet. Step from the top of this to the steep right wall, and so, shortly, to the top. This name was due to the fact that, being the first climb on the cliff, they did not realise that there were prickly things to push through on nearly all the routes up it. Further to the left again are three fine columns. Of these the left hand is the easiest. It is called Parchment Passage for aesthetic reasons, and it is covered from head to foot with prickly things through which duty carries one. On this and the next climb it was a very hot day and they only wore shorts and gym shoes. The protection was inadequate. For the benefit of those that come after they wish to state that if you want to sit down, find some rock somewhere, shorts are not enough for

'It is to S.B. Donkin that the club owes the provision of electric light, cooking and water heating at Helyg.'

sitting on holly: as a method of blood letting leaches are much superior. In case anybody else has to get through a holly bush and is not sure how to start, it is a good sound policy to get the back of the head through first, and then follow up en masse quickly and snakily. Vision is less acute perhaps, but there's not much in it — especially if you map out the snags first. It is useful to get No. 2 through between the same branches for the sake of the rope, which may otherwise take a fancy to things you have passed, and become a bar to further progress. No. 2 is almost certain to try the wrong "gap" if left to his own devices, and I know of nothing more difficult to arrange tactfully than No. 2 in the wrong part of a holly bush. There is no other type of difficulty. The middle column starts with a little overhang: it is called Pharaoh's Passage. After a short struggle against the forces of nature one can grasp the top of his nightcap (extinguisher pattern), and pull out on to holly leaves again. The right hand column is the hardest of the three. The route goes up the large pockets in the steep right wall. After a short climb a cubby hole is entered where one can go into residence for a time before traversing over to the left. The rest is simple and as the holds are big and clear throughout, there is minimum technical difficulty. This all sounds ridiculously easy and doubtless is, but Columnar Cliff is a steep place and here and there still the strong aroma of excitement breaks in upon the hills. Sometimes it is made clear by the heavy breathing of No. 2 striving after a sign, and perhaps there is this sign given him that where he asked for a handhold from above there was given him a rope around his middle. It is, indeed, pleasant for the leader to hear the hard grunting of effort give place to the more calmly audible expirations of one who, after a long and laborious career, has found peace of mind at last in a gracefully-executed retirement. One must, though, realise that it is not only No. 2 who is fallible. Sometimes even the leader has happened across some miscalculation, perhaps only slight, which had a sudden and profound influence upon his future course. He realises with a start that something radically unsettling has occurred, something which completely upset his balance. Perhaps the body politic has been let down by the toe-nail of temerity, and there is borne in upon the prime actor, that beyond the protection of the scant coverings of custom, there is, suddenly unfolded, a fast and glorious stratosphere, punctuated, alas, by occasional primordial objects of stone. Like when you are sliding down snow that gets steeper than you had thought, and, after a brief period of indecision, you sort of come among rocks. There is a very deep-seated sense of conflict with the aims of nature. The Columnar Cliff is interestingly steep in parts for exploration. Not that these are the only dangers attaching to the sport: there is that terrible over-confidence that may attack one after a good route. I remember the car got that once. It drove us faster and faster through the wilds of Denbigh until, screwing its accelerator to the sticking point, the graceless vehicle turned against the

Gribin Facet - The Zig-Zag.   *Photo: R.J. Collinson.*

hand that led it, and after a short, decisive battle, pitched us head first out on to the road. But that is quite another story. Incidentally, it was rather a famous car on account of its small size and curious appearance. I hear that only a week or so ago, in a like mood, the little car charged into the back of a sheep, and, unhappily, with fatal results. The car never regained consciousness.

Then there are the climbs on the right of Cenotaph Corner. The first steep corner to the right has not been climbed, but just beyond that is a steep, loose-looking gully crack, facing out to the left. This gives a good pitch of its kind, and with adequate use of the rope there can be no sort of danger. It gives out on the Crawl section of the face, which lies back a good deal and is covered with grass and other such things. The route carries on to Happy Valley, just by the left of the crawl route. Happy Valley is the large, long ledge crossing the cliff three-quarters of the way up. It was given this name in a Romantic Moment, when one was not feeling very well, and one rather wished to live there for always — which, indeed, one very well might if it did not get too cold, or rainy, or something. It is really a very beautiful spot and we have tried to take a great many photographs of it. With a little luck one can trundle right down to the wall of the road. When playing about here, however, one should avoid tripping up in the rather thick vegetation: but there is nothing to prevent a resolute body of men from really going up there and making a firm stand against the pressure of modern life and the burden of over-civilisation. No. 3, before setting out from Helyg for the climb in question, discovered that it was cold, and put an extra coat in his sack. It started hailing during the first pitch, and No. 3, finding that his several waistcoats, coats, and cut down macintoshes afforded insufficient protection, took the coat out from the sack and by a skilled acrobatic manœuvre added this garment deftly to the pile upon his shoulders. It was a black tail-coat, and would probably have fitted him very well if it had not been made on far too small a scale, and unhappily the sleeves, for their part, did not extend far beyond the elbows. It got on much better when the pressure of circumstance discovered extensive outlets down the seams. The route was called Sexton's Route. To the right again, are, a gully in the cliff, a rib extending after some vicissitudes to the top, and a gully carrying definitely to the top and limiting the cliff on the right. There is a climb keeping just left of the first gully, up the easy, sloping, vegetative bit of cliff referred to as the Crawl section. It starts up the immediate left wall of the little gully and arrives at the right hand extremity of the valley. It would be tedious to describe in detail the types of turf to look for en route. The name is Nebuchadnezzar's Crawl; Nebs Crawl for short. It will be remembered that, during a period of mental aberration, this old gentleman went on his belly seven years with the beasts of the field, size not specified, and his face he buried in the grass. There was an amusing incident on the Crawl when we got into a corner and then got out again. The Flying Buttress is the name of the rib, after the gully, because the upper part of it does rather. The lower part may be taken as such or via the little gully on its left. The flying part is started on the right corner, and then an easy traverse is made up to the left, then up and back again to the right, along obvious faults. It is easy, but there is a tiny tree which should be treated with respect in view of the important position it will fill when it grows up. The Valley itself may be approached easily from the left side of the upper part of the Columnar Cliff. Coming to the right end a connection can be made with the Flying Buttress and up it to the top. This makes the easy Valley Crossings. The far right gully was climbed with a most improper amount of aid a very long time ago. It does not look very funny.

On the other side of the Valley, Dinas Mot shows a Girdle at three-quarters height which is a nice Difficult with good rope technique, but the technique is not absolutely simple and one should remember when explaining about it to the other man that a cord around the neck of a good knave is better than ship's hawsers round the belly of an ass. Just left of the West Gully is the Western Slabs route. On the first pitch it is customary to start by going up to the right and scratching about a bit, before coming down to start again. The second pitch is long and interesting, especially at the top. The West Rib, Kirkus's climb, keeps just left of it throughout. The difficulty is maintained right to the top and it is probably harder than the Slabs, a little all round.

Half way along the line between Dinas and Cyrn Las is a steep, stiff-looking crag, made of unusually rotten rock. Gimmer Crag is popularly credited with the excellent idea of standing out on all sides, so as to have no more than its own rainfall to dispose of. Craig Rhaiadr stood out pretty well, but overlooked a little stream running down over its middle. So stand it never so well, in fine weather it is wet, and in wet weather it is pouring: and when we went it was coming down in bucketfuls all over the place, and even so the stream stood out strongly by comparison, falling sheer on to a narrow ledge half-way up. The first pitch was a corner beneath this and it brought home to one at once the significance of that phrase "the ominous cessation of the noise of running water." This often occurs in the good old gullies, and it means that the aforesaid water is being soaked up by the body of the leader in mid-stream: like a sponge. And the irony of the situation is that the poor lad cannot do otherwise, he may be absolutely unwilling to vacate his absurd position; as like as not he has been nailed to the rivulet by the hand of fear. Then, of course, the route led across the narrow ledge in question. "It sometimes comes upon one as a direct shock — this mighty force of water in its natural surroundings." The next pitch was very long and No.2 remained on the end of the ledge in a "comparatively sheltered" position. The grass on this pitch is long and

rank, and serves admirably to hold the rock together: but really, it is a fine cliff, and gives one an excellent swim in bad weather. There is no other technical difficulty, and if umbrellas were stored at a few critical points, and a steel shelter erected over the narrow ledge, it would no doubt become suitable for a wider public than the few expert freshwater fish in these parts. Also a telephone might be installed over the 180-foot final pitch, thus rendering unnecessary the perilous task of the original No. 1, when he had to make the long run round to the foot of the cliff alone, to find out whether the original No. 2 had escaped notice drowning, and to tell him that he was not yet ready to take him (the original No. 2) up. The rain was very rowdy that day. We simply could not think what to call the climb.

Then there is fine old Clogwyn Du'r-Arddu: that thick-headed old friend. We are not allowed to call him Cloggy in deference to the older University tradition. They seem so forcibly reminded thereby of the devastating popularity of the words and accents that it held so sacred to it. Kirkus has done a lot of new stuff there, of which I have no first-hand knowledge. The older climbs continue to be popular, and the long first pitch of the Great Slab route has been ascended and descended under regulation greasy conditions. The grass seems to be settling down for a long and useful career. All the routes on this cliff are first class, and exploration at such an angle entails a severe strain on the neck. It is the sort of place where the guide-book has an unfair advantage. It says "rise fifteen feet to a grass patch." Just like that. But you never know: you may get involved in all sorts of the most dreadful difficulties whilst rising fifteen feet. Once I distinctly remember reaching a glorious position lying down on a small ledge only fifteen feet from the green grass, and yet I am sure that there was no way up at all. Linnell has made a new route up the West Buttress which sounds rather like this. One gathers that you float out a bit, jump fifteen feet, then rise up the West Buttress. Before finishing I must issue a word of warning about that Curving Chimney. It is certainly a fine climb, but I am not sure that it is worth it. Definitely it is not if there is a terribly energetic little man swearing about above you on the rope, and a tremendously heavy tall man swaying about below you on the rope. *Eheu fugaces* — we had better untie.

Introversion: retrospection: the cliffs were made for failures rather than for success. Alas! had we better untie?

Bill Stallybrass and Max Wirth on Crib Goch Buttress, September, 1938.   *Photo: John Buzzard.*

Photo: R.J. Collinson.

Above: The Helyg Boulder.
Below: The familiar and the unfamiliar at Helyg.

Photo: W.W. Stallybrass.

EARLY DAYS IN HELYG

T.A.H. PEACOCK

My first visit to Helyg was in March 1931 with an O.U.M.C. party of eight. The party consisted of John Bingham, George Meade-King, John Philpot, David Hodgkinson, Patrick Greeves, John Gairdner, myself and one other whose name I forget. Seven of us stayed in Helyg, but John Bingham preferred the fleshpots of Pen-y-Gwryd and the company of the Lockwoods!

Four of us arrived a day early, travelling in George's car. Next morning we set off to climb Lockwood's Chimney, but failing to find it we made the laborious ascent of Lliwedd from the Power Station. We had taken the key of Helyg with us and on our return we found the remainder of the party had arrived and were attempting to force an entry via the skylight.

The club had built the garage which was in better condition than it is now. Nine bunks had also been installed in the outer room of Helyg and two camp beds in the loft. To enter the loft it was considered unsporting to use the ladder (At the top of the ladder was a door bearing a notice, 'Reserviert für der Huttenwart', which notice had obviously been removed from a Swiss Hut.) and you were expected to do a straight pull up. With the door closed this was a good V.S. Whether Mr. Jones used this method of entry is doubtful. Cooking was with primus stoves, and an Aladdin lamp cast its fitful gleams in the kitchen, when it was not sooted up. Outside there was a coal shed and the lavatory consisted of an Elsan. This had to be emptied periodically and the two medical students in the party were elected by a majority of five to two to carry out this task, which they did to perfection.

On the lavatory door was fixed a remarkable notice which some enterprising member of the C.C. had removed from a foreign hotel. It read as follows: 'On est instamment prié de ne jeter aucune object obturante, tel que tampon ou autre carton dans le lavabo'. This was followed by an 'English' translation, 'You are instantly recommended to don't throw any obturating materials such as pad, cotton wool into the closet'.

The walls of the kitchen were decorated with some brilliant caricatures by a member of the C.C. named French. I remember two in particular; one of General Bruce and another of A.B. Hargreaves frying the Helyg rat, and entitled 'The Epicure'. We never actually saw the Helyg rat, but we heard him at night gnawing the floor boards. I am glad to say that he never attempted to gnaw our toes!

The inner room could be heated by a coal fire, but the chimney smoked so badly that we never used it. Drying facilities were distinctly limited, but the weather, fortunately, was gloriously fine throughout our stay with much snow in the gullies, but the rocks were clear on Tryfan. The whole scene, in fact, was Alpine. Outside we found the Helyg Boulder a challenge for using up spare energy. In the late thirties J.M. Edwards wrote up in the Helyg book a guide to the boulder with 47 routes on the face! No doubt this triumph is preserved in the archives of the Club.

We were all novices to Welsh climbing except our leader, John Bingham. Being the only other officer of the club and having climbed in the Alps, I was appointed leader and on the first official day of the meet we started traditionally with the Milestone Buttress, Ordinary Route, four on a rope. We then moved round to the East Face of Tryfan to do the Pinnacle Rib. Having found little difficulty and suffering from a swollen head I ventured to tackle the final chimney which John had wisely avoided. The small stone, which I believe had previously been jammed in the crack, was missing and I could not get started. Having read in George Abraham that in such circumstances the leader should take a shoulder, I positioned the third member of the party, wedged in the lower part of the chimney to belay me, and attempted to stand on the back of my second. His back proved unstable and I fell off backwards, but luckily landed feet first in some soft snow. I say luckily as the previous man to fall out of this chimney was reported to have killed himself. After this abortive attempt we by-passed the chimney.

Next day we did the Idwal Slabs and then six of us followed John up the Holly Tree Wall belaying traditionally on the Holly Tree. We were all of course using Clinkers; rubbers would have been considered bad form; the holds, though small were less polished than now. We then attempted the Central Arete of Glyder Fawr, but found too much snow.

We had another day on Tryfan doing Grooved Arete and Gashed Crag and on the last day John took a party up Parson's Nose while I did Slanting Buttress on Lliwedd. This was in real winter condition and the final chimney was so choked with snow that I had to jam my ice axe in the upper part, pull up and finally stand on it! All somewhat unorthodox.

Thus ended the first of some fifty visits to Helyg, the last being in 1975. Two members of the party became life-long friends, George Meade-King and David Hodgkinson, and we climbed together for many years. It was a memorable holiday and the recollections of it are as clear today as they were fifty years ago.

A GREAT WALL OF ROCKS

J.E.Q. BARFORD

THE first time I went there was in July 1936, the day after a visit to Cwm Du of Mynydd Mawr and a feast of bilberries. This was to prove our undoing as by the time the leader had reached the top of the first pitch of Pigott's, the second's stomach had remembered the previous day's feast and the climb had to be abandoned. A week later we were aroused from our sleep at 1-20 a.m. by insistent and clamorous knocking at the door of Helyg. Our visitors were two members of the Rucksack Club from Talybraich who explained that they were seriously worried because two of their guests had not returned from a visit to the cliff, where their stated intention was to climb Linnell's Narrow Slab route. This sounded grim, so we collected the First Aid kit, piled it into the cars and drove round to Llanberis. We called at the police station, succeeded in rousing a sleepy sergeant who had heard of no accident, and we therefore set out up the Llanberis path to the cwm. The night was black and very wet, as it always is on these occasions, and by the time we had climbed up the scree to the foot of the West Buttress our spirits were low indeed. We raised our voices and hailed the deeper blackness above. There was no answer except for the croak of a raven annoyed at being disturbed at such a time. After a few minutes of this futile occupation we crept into one of the disused mine adits at the foot of the buttress and spent a cold and wet two hours waiting for dawn. This came at last and disclosed no corpses at the foot of the buttress or climbers on it, so we returned to Helyg to breakfast and bed. About midday we were woken to listen disgruntledly to the apologies of the two men we had set out to rescue. They had had a minor accident in roping down from the climb which they had been unable to complete, but had rescued themselves, had their wounds dressed in Llanberis and returned to Tyb in the morning. They said that they had climbed many Very Severes in the Lakes and had not expected any serious difficulty with the climb. There are two morals to be drawn from this little story.

Two days later in dampish conditions three of us went there again intending to do Longland's. The place had now a considerable reputation with us and the party became distinctly lukewarm when it was found that the initial chimney was very hard and greasy. By common consent it was left.

Nearly a year later on the second of August 1937 I went there again with a better leader, Jim Joyce. We first tried the Curving Crack, but to my discontent found that the first pitch was very hard, left it alone and instead climbed Longland's without incident or special difficulty. This was a most enjoyable day and changed my feeling of horror of the cliff to one of friendship. A few days later I had the pleasure

John Barford leading in Wales.   *Photo: John Buzzard.*

of leading Steuart Palmer up the climb, during one of his infrequent but always stimulating visits to Wales. He had never climbed on the cliff before.

Easter 1939 saw a large party from Helyg there again with the Curving Crack as the specific objective. I made such a noise leading the first pitch that no one could be persuaded to follow me. As I had little stomach for doing the rest of the climb solo I ordered the others to go up the terrace in force to the top of the climb and lower me a strong rope. This they did and with this re-assurance I climbed the rest. In September, I returned to Longland's once with Nea Morin and once with a comparative beginner and again felt the awkwardness of the little chimney crack at the start of the slab; the keen pleasure of the slab itself in both its sections; the joy of having accomplished the difficult step modified by doubt at Faith and Friction; the short fierce tussle with the final overhang and the peace of the long walk home in the dusk.

In 1940 work on the Llanberis guide kept me away but in September 1941 I returned with Nea Morin. The climb chosen was the Curving Crack and I had fair confidence in my ability to climb it. It was not to be; the rocks of the first pitch were dampish and when I was three-quarters of the way up I realised I was not going to make it. I started to descend — but my strength failing, I fell off, not suffering much damage. I am quite convinced by this experience that if this pitch is laybacked any climber with insufficient strength to complete it will fall off if he tries to descend — the layback is almost as strenuous in descent as in climbing. Nea decided after this exhibition that the crack was best climbed by jamming and went up quite quickly and neatly. She led the more difficult parts of the remainder, the first time this had been done by a woman. We stayed in the corner the whole way up, not moving out on to the edge to the right at the top.

Three days later we returned with Menlove Edwards to the West Buttress. An attempt was made to get on to the buttress over the initial overhang at a point below the foot of the Concrete Slab (otherwise known as the Hourglass)*. This failed although the possibility remains and should be tried again some day in really dry conditions. We retired to the Terrace and walked down it to the beginning of the Narrow Slab. We went round and up past a little ash tree and started to traverse to the right. We were soon stopped by a smooth and untraversable groove-wall with a rib surmounted by some large blocks on its far side. At this stage Nea and I were prepared to call the whole business off — not so J.M.E., who is made of sterner stuff. He gathered in the spare rope and lassooed the further and finer block, then swung on the anchored rope across the impasse and climbed up the rope to the continuing ledge. Nea and I joined him by the same method.

Menlove continued round to the right, until the ledge finished in a steep corner, then up this to a point on the Narrow Slab traverse just above Linnell's jump — a

* Now again re-named White Slab.

pitch of 100 to 110 feet and a very fine lead as we found when we came to do it. The crux is a little extremely delicate overhang in the crack with tiny and widely spaced holds. Without knowing at that time that we were, in fact, on the Narrow Slab route, we continued round the cliff until we were at the foot of the Narrow Slab itself. Then we held a council of war. We had started late and seemed to have been climbing for a long time. There was about an hour of daylight left. Should we bivouac and complete the climb the next day? After a little discussion we agreed to go down, but not by the way we had come. We returned to the grass ledge on which Linnell's jump lands. Menlove climbed up the thin little slab to the edge and then stepped round out of sight to the ledge at the top of pitch (1) of the Narrow Slab. It all looked very difficult and I safeguarded myself by using a doubled rope. This stuck and Menlove had to climb back to retrieve it. We then traversed to the foot of Longland's slab and so home. This was a day of great climbing and a good introduction to what were then the wilder parts of the West Buttress.

At about this time the editor of this journal conceived, rather lightly, the idea that it would be a good thing if an article on the cliff were written for him and Menlove agreed to do it.

So in June 1942 Menlove and I were back again stopping with Mrs. Roberts at Hafotty Newydd, with the intention of spending all our time on the cliff. The weather had other views and we only had half a week on the rocks, one day being wasted, as has already been related, in looking for our ropes which we had hidden too well.

We tried the Sunset Crack on the East Buttress, a very nice climb, but with a stubborn last pitch to which we could find no solution. Another climb was not led — the Pedestal Crack; this was done on a rope by Menlove, the indications being that it is very difficult especially by the direct start. This climb is probably as hard as any climb on the cliff, in North Wales, or the British Isles. It has only been led three times. It would be difficult to imagine any more direct way up the cliff; it is possible to drop a plumb-line from the top to the bottom of the crack.

The Birthday Crack was also done on a rope, unnecessarily since this climb is nowhere near as difficult as the East Buttress ones. It is a good way of getting to the terrace and it is strange that it is so rarely done. The first pitch is a delightful wall of rough, jug-handled rock. The crack itself is hard and of considerable technical interest.

Pigott's I did for the first time — Menlove had of course done it before. I was allowed a shoulder in the little corner. The crack itself was full of rope slings and inserted chockstones which I was only too pleased to use; Menlove, following, cast them all down and climbed the place clean. The last bit of this pitch is as memorable as anything on the whole cliff. From a wedged position too comfortable to be easy to leave, near the top of the steep crack, a delicate step to the right is immediately followed by a delicate step up to the next ledge. The last pitch was done round on the right, safeguarded by a lasso over the corner. Hoyland's direct finish was tried and found to be too difficult in the prevailing conditions.

The greatest pleasure was reserved until the end of the week — the Great Slab. It is not possible to praise this climb too highly and together with the Dinas Mot Direct is probably Colin's finest memorial. The precision of the qualifying step which tries to bar access to the Green Caterpillar; the traverse across to the first field, apparently the only key and that a subtly hidden one; the safety and delicacy of the hardest move are a fitting approach to the culminating glory of the Great Slab itself. The climbing here is not very hard, but the position of the place would be difficult to equal and the climbing and lack of good belays are such as to call into full operation the mutual confidence of the members of the party in each other, which is the key to success and pleasure on this buttress.

The next year we held the first wartime summer meet at Helyg, at the same time as the Alpine Club were holding their first meet at Penypass. The Alpine Club at its expensive dinners in London had several times showed considerable interest in the Black Hollow and the cliff which encloses it; and it was partly to redeem half promises to them that on June 28th a large party cycled round to Penypass from Helyg. Later, three ropes went up Longland's and the peace of the cliff was decisively shattered for many hours. The weather was perfect and the return walk to Penypass was as satisfying as it always is after these days.

A few days later a party including this time only two members of the Alpine Club returned and did the Great Slab and the modern division of the pitches was firmly established as the best way.

In September 1944 it was felt that the Chimney route might be feeling neglected, so we set out from Penypass to try it. The first pitch was a fair imitation of a waterfall and so the climb was abandoned.

Two days later the cliff was thought to have dried sufficiently for climbing and I climbed the Narrow Slab having selfishly discarded two members of the party before they had properly started. On pitch (2) much effort and time was wasted by the leader in trying to get to the corner at too high a level. Scotty Dwyer and Dick Morsley who were on the East Buttress called across correcting instructions and the corner was reached. The leader is here faced with the problem which Linnell solved by jumping. The jump is not a nice one as it is backwards and sideways and some people prefer to climb down and across on excruciatingly small holds. Not so the leader on this occasion. There is rather a good handhold high up — which is actually the key to the step round the corner itself. This is so good that a line sling can be put round it. With this sling as a handhold it is possible to face the direction of the jump and the whole affair is made much easier.

The first pitch of the Slab itself, pitch (4) of the climb, is the great one. It gets progressively harder until the final move, which is the hardest of the lot and fifty feet above the belay. For a leader in good condition it is very enjoyable, as there are just sufficient holds to make it justifiable and these though small are of good quality. The next pitch is perhaps as hard towards the top, but it can be so well safeguarded that there is not the same quality of excitement about it. The remainder is good scrambling in an enjoyable position. This climb as a whole is harder than Longland's or the Great Slab, in fact the true grading is probably VI, VB, VA, respectively. The position of Bow Shaped Slab must be considered indeterminate as no one, except its inventor and one rumoured other party, has led it right through.

Another incident of this day deserves record. Scotty Dwyer and Dick Morsley had been busy all day on the East Buttress and during the long period of delay at the top of the first pitch of Narrow Slab, they appeared in an incredible position in the ·middle of one of the large sheer walls of the buttress. After some consideration this was identified as the outside finish of Pigott's, but instead of finishing up the chimney they kept left and connected with variation *(c)* of the last pitch of Pigott's. They were the nearest approach to the 'flies on a wall' simile I have ever seen.

Towards the end of 1945 I stole an extra fortnight's holiday and settled accounts with the Chimney route, did the direct finish to the East Buttress and repeated the Great Slab for the joy of it. The Chimney route in good weather falls below VI and is very nice in the style of the Holly Tree wall — pleasant gymnastics on good rock. The rickety innards are no longer very rickety.

I wrote a good ending to this article, but the editor thought it was too didactic, so we must finish here with no ending at all.

WALES REVISITED

E.E. SHIPTON

THAT night Cwm Silin was very beautiful under a large, clear moon. We slept in the open on the grassy slopes above the lake. I awoke at about five to find the sun shining over a bank of white mist. At seven I was awakened by rain falling on my face. We crowded together in one of the tents and occupied ourselves happily with breakfast until about ten o'clock.

My companions had promised to take me to Clogwyn du'r Arddu that day to watch the experts at play on the Very Impossibles. I had been looking forward keenly to this as it was a sight I had never seen. My anticipation of enjoyment was not even damped by the possibility that I might be invited to tie on to one of their ropes. However, the rain had obviously come to stay and Clogwyn du'r Arddu was out of the question. I was bitterly disappointed. Now it may be another ten years before I get a chance to witness the spectacle of first-class rock climbing in Britain, by which time no doubt Clogwyn du'r Arddu will have ceased to attract the expert and will be used as a training ground for novices.

The delights of breakfast at an end, the rain showing no sign of relenting, the atmosphere inside the small tent became somewhat squalid and we decided to move to Helyg. We arrived in nice time for an early and protracted luncheon. I had last visited the Hut early in 1928, and, though of course I had heard of its renovations, I was most agreeably surprised. A brief clearing in the weather in the afternoon encouraged us to emerge, and, feeling at first somewhat bloated, we climbed Tryfan by some nondescript route, which, however, I enjoyed enormously. There was a fair number of people in the Hut when we returned, and after dinner we were treated to a discourse by an Austrian climber on some recent developments of climbing in the Eastern Alps. It was illustrated by some startling photographs, mostly of men suspended from pitons, looking rather like sailors engaged in painting the side of a ship. I retired to bed with a heavy sense of my obsolescence.

The next morning I awoke at six in time to see Barford stripped to the waist setting out to dig a trench. Satisfying myself that he was in the minority I went to sleep again until a more reasonable hour. It was still raining but we spent an instructive morning watching a demonstration of various methods of abseiling from one of the top bunks in the Hut. The show was admirably staged. It led its expectant audience from the simpler methods of getting down, which even I could understand, through the more complicated, to a way of abseiling uphill which seemed to call for a prodigious output of strength and ingenuity to gain a couple of hard-won feet. The climax was an exposition of how to abseil with an injured man on one's back. The conjurer asked for a volunteer from among the audience, and with some natural hesitation Michael Ward stepped forward to take the part of the injured man. The preparations on the top bunk took a long time, while the performers wound themselves into an inextricable cocoon. At last the descent was launched. It was agony to watch. Eventually both rescuer and rescued reached the floor head first. It was explained that the manoeuvre would have been more impressive demonstrated from the top of a 100-foot cliff. Of this there could be little doubt. I made a mental resolve to do all I could to avoid breaking a leg in the company of the experts.

Among those at Helyg I had been delighted to find Gilbert Peaker. It was a curious circumstance, for it was with him that I had stayed there the only time in my life, more than eighteen years before. Now he was there alone, and, as my companions had to leave that day to return to their labours, I decided to seize the chance to revive the memory of a very pleasant mountain companionship in such an appropriate setting. We set out together in the middle of the afternoon. The rain had stopped except for an occasional shower. Had I been able I would not have exchanged the wind and cloud for warm sunlight. We climbed Tryfan by one of the ordinary routes, dallied on the summit and descended on the other side. A sharp hailstorm hit us as we reached the foot of the rocks of Glyder Fach. But it stopped as suddenly as it had come, and we climbed comfortably up the Direct route, reaching the top of it in thick, drifting mist. As we were nearing the summit of Glyder Fach at about ten o'clock (Double Summer Time) the mist lifted, the light of the setting sun struck up beneath it and glistened upon those great boulders, that a moment before had been dark, looming spectres. As we reached the top the mists dissolved and we looked far across the Menai Strait and the sea, through a vast frame of flaming colour. This was reflected over the hills as we swung gently down. It was almost dark by the time we reached the farm where we drank the best part of a gallon of creamy milk.

The next morning we went to Craig yr Ysfa to renew our acquaintance with the Great Gully. After so much rain we expected to find it impossibly wet, and, as we had slept late, there was the added interest that to climb it and get back in time to catch our train at Bettws-y-Coed that afternoon meant working to a fairly tight schedule. The Gully was wet, though not unpleasantly so, and it did not rain while we were in it. It was strange how each feature of the rock structure, so long forgotten, emerged one by one out of the past, some magnified, some dwarfed, the positions of some transposed, but each, like a tune or a smell, recalling its special sensations. Getting out of the top of the big chimney was a more strenuous business than I had remembered, the last pitch very much easier. We reached the top with plenty of time to spare for a gentle stroll back past the lake, while our wet clothes dried in the sun. Ten minutes before we reached the Hut a torrential downpour soaked us to the skin. This upset our time-table as we had to strip and dry our clothes against a night in the train while we ate our lunch, washed the dishes and tidied the Hut. But despite the fact that a tyre of Peaker's bicycle burst under its quite unreasonable burden, we caught the train.

The long night journey via Bristol to Warminster, standing in countless corridors and waiting on crowded platforms ready to do battle for a tiny space available on each belated train, was a sad contrast to the swift comfort of my outward journey. But even in the darkest hour I did not grudge the price I was paying for my extra day. The week-end had been commonplace enough. But, to those of us who spend much of our time abroad the memory of days spent among British hills remains fresher and provides more satisfaction than many of our ventures in grander and less familiar ranges of the Earth.

Photo by
A. M. Uttley

MICKLEDORE GROOVES — THE TOP PITCH

Below the final groove and just above the overhang

A TRAINING CAMP AT HELYG - 15th-29th MAY, 1942

JOHN HUNT

THE choice of North Wales as the location of a Toughening School for one of our Armoured formations was made possible mainly owing to the generosity of the Club in placing Helyg at my disposal for the first Course, which took place in the second half of May.

The objects of this Course, in addition to the training of a more specifically military nature, may be summarised as follows:

(a) to test reactions of leaders to arduous physical conditions, and also to circumstances sometimes trying to the nerves and temper;

(b) to prove their readiness and adaptability to share hardships and "muck in" regardless of rank — to live communally without loss of discipline and respect for authority.

(c) by encouraging them to do things concerning which they may have doubted their ability, and have felt reluctance about attempting, to help them gain in self-reliance, and to experience the satisfaction of triumphing over difficulties.

The programme was planned, with these objects in view, on "Commando" lines, and was a somewhat ambitious one for students whose normal training is concerned with Tanks, Trucks, and Carriers. Broadly, it was divided into seven main parts:—

Part A. Ridge Walking and Cross Country Work.

Part B. Map Reading and Reconnaissance.

Part C. Stalking and Observation Training.

Part D. Fell Racing.

Part E. Route Finding by Compass.

Part F. The Expedition.

Part G. Rock-climbing.

Students were organised into Regimental Patrols of four, and at the end of the first day each Patrol was asked to choose its own leader, on the team principle that the man most adapted to this type of work should lead, irrespective of rank. For rock-climbing we worked in half-patrols, and owing to the small number of leaders available, the programme was "staggered," so that only half the students were engaged on this training on any one day.

I was, however, more than fortunate in my instructors. Among them were such able leaders as A.W. Bridge and Lieutenant C.W.F. Noyce, both of whom joined the School for part of the Course. In addition, instructors were lent by a rock-

Ivan Waller following Colin Kirkus on the 1st ascent of Mickledore Grooves.   *Photo: A.M. Uttley.*

climbing Troop of a Commando unit billeted in the neighbourhood, and among them no less a celebrity than C.F. Holland (Lance-Corporal), who was with our ropes on several occasions. From Capel Curig, M.G. Bradley and the Aitchesons *pere et fils,* came out to assist on one day, so that we did not lack willing and well-qualified assistants.

We lived entirely the communal life, which while being incidental to Helyg, was also by design, on the principle that in this type of training at least, the more stereotyped military regime can, and should, be replaced by the "Expedition" spirit. We had, in fact, all ranks on the Course from Major to Trooper, and all worked, fed, and slept together, sharing the same hardships in training, and the same fatigue duties. The mountains and Helyg between them, certainly succeeded in producing a fine spirit of comradeship among all concerned.

We worked to a fairly "set" routine.

7 a.m. — P.T., followed by a bathe in the stream.

7-40 and 8 a.m. — Breakfasts in two sittings.

8-45 a.m. — Patrols started out with haversack rations for the day's training, no matter what the weather was doing. In the course of the day, and whatever the nature of the training, Patrols had two additional obligations: (a) to bathe in one or other of the lakes; (b) to carry out Unarmed Combat practice. The return to Helyg was scheduled to be at 5-30 p.m., but we were often later than that.

5-30 p.m. — Dinners.

6-30-8 p.m. — Further parades for Wrestling, Unarmed Combat, and for Lectures and Discussions.

8 p.m. — Light supper before "bedding down."

Even allowing for a normally high proportion of wet days in Snowdonia, we had exceptionally bad weather throughout. It was part of the underlying idea of the Course to persist with the programme at all costs, and with one exception this principle was maintained. But it was not an easy job, the drying of repeatedly drenched clothing being one of the major problems.

I give below in diary form, our activities from day to day:—

17th May. — Ridge Walk. Route from Helyg to Helyg via Tryfan — Glyder Fach — Glyder Fawr — Y Garn — Foel Goch — Elidir Fawr — Pentre and Ogwen.

This was a stiff introduction for men quite unused to this type of country, but all Patrols finished except one, which did not make the summit of the Elidir. We had heavy rain from mid-day onwards, and arrived back thoroughly soaked.

18th May. — Route Finding and Reconnaissance. The route given was Bwlch Tryfan — Saddle on Gribin Ridge — Devil's Kitchen — Llyn Clyd — Ogwen — Ffynnon Lloer — Helyg.

Heavy rain delayed the start for an hour, and as a consequence the visit to Llyn Clyd was cut out. Even so, Patrols found this cross-country traversing at the lower level, more taxing physically, and more of a test of route-finding than their longer ridge walk of yesterday; an interesting contrast.

19th-20th May. — Patrols were in turn carrying out stalking exercises, under fire, and being initiated to rock-climbing. The latter training took place in Cwm Idwal, with a number of Commando Instructors to assist. Students sampled various routes on the Slabs, and some ropes were later introduced to some of the ridges — Pinnacle Edge and Cneifion Arete on the Gribin, and the Central and East Aretes on the Glyder Fawr.

While some students showed immediate aptitude, others had clearly not overcome their preconceived fears by the end of the day; confidence had yet to come.

21st-22nd May. — Half the Course was on rock-climbing, while the remainder were sent to carry out a reconnaissance task on Snowdon, involving the traverse of the "Horseshoe" — in turns.

Climbing was on the Tryfan Buttresses, all of which were fairly well covered in the course of two days; the work included instruction and practice in abseiling.

Students took very readily to the abseiling, and there was a marked improvement in individual confidence on steep rock; not entirely due to the "pull" holds provided by the mountain. We had a certain amount of rain each day, particularly in the case of the Snowdon parties.

On the 21st evening we had a minor excitement, when two Instructors sent out to place clues for a Compass Route failed to return by 9-30 p.m. Noyce and I set out carrying food, blankets, and first aid kit, and made for Moel Siabod, in case the compass bearing between that summit and a small lake to the west of it might have led them into trouble on the crags. We failed to rouse any response to our shouts and whistle blasts in the moonlight, and on return at 2 a.m., found that they had come in only one hour after we had started!

23rd May. — Fell Race from Helyg to Ogwen Cottage over the summit of the Glyder Fawr. This was an individual affair, with points counting towards a Patrol aggregate. Various routes were therefore taken to the top, and in the mist and drizzle a few did not find it. The best recorded time was 111 minutes.

24th May. — A rest day. Casualties had been fairly high, and there were signs of further ailments; the pace had, in fact, proved a bit "hot" for some. I therefore cut out the strenuous Compass Course, and the only training done that day was a night stalking competition in Cwm Llugwy, between 9 p.m. and 12-30 a.m.

This was the only large departure from the programme, but on this day it was also learned that the Course was to be curtailed, and would finish on 29th instead of 31st May. By dint of combining the Expedition with the Endurance Test, however, no major alteration was involved.

25th-26th May. — Patrols in turn on rock-climbing and a traverse of the Carnedds (including Foels Grach and Fras, and return via Llyn Dulyn and Llyn Eigiau). On the 25th it was blowing a gale, with torrential rain which later turned to hail and snow. Climbing was out of the question, so all students were "switched" to the Carnedd walk that day in the hope that all would be able to climb on 26th. The first part of this was an inter-patrol Fell Race to the summit of the Dafydd. On arrival there we found conditions little short of terrible, with a violent wind blowing which bowled several of us over; it was extremely difficult to stand, and impossible to make oneself heard. In these circumstances it was unreasonable to continue the whole route, and a return was made over Llewelyn and down via Llyn Llugwy; we were all feeling distinctly battered; the best recorded time was 1 hour 14 minutes to the top. A powdering of snow lay on the fells to below the 3,000 contour.

Despite dull conditions and some rain next day, all of us had an excellent day's climbing, with parties on the Glyder Fach, the Milestone and Bochlwyd Buttress. Some of the ropes fitted in a considerable number of routes during the day.

27th May. — The morning was spend in stalking and map-reading competitions. Students were then given the afternoon to prepare for the Expedition-cum-Endurance Test, which consisted of a trek across country to a pre-fixed bivouac site beneath Lliwedd, where Patrols were to bathe in Llyn Llydaw and bivouac for the night. Next morning an ascent of the cliff was to be made by various routes, and from the summit students were to leave on a timed race on the following route: — Snowdon — Crib Goch — Elidir Fawr — Y Garn — Glyder Fawr and Fach — Tryfan — Helyg.

Hardly had our Patrols started out at 5 p.m., however, than the deluge began! By 6 p.m. we were all so thoroughly saturated that I had to decide, very reluctantly, to retreat. I accordingly returned from near Bwlch Tryfan to Helyg, and brought our lorry round to Pen y Pass to pick up the parties there. The possibility of sheltering for the night in the hotel outhouse was considered, but abandoned in view of the condition of most of the students — it was a bitter but necessary decision. We went back to Helyg, with the orders altered to the extent of returning early next morning by lorry and carrying on from the Pass.

28th May. — This we did. It was still raining fairly hard, and as we had lost time by this arrangement, I cut out the Elidir from the Test Route. We climbed by three routes on the West Peak on five ropes — most of it in a thorough downpour! — and became unpleasantly cold on the way up. Progress in the case of some ropes was slow, and as I had placed all decisions subsequent to the start of the climbs in the hands of leaders of ropes, not all students actually started the race. Two ropes were in effect on the crag most of the day, taking a devious route (partly new), worked out by Alf Bridge. The best time for the test was just under eight hours. Competitors were met on the summit of the Glyder Fawr by an Instructor with hot tea and chocolate. Despite the conditions — or perhaps because of them — this had been a great day's training.

29th May. — The morning was spent winding up training by various tests, including rope technique, which had been very well mastered in the course of the fortnight.

This brought to a close the Toughening Course. If, as I believe, it had succeeded in the objects set out at the beginning of this paper, then there is no doubt that the Club has rendered a very real service to the Army.

WARTIME EXTRACTS

'War has one mighty disadvantage. It is seldom that friends can fix days together, and the climber rushes to Helyg or Wastwater alone, to snatch what he can.'

C.W.F. Noyce, 1942.

'Let's go to Wales; Helyg, I should think. One's so much freer there, and it isn't likely to be crowded...'

D.M. Murray-Rust, 1942.

Squadron Leader John Mahler who was eventually killed on active service with Bomber Command paid his first visit to Helyg and joined the Climbers' Club in 1933;

'Naturally strong and full of energy, he quickly showed great possibilities, though his complete disregard for danger threatened to get him in trouble on more than one occasion. Some alarm was felt by those staying at Helyg when he made an ascent of the Holly Tree Wall after dark on a January evening with the aid of a torch!'

'Our thanks are due to the F. & R.C.C. for the use of their cottage, especially as we felt that we were regarded in that place as definitely wild, and rather uncouth, men from Wales. From an inspection of the visitors' book at Brackenclose, it seems that the reciprocal arrangement is of more benefit to members of our club than to the F. & R.C.C. members. At least the latter seem less ready to try the unknown horrors of Wales and Helyg, than we are to take advantage of the more civilised hospitality of Brackenclose.'

J.E.Q. Barford, C.C.J. 1942.

'Geoffrey Young replied in a most interesting speech, tracing the history of the club from its early days. It was delightful for the younger generation to be introduced personally, as it were, to so many great figures of the past whom one had known only as a name to be revered. In the early days the Climbers' Club was the only junior club in the country, and flourished exceedingly, but the formation of many other clubs with close local associations began to threaten its very existence as

Quartz Ledge, Pinnacle Wall.   *Photo: J.M. Bechervaise.*

an active body. Necessarily there had to be a change of focal point from the original group of A.C. members, and the committee sought other fields for recruitment, even resorting to the time-honoured method of the last war as shown by those fine journals produced during the presidency of Mallory and Arnold Lunn, when a peak of literary achievement was reached which has never been surpassed; but somehow, the new focal point was never discovered until the foundation of Helyg.

F.A. Pullinger, 1942 C.C.J.

'Broadly speaking, the normal method of recording a climb in the Helyg Book has been the Fell and Rock method, a little less cut and dried, perhaps, and a little more talkative.'

Craig yr Ysfa supplement 1943. A.D.M. Cox & H.E. Kretschmer.

'... You may change the classification of climbs to your scientific and horrid figures - (I will still like to think of some day achieving again a "mild severe" - not a IVB) - but as long as the literary conventions of climbing guides remain unchallenged, I will still look forward to a return to England, Home and Helyg...'

R.M. Hamer, 1943 C.C.J.

'Helyg and Bosigran have continued to be used at regular intervals. The university clubs have held meets there and Helyg has also been used by the army. Indeed you are not likely to suffer long from peaceful illusions there for your morning sleep is frequently broken by the irritating spatter of machine guns and attendant alarms and excursions.'

1943 C.C.J. edited by F.A. Pullinger.

'Flying Officer D.F.H. Biggane, D.F.C. was killed in action over Germany in December 1942.. He was a first class climber, and the Helyg log bears ample testimony to the standard of his achievements in the early war years when he was up at Cambridge.

... He was indeed a curious mixture of efficiency on the rocks and haphazard lack of concern about his equipment. He would walk from Scafell to Langdale in his Sunday shoes; he seldom carried a rope, and when he did, he did not expect other people to trust it, so we took our own. He would do similar odd things in everyday life at Cambridge, and his eccentric ways led to the weaving of numerous comic tales about him, which only served to amuse him, and to make everyone like him the more. On one occasion he set off from Helyg for Dinas Mot, for which crag, remote as it is from Helyg, he had such an affection that it became known among us as "Denny's Mot". He took with him an old envelope on which he had scribbled what he could learn of the route, and an ancient rusty piton from the tool drawer in the hut, "just in case". At the top of the first pitch the envelope blew away. A little later, the stone which had served as a piton hammer split in half and nearly dislodged the second man. Despite these mishaps they accomplished the climb successfully, but with some doubt as to the route taken.

C.F. Rolland, 1944 C.C.J.

'Meanwhile, Helyg continues to fulfil our needs adequately. It is not easy to keep it as clean and tidy as we should wish (for that matter this applies to all club huts just now); sometimes this gets a bit beyond the superficial titivating of the amateur char, and this has evoked truly self-sacrificing efforts and most exemplary purges by a few, and self-righteous entries in the log by others. All previous efforts, have, I learn, been recently surpassed by John Watson and Maurice Eggleshaw, who have virtually repainted the hut and left it, to quote Stuart Chantrell, "better than it has ever been since 1933".

F.A. Pullinger, 1944 C.C.J.

'Michael Bulkeley - "I remember how, after walking over the hills from Colwyn Bay to Helyg to join a winter O.U.M.C. Meet, he appeared at breakfast time and, notwithstanding the little sleep he had managed to snatch lying in the open on the way over, insisted on joining the day's expedition... Aged 23, he was killed in action in April, 1945.'

H.J.F. Cairns, 1946 C.C.J.

'W.R.'s (William Russell Reade) work for Helyg is too well-known to need reference and he was equally enthusiastic over Ynys Ettws.'

Geoffrey L. Bartrum, 1946 C.C.J.

'Users of Helyg are reminded that the log is intended to be a record of their climbs and expeditions and of their observations on the hills. There is no harm in gilding the bare factual record if there is anything interesting to say, and in the past the book has maintained a high standard both as a record of achievement and as good reading. Recently, however, the standard has been declining, there have been too many entries, mainly facetious, which are of interest to none but the writer. Another irritating form is the extolling of self virtue in hut cleaning, which has in any case been indicative rather of the normality of sloth, than any peak of virtue. Above all, if there is anything wrong with the Hut don't grumble about it in the pages of the log, do something about it.'

F.A. Pullinger, 1946 C.C.J.

'Our new Treasurer, with less than his usual admirable caution, reports that the Club's annual accounts show an insignificant loss on the year's working, and he also draws the attention of members to the fact that the last premium of the Helyg Sinking Fund will be paid in December, 1946, that all the Helyg bond holders will be repaid during 1947, and that thereafter the cottage will be shown on our Balance Sheet at a nominal figure much less than its real value.'

J.L. Longland, 25th January, 1946.

'Helyg is already uncomfortably full at summer weekends.'

F.H. Keenlyside, 1947 C.C.J.

'Burglary and overcrowding have caused some tightening up of the rules about the use of Helyg this year.'

A.D.M. Cox, 1947 C.C.J.

The very treacherous Alpine season of 1947 has brought the Club two heavy blows. On 23rd July, J.E.Q. Barford was killed by a stonefall on the Col Coste Rouge, below the Ailefroide. The other members of the party, W.H. Murray (S.M.C.) and Michael Ward, were severely hurt and only got down to Ailefroide village by a remarkable display of courage and toughness. On 7th August H.E. Kretschmer and J.R. Jenkins (Rucksack Club) lost their lives through a slip on ice when descending the upper part of the Brenva ridge.

John Barford and Nully Kretschmer were two of the outstanding mountaineers of the younger generation, and each played a very active part in the life of the Club. Much of their climbing in this country was done from Helyg. Between them they were responsible, wholly or in part, for all the three Welsh guidebooks published

THE KNIGHT'S MOVE, GROOVED ARÊTE   *R. Gorbold*

during the war. Barford was Hon. Secretary of the Club from 1939 to 1946, when he resigned in order to be able to give more time to the B.M.C. During all the war years he was the very efficient compiler of "New Climbs and Notes" for the Journal, to which he also contributed several articles. Kretschmer was the Journal's Assistant Editor for two years, and, as Guidebook Editor since 1943, had recently completed the re-publication of all the pre-war guides. A very typical article and a review by him appear in this number of the Journal. It will not be possible to print obituary notices until next year, but the Club will wish to offer its deep sympathy to the relatives in a loss by which it is itself so deeply affected.

'Most of Marshall's rules (unwritten) were jolly good ones including that all occupants should contribute towards the efficient work of the Hut and that the youngest or most junior members (whether they were tigers or rabbits on the rocks) should do the tiresome and dirty jobs.'

A.B. Hargreaves, 1948 C.C.J.

'Before breakfast I would do the Great Gully on Craig yr Ysfa and then, after some breakfast, on to Idwal Slabs - Holly Tree Wall - Central Arete - Glyders -Bristly Ridge - Tryfan - down Grooved Arete and back to Helyg. Every precious moment was squeezed out of our week-ends - youth, vigour, ambition and the joy of living in our mountains meant so much to us.'

Alf Bridge, 1949 C.C.J.

At the opening of Ynys Ettws on 20th May 1950:

'... there can be no doubt that the hut is worthy of the Club and of the years of hard work put into its planning and construction. Some conservatives pined for the sunlit lavatory of Helyg, and all viewed the palatial electric drying room with a profound suspicion, which was deepened by the fact that it had short circuited the better part of North Wales on the previous evening; but among the innovations the shelves in the dormitory, the bath of normal shape, and the large kitchen with its fine fireplace were particularly admired. The bunks are comfortable. The hut has nothing that can quite compare with Helyg's view of Tryfan...'

R.M.V. in the 1950 C.C.J.

'Dear Sir,

I read with horror the proposal that all the rocks of Wales should be explored and described in the same detail as the climbs round Helyg...'

J.N. Mills, 1951 C.C.J.

'Geoffrey Winthrop Young was living in Cambridge in those days. His influence, combined with that of the Climbers' Club and Helyg directed the attention of a particularly brilliant generation of Cambridge mountaineers to North Wales. The flourishing of the Cambridge Club, coming on top of Pigott's exploits, gave a great impulse to Welsh rock climbing.'

H.E. Kretschmer. The Mountains of Snowdonia, Second Edition. 1948.

'When staying at Helyg a venerable C.C. member once criticised Harding for climbing continually to the exclusion of mountain walking. On returning late that evening Harding and Dyke announced that they had been over Tryfan, Glyder Fach, down to the Pass and back over Glyder Fawr. "Very good", was the reply, "but you have taken a rather long time — a good walker would have been back in four hours". They had in fact done thirty climbs up, and sometimes down, routes on Tryfan, Glyder Fach, Craig Nant Peris, Dinas Mot, Carreg Wastad - up Bryant's Gully, down the Idwal Slabs and up Bochlwyd Buttress, finishing up Soap Gut in the dark. But it was not opposition of this type that deterred Harding. Guide-book work was the cause:

"Cloggy had faded into the background. The little crags and easy routes (of the Pass) had to be surveyed: some eighty in all... On our last day we took a holiday and raced over to Cloggy after tea to climb Curving Crack; it was a sheer pleasure to climb for once without the inevitable notebook and pencil".'

The Black Cliff. Crew/Soper/Wilson, 1971.

Above: Peter Harding and Alf Bridge.
Below: Peter Harding (snoozing) and Tony Moulam (with glasses).

A WELSH THREE-THOUSAND

PETER HARDING

THIS is the result of one of those very persuasive letters which one receives occasionally from a journal editor.

An article please, but what shall I write about? What can I write about? Wales or the Lake District? How long shall the article be? Something like 3,000 words; it sounds simple enough. And yet I have had no hair-raising escapes, no incredible falls. It is going to be difficult. Some climbers seem gifted to write whole chapters on 'My Most Difficult Climb' or 'A Day on the Milestone.' When I set off, pen in hand, on such an expedition I invariably wake up a few hours later having had a wonderful time; but with the paper in front of me still blank. But let's get started. Only a number of words fit together into some sort of sense or nonsense. Let's start with my first real visit to Helyg.

It was before Whitsuntide, 1946, when I met Richard Myers at the Black Rocks, near Matlock. That was my favourite week-end spot when I wasn't in Wales or the Lakes. A few hours' climbing kindled a strong flame of friendship and we were planning a holiday together. What about going to Wales at Whitsuntide?

Normally, guests were not allowed at Helyg during Bank Holidays, but this one promised to be slack: it might be arranged. All went well and I had high hopes as I set off with Tony Moulam on my motorcycle. The weather was perfect. Tony was staying at Tyn-y-Weirglodd, the Manchester University hut near Llyn Quellyn. It was late that afternoon when I wished him 'good climbing' at the gate of T-y-W and turned towards Helyg. I met Richard a few hundred yards from the hut, pushing his overladen cycle along the road. In a few moments Helyg was unshuttered and a mighty meal was being prepared with the aid of the North Wales Power Co. The remainder of that evening sped by with photographs and climbing talk. We were the sole occupants until John Barford's party arrived in the early hours. Another brew of tea and with thoughts of Cloggy we turned in.

The morning fulfilled the promise of the evening; weather perfect. A large breakfast was quickly put away and we were crammed in Peter's car, bound for Llanberis. It was my first visit to du'r Arddu and I had a queer feeling in the pit of my stomach. I still experience that same feeling before tackling the crux on a hard 'V.S.' As we ambled up the long track by the side of the Snowdon railway I listened to the experts talking. I chanced to overhear John's question to Richard. "What's the new chap like?" Richard's answer was embarrassing: I should have to give good account of myself.

Eager eyes waited for the crag to appear and when it did finally rise into view above the gentle slope of Cwm Brwynog, the impressions made upon me by the guide book were deepened. Here was Cloggy, in the rock, more vivid, more impressive than ever a camera-captured image could be.

We rested by the tiny llyn and ate our sandwiches and chocolate, gazing across at the awe-inspiring slabs of the West, the sheerness of the East. I could hardly wait for the pundits to announce the name of our route. It was to be the Great Slab, with a look at the recent Central Rib.

At the top of the scree, below the crag, we all changed into rubbers and Michael Ward led off for the first party. The smooth way in which he flowed across the 'qualifying step' gave no hint of its latent difficulty and the others followed quickly and with no fuss. Richard tied on the business end of our rope, and with a grin and a long stride was out of sight. Then my turn came. I found the step across more awkward than it had been made to look, but the rope above made things friendly.

Once one is off the ground on Cloggy, the angle seems to relent; the cliff appears to yield after the initial advances and give one time to pluck up courage for the next moves. The view down past the Llyn into the peaceful Cwm is relaxing and the comical little engine with its queer carriages and faintly discernible heads, relieves the seriousness of the position. I have grown to like that engine from the Cloggy viewpoint.

I was invited to lead the next pitch, up by the edge of the Bow-Shaped Slab. It was easy work. Richard came through and across the traverse to the pastures. That looked more difficult, I thought, and it was perhaps due to my thinking that I didn't find it so.

The advance party was already up the difficult corner and I discovered that it was again my turn to lead. One look at the wet and greasy corner and I decided rubbers were best attached to the waist loop. The pitch wasn't made any easier by the audience of experts on the ledge above and their gasps intimated that I was not paying enough respect to the crux. It went without too much bother.

The whole party gathered on the ledge while John tried the fierce looking crack leading onto the Central Rib. After one or two playful attempts he retired through lack of 'zip' as he put it. Peter took over from the rear and quickly disappeared from view. From time to time tufts of grass floated down; the only indications of his progress. Suddenly the rope ran out more quickly and a faint shout heralded victory. The others followed leaving Richard and myself. It was an impressive place. By some odd mishandling of the rope I was still attached to the business end. Richard belayed meaningly and I went into a clinch with the crack. It proved to be much easier than it looked but the greasy groove above had a disconcerting tendency to push one back onto the Great Slab. The lead was a fairly long one, ninety feet; with the usual amount of vegetation. How grand it was to emerge onto the rib and see clean grey rock stretching towards the summit. Richard joined me and, after a scathing remark about my belay, which he lifted from its grassy perch with one hand, we set off towards the sun. The rest was sheer delight.

I was thrilled with my first acquaintance with the cliff. My appetite was whetted, so we gathered in coils and followed the others down by the Eastern Terrace. We all scrambled round to the foot of the Curving Crack. This was a climb which I had longed to see and I was just a little disappointed. From the pictures I had seen of the notorious crack, I expected it to be halfway up the cliff, exposed, with scree beneath, hundreds of feet away. And it was the first pitch — with a soft grassy landing. We all sat down to watch Michael perform. A very smart line in laybacks saw it go in a matter of seconds; Peter followed and John descended into the sun for an 'armchair ascent'. Richard and I tossed a coin to see who should lead. I won, but after a very rigid mathematical proof that I was really on the leading end of the rope, I gave in and jammed up the crack marvelling at the wonders of applied mathematics. First pitch or not, it is a fine crack and the whole climb made a perfect finish to a grand day. I shall always enjoy, as I have done many times since, those gloomy middle pitches followed by that exhilarating arête at the top and the exit onto the sunny slopes of the terrace. It was a happy and somewhat tired climber who sat in P.Y.G. that night, drinking and listening to the technical conversation of 'les chefs de cordée'.

The next day accentuated the fineness of the previous one. It was perhaps more typical of Wales. The good weather had broken. This time it was to be the Llanberis cliffs; Richard and I took the motorcycle round to Pont-y-Gromlech while the others came by car. Dinas Mot was the first objective — another new acquaintance for me. The weather dictated boots, John dictated Western Slabs (in rubbers!) and after hearing a vague verbal description we were left alone to decide. They were going to do The Cracks. Not knowing any better, Richard and I ascended directly from the left-hand side of the wall. We found afterwards that we had added the Direct Start, but it was no more difficult than the rest of the climb. It was indeed a very attractive route and I came across my first piton in a crack above the first ledge. I made a resolution to return and extract it. Near the bridge of the Nose we met the other party coming round on the Girdle. They descended Western Gully and disappeared in the direction of the 'three cliffs' while we put on the top pitch of our climb. By that time it was raining heavily and we rapidly descended to spend an hour talking and shivering beneath one of the large boulders. Then, resigned to a soaking, we walked across to the 'Grochan,' to watch John and Co. at work on the Bluebell Traverse. There was no sign of them when we reached the foot of the cliff so we ascended by a route called Nea. It turned out to be an ideal climb for that day; harder than Western Slabs we thought, under the conditions. Its many trees completed the job of soaking us.

Before returning home the next day, amusing hours were spent in Helyg watching the rope tricks which are so wittily described by Eric Shipton in last year's *Journal*.

It was a memorable holiday, for it was the beginning of many things; climbs and friendships. The rest of the year was full of both these things.

Two months later I was again at Helyg, this time for a longer stay. Craig yr Ysfa was visited and the Amphitheatre Wall remembered for its Pinnacle and the effect of the rough work on bare legs. With Tony I scrambled all over the Nose of Dinas Mot, removing my piton and climbing everything except Diagonal Route. Cloggy was in perfect condition after a dry spell and Longland's was ascended when a rescue alarm was found to be a damp firework. The Narrow Slab, on a day when we considered Pigott's too serious an undertaking for a party of two. A remarkable day! It was then that I first learned to appreciate that funny little engine. We were alone on the cliff save for an unseen party on Longland's. Tony was patiently sitting at the foot of the Narrow Slab proper, secured to the Dinas Mot piton and little else. I was on the slab with nearly fifty feet of rope out; on the difficult part. And I *was* finding it difficult. I sensed the seriousness of the position, the exposure, the minuteness of the holds. My finger tips started to perspire. Then I looked across the Cwm. Without warning, the little engine chugged noisily and painfully into sight, and I started to laugh. That comical contraption had relieved the stress; lightly I stepped across to the corner and up, further to the very edge then onto a stance. I mused what a brilliant lead it must have been when Maurice Linnell first did it, and I looked at my engine and laughed again.

The days flashed by, crowded with climbs hard and easy. The last few were a fine climax.

All my friends had returned and it was during a solo day in Cwm Idwal that I met Nic. It was not our first meeting, but we had never climbed together. A day on Glyder Fawr was planned. The weather was rather grim, cold and squally, as Nic led the way towards Bochlwyd. I guessed that he had mistaken my clumsy pronunciation of Fawr and followed without comment. On Glyder Fach we started up the Chasm route, with occasional hail. I was very much impressed by the steep groove on the left, and tried to study it as we ascended. So this was the notorious Lot's Groove. Even the weather couldn't damp my enthusiasm for attempting it and tried to persuade my companion that it would go easily. He was not convinced, but tied on at the foot of the Chimney. The next few moments went by quickly. I was so absorbed with the delightful technicalities of the climb that I didn't notice the wind and the rain. Running belays on the spikes below the overhang, curious

spiral bridging movements above, then I was at the top. It started to rain again, the wind howled and hail stung my face and hands. I yelled for Nic to follow. He answered that it was no climb for a man nearly fifty, in boots, in bad weather. But he was of stern stuff and really wouldn't have missed it. At thirty feet he stopped for some time then started to descend slowly. I think he must have started on the wrong foot. It was so cold that I could hardly hold the line. I daren't open my eyes for the hail beating at my face. I said an inward prayer and hoped he wouldn't fall off. He didn't. He rested in the Chasm then announced that he was coming again. This time he meant it and I could hardly take the rope in fast enough. His face appearing above the overhang was a sight which matched the roughness of the day. I shall always remember Nic coming over the top, his shirt tails flying and one leg of his tattered plus-fours completely torn off, flapping round his ankle. A satisfying climb: the last I was to do with him.

Back in Helyg I met Charles. He, too, had stayed on after his companions and the next day we climbed the Hanging Garden Gully together: a lazy ascent, talking, smoking, admiring the scenery and getting damp. Later we descended into the Devil's Kitchen to have a look at Advocate's Wall. It was a proper climber's look and landed us at the top of the first pitch! The route ascends the right wall of the Kitchen directly from the Waterfall pitch, in magnificent position. The outlook is superb and this, coupled with the seeming doubtfulness of the rock adds up to perhaps the finest climb on these cliffs or in Cwm Idwal. There wasn't much of a belay on the first stance, but Charles encouragingly tied a loop in the rope and sat on it. I must confess that I didn't like the look of the next few feet which consisted of a steep traverse beneath a large block. I speculated on the stability of the structure. That pitch was led morally by Charles and only physically by me. Once across I felt happier and the short ascent to a good stance and belay was much easier than I had anticipated. The whole thing does not demand a very advanced technique but is quite intimidating to those not familiar with Clogwyn y Geifr. Charles followed and led through to the foot of a short, overhanging chimney. This looked hard, but the thought of things below melted any difficulty and I was soon scrambling up a groove which must be a botanist's paradise. It was dark when we descended by the llyn to the road and dear old Helyg.

Shortly after midnight the peace of the hut and its two occupants was disturbed by the arrival of a large car containing Ivan and Mac. They were there on business and it was unanimously agreed that the ideal place to test back-axles was a little track up to Hafotty Newydd — en route for Cloggy. That settled it; the occupants were to be tested on Pigott's. The drive round to Llanberis in the morning decided me that climbing, even on du'r Arddu, is not thrilling at all. I wondered what Dr. Johnson would have said, if while riding in his carriage below the horrifying slopes of Skiddaw he could have seen a monstrous car approaching along the narrow road, with Ivan at the wheel? Perhaps it would at least have been more printable than the expression of the Llanberis bus driver as he came widely round a corner of the pass to be confronted, for an instant, with such a spectacle. A white face, a frantic, belated effort to pull in, a whirr of stones and we were past with no more than an eyelash to spare on either side. Child's play to Ivan!

We were very fortunate again with the Cloggy weather. The delightful stroll up Cwm Brwynog and across the Maen d'ur Arddu put us in good trim. We donned our rubbers at the grassy foot of the East Buttress.

Pigott's is a grand climb for a large party. The green bays between pitches enable the rest of the party to watch the antics of the leader in mental and physical comfort. Those final pitches stamp the route as the classic of the East. It makes a fitting finish to the route and the day to take the continuation to the summit of the East Pinnacle. And a glorious finish to one's holiday to stand there with Llyn du'r Arddu a tiny pool far below.

The walk down to the farm, and further in the car to Llanberis was very different from the walk up. The leader's condition was then of no concern; he carried the rucksacks, he opened the gates.

But how are the words going? I must return from dreamy wanderings in Arfon. The object is achieved: the editor's whim is satisfied, I hope.

We have exactly the right number; three thousand words.

EXTRACTS FROM
THE GREAT ESCAPE

TONY HUSBANDS

It may seem hard to believe but when I was at Cambridge I never knew there was a Mountaineering Club. I associated mountaineering with people like Smythe and Odell and Mount Everest and not a youth like myself whose only contact with a mountain had been to be taken up Snowdon on a train one very cloudy day.

Robin Plackett was on my staircase but being a year senior I did not really get to know him very well. I hope he will forgive me when I say that, from time to time, someone would mention that he was a climber and this seemed very funny to us. Apart from the fact that it was rumoured he could climb into his room after the gates were locked we couldn't see any point in it. After all it could not be a serious pastime such as rowing was to us with our first boat Head of the River and five Blues in the University VIII. I should have thought it even more of a joke if someone had suggested to me that within five years I would be climbing in the Alps with Robin on a C.C. meet.

Being supposed to have a little knowledge of chemistry and not exactly perfect eyesight I was sent from Cambridge to Runcorn. It would be difficult to imagine a greater contrast. Apart from anything else the air at Runcorn had a perpetual odour of leather tanneries and chemicals but there was no point in bothering about that when people were being killed all the time by enemy action.

Paul Burt was one of the chemists. He had been in the C.U.M.C. and was a member of the C.C. As he had no one to climb with he had persuaded John Whittaker to try but they needed someone else as the afternoon shift always caused a problem and one evening when we were on morning, day and night shift respectively they persuaded me to cycle out to Helsby with them.

We did a few easy climbs which I found rather enjoyable and even led a V. Diff. They pointed out a fierce looking crack and said that Menlove Edwards and Colin Kirkus would cycle over from Liverpool and lay back up it. I didn't know who they were but they sounded like super-men.

We went again from time to time but they said it was not really like the proper thing in North Wales and John said he would arrange to take me there one weekend if I could get a pair of boots. This was a problem because it meant parting with some clothing coupons for something one could only use a few days each year. Anyway I decided to take the plunge and wrote to Robert Lawrie at Newark to ask if

140

he could help. He wrote back to say that he could make a pair for £4.12.0. (£4.60) and I accepted.

A novice climber was not faced with any problem with regard to equipment. There wasn't any. Lawrie had nailed the boots with something new he had managed to make as nearly as possible like a number 5 Tricouni which he hoped would be an improvement on a clinker. In fact the steel was too soft and they wore down rather quickly.

We were allowed nine days leave each year and on the basis of a 5½ day week (although we always did a full six days minimum 54 hours and 70 hours on the night shift) it meant you couldn't have two weeks holiday a year unless you worked Christmas day and Boxing day which would enable you to have two more days in lieu. Most of us preferred to have one week's holiday and two three-day week-ends and one three-and-a-half-day week-end. We had a two-day week-end every other week-end as the Saturday was taken as the day off at the end of one week but this wasn't enough time to get to Helyg and back so John and I took a day's leave to make it worth while.

I remember we took a train to Bangor and one from there to Bethesda (who will believe that today?) and after surprisingly managing to get a good lunch at a pub — it should be remembered that food was strictly rationed and 'meals out' were very difficult to get — we pushed our bicycles up the Nant Ffrancon and did one or two climbs on the Milestone before pedalling down to Helyg.

The next day we spent on Tryfan and the day after on Glyder Fawr culminating in a successful ascent of Central Arete (Grade D) which we thought a great achievement considering how desperately cold it was as it snowed.

After that week-end I thought I ought to try to obtain a rope and there was a rumour that Brigham was occasionally able to supply cotton ropes. Not exactly ideal because to have the necessary strength they had to be about ¾", say about 18mm., in diameter but there was nothing else so I wrote to Brigham and he said he would let me know when he could supply one as it might be anything up to a year. I was pleasantly surprised when he wrote about three months later to ask if I would like a 120' rope which would cost £1.15.0. (£1.75).

Glad as I was to have it I can assure younger readers that on wet days it picked up moisture very readily and so it is perhaps not so surprising that when it was wet we seldom climbed anything much harder than Severe because of the sheer weight of the rope at the end of a 100' run out, coupled with the fact that we had no runners. In any case we hadn't any karabiners.

If we didn't feel too happy on wet rocks we sometimes took our boots off and did a bit in socks although this was a last resort as it wore holes in them and that meant using up more clothing coupons to buy new ones. If the rocks were dry we would put on an old pair of gym shoes.

Paul used to say that nice as North Wales was one needed to go to Scotland in winter to get some experience on snow and ice so I put an advert in the North Wales Weekly News for an ice axe. Happily Frank Lockwood saw it and offered to sell me his Simond for £3 so the next time we went to Helyg we cycled up to his house beside Pen-y-Gwryd and collected it. I still use it occasionally.

We had been working all this time on poison gases and although it was difficult to conceive that there could be anything worse than mustard, which is in fact liquid, rumours were reaching us that there was something infinitely worse and we realised that production was being slowed down although we weren't sure if this was due to the fact that we already had huge stocks and the tanks in the underground stores in the Flintshire hills were getting nearly full to capacity.

Anyway much to my annoyance I was suddenly told I was going to be transferred to Woolwich Arsenal. This meant that I was parted from my friends and put at a still greater distance from the hills and to start off I knew no one.

However I met John Barford and he took me to Harrison's rocks and by using the night trains we did get to North Wales occasionally. The trains up were not too bad but on the return they always seemed full. We seldom got a seat and had to sit on the floor in the corridor or in the guard's van and on at least two occasions had to stand all night.

Climbing with John was an education because he had one or two karabiners and so could use runners. He also had the ability to make one climb better than one thought one could. Lliwedd was still popular then and on a fine day John used to like to sing on this cliff and I can hear him now singing his way up Bowling Green Buttress and the Sword but his real interest lay in the Pass.

His guide to the Three Cliffs appeared in the 1944 Journal but he wanted to produce a pocket guide to all the cliffs in the Pass and we spent some time checking the lengths of pitches of known climbs and trying new ones. Sadly he never lived to complete the work. He was convinced that the cliffs in the Pass and Cloggy would become more popular after the war and that there would be a need for a hut and we visited the ruins of Ynys once or twice to measure the walls in order to experiment with plans. In spite of the short stays and the deadline of having trains to catch we always allowed time to give Helyg a clean before leaving. John was Secretary of the C.C. from 1939-1946 and the first Secretary of the B.M.C. His death was a great loss to British climbing and not least to all his many friends.

1981 C.C. Journal.

EVEREST MEMORIAL AT HELYG

EVEREST PLAQUE AT HELYG
K. A. Crowther

To the Editor, "Climbers' Club Journal."

DEAR SIR,

The part that members of the Club had played in the assaults of Everest deserved, I felt, some permanent memorial and the Committee agreed that the walls of Helyg might most fittingly display it. When approached, my handicraft master, Mr. Eric Saunders, accepted the job with enthusiasm, and his finished work is seen on the opposite page. The board is of fumed oak and the carving is copied from the air photograph which was printed in the Journal of the R.G.S. Our intention was to follow the chronological order of the expeditions from the top to the bottom of the board but unfortunately my original list was incomplete and it was necessary to add the names of Kempson, Wood-Johnson and Finch after the other names had been carved: the error in the spelling of Wood-Johnson (due to reliance upon the index in W.H. Murray's 'Story of Everest') has now been corrected: as has also the omission of a year in Shipton's long sequence and of a second year for Warren. Mr. Saunders has shown the greatest patience and skill in making these amendments. I hope the board will be of interest to those who 'come after.' I believe that during these 32 years, between 60 and 70 Europeans (including the solitary eccentrics), shared in the great adventure, so that the Club has a record of which it may well be proud.

Yours sincerely,

Harrogate Grammar School.   H.R.C.C.
20th December, 1954.

HELYG FROM THE FIFTIES

'On 13th August, 1950, Philip Harvey fell and was killed when climbing Tennis Shoe climb alone..... after completing his period of military service was about to begin his training as a doctor, the profession of his father.

He had a deep and sincere love of mountains, of their solitude and beauty, and great affection for the companionship and the sense of common interest he found at Helyg.'

W.E. Radcliffe, 1951 C.C.J.

'H.P. Koch was killed in an accident in the Central Trinity Gully of Snowdon on Easter Saturday, 1951.....

.....After the war, he started to climb afresh, trying to take up the threads where he had left them as a boy, in the Dolomites. He joined the club in 1945, and took part in an A.C. Meet. I met him on crags in the Lakes and Wales, and we shared a Christmas search party on Snowdon. —

But the come-back gathered momentum and purpose only when he met G.F. Peaker at Helyg. Climbs in Wales were followed by an Alpine campaign culminating in the great West-East Traverse of Mont Blanc, and a friendship developed that meant a great deal to Peter, not only in mountaineering terms. Among those who philosophise on climbing it has long been a bone of contention whether climbing is more a means of escaping oneself or of finding oneself. It may be that the two are inseparable.'

R.E. Meyer, 1952 C.C.J.

Talking of Will McNaught:

'He was often at Helyg from the start; in the photograph of the opening ceremony he stands beside the tree, looking down upon the rest of us, no doubt with a merry twinkle in the eyes behind the spectacles and with a sly dig at old Marples coming from the lips. On one of those early visits he walked up from Dolgarrog an hour or two before the Cowlyd dam burst causing terrible destruction in that valley; it was a lucky escape for him.'

H.R.C. Carr, 1954 C.C.J.

Even in humour Helyg is always there:

'That night there was a green sunset, and great snakes wormed out of their fastnesses on the Cliffs of Llewyd as all nature stood hushed while the Spirit of the Mountain brooded over Capel Curig. "Cor ad cor loquitur," murmured Hargreaves, as he set off on the lonely walk to Helyg. He was deeply moved. We were all moved. Even Longland who had walked over from King's Lynn to collect a forgotten pipe was moved. It was a moving experience.'

Kevin FitzGerald, 1954 C.C.J.

'To celebrate the ascent of Mount Everest by a party containing seven members of the Climbers' Club, all members of the successful expedition were invited to spend the week-end of the 17th October in Wales as guests of the Club..... The hardy Himalayan mountaineers with sybaritic unanimity declined the offer of accommodation in the Club huts and stayed at P.Y.G.

R.M. Viney, 1954 C.C.J.

'From Helyg, Youth Hostels and camps, the post-war climbers practised their craft, and the last of the army mountain training school pushed up the limits, culminating in Preston's Suicide Wall.'

A.J.J. Moulam, 1955 C.C.J.

'At Helyg in March, Tony Moulam was the host; there was a lot of snow, and some ascended the North Gully of Tryfan. However, rather too much food was provided.....'

Alan Blackshaw, 1956 C.C.J.

'As a memorial to Tom Bourdillon and Dick Viney, who were killed in the Alps in 1956, a framed and mounted map has been hung on the wall of Helyg.'

A.K. Rawlinson, 1958 C.C.J.

'We must record also the retirement from office of Stuart Chantrell, custodian of Helyg since 1928. No man has served his fellow members, and indeed all those, notably the university clubs, who use Helyg more devotedly or for a longer period. His retirement seems scarcely credible: Chantrell has been as much part of Helyg, and Helyg climbing, as Adam and Eve of Tryfan. We thank him, both for making for us at Helyg the beloved base of many of our happiest Welsh days and for his counsels in Club affairs over so many years. Moulam succeeds with all our good wishes.'

A.K. Rawlinson, 1957 C.C.J.

It would be hard to name anyone whose absence will be more sadly felt in the mountaineering world than General Bruce. To everyone he will be remembered for his Himalayan achievements, but to many in his club there will be the more compelling memory of personal friendship at home. A splendid raconteur, no mountaineering club dinner could be considered complete without him; typical was the remark heard at a Northern dinner which evoked French's cartoon in the 1931 journal, "When in London I go to Richmond Park, and don't return till I have put a chalk-mark on the tails of at least three deer." Above all he was fond of his native Wales, and he took an active part in the foundation of Helyg and was, of course, present at the opening ceremony of the extension in 1933. The kindliest and happiest of men, he was never happier than when introducing novices to the hills.'

'My descent to the road was literally painfully slow in the near dark but later, at Helyg, I contentedly deciphered my notes from this last day's fieldwork for the Cwm Idwal guide.'

'A long summer holiday before I became a student at Manchester University gave me a flying start and I had sufficient time thereafter to keep in good trim. Thus the originally long walks to the main crags soon seemed commonplace and I thought nothing of going from Helyg straight over the summit of Carnedd Dafydd to reach Cwm Llafar. It is perhaps not surprising that I had difficulty in persuading friends to come scratching in the mud and heather for routes old and new, particularly as the Three Cliffs were so near the road and exciting things were going on there.

A.J.J. Moulam, 1959 C.C.J.

'No one would recognize Helyg to-day from its earlier description, with its bright paint, several rooms, library, ghost and electrical appliances, and there is even a form of religious faith abroad that one day the chimney will stop smoking. The bath too, is a highly efficient instrument of torture. Being square, it forces one to sit bolt upright, and as it is supplied by a completely inadequate hot-water cistern the hopeful newcomer is left shivering in a chilly three-inch puddle of water. At present only Thomas in the Climbers' Club is of sufficient stature to fill it by displacement. Similar blessings can be enjoyed at the Climbers' Club hut at Ynys Ettws in the Llanberis Pass, and at the Rucksack Club hut at Beudy Mawr in the same valley: and the innumerable other huts owned by these and smaller clubs all over Wales are only slightly less luxurious, which may account for the rumour that climbers seldom wash.'

The Greased Pole, Snowdon Biography. Geoffrey Sutton, 1957.

'There is an entry in the log-book at Helyg in which Edwards described nineteen routes for ascending the little boulder in the Helyg grounds. This includes every possible way, every permutation by which any more or less normal human being could possibly ascend this rock. This painstaking thoroughness is typical of the man.'

The Greased Pole, Snowdon Biography. Geoffrey Sutton.

'Those who know only the present Helyg with its spacious dormitory added in 1933, with its electric lighting, heating and cooking, and with hot and cold water laid on, would hardly recognise the original one-room Helyg with a river flowing across its stone-flagged floor in any weather, except after prolonged drought.'

Bryan Donkin.

'After the first World War, at the instigation of Herbert Carr, the Climbers' Club bought an old cottage called Helyg and turned it into the first successful climbing 'hut' in the country. It was the beginning of a new era.....'

Charles Evans, 1958, in 'Snowdonia'.

FRIENDSHIP IN THE MOUNTAINS

M. BORUSHKO AND E. GIPPENREITER

(translated from *Soviet Sport*, 21-22 July, 1960)

In a few days, in the mountains of North Wales, John Hunt will solicitously place on the cold jutting edge of the rock little squares of chocolate and turning to the Soviet climber behind him will repeat with a friendly smile the words from the film, spoken by Ushba: "An inexplicable people. Do you always look after each other, or only in moments of great trial? This question gives me no rest whenever I see people on these cliffs."

On the way to North Wales we visit the ancient University town of Oxford, we have a look at the little house-museum in Stratford-on-Avon which is Shakespeare's birthplace, become acquainted with the scientific research laboratory in Wolverhampton where one of the English mountaineers, John Neill, works.

In the Ogwen Valley (sic)

The mountain hut in the Ogwen valley is even comfortable: comfortable two-tier bunks, a kitchen/dining room with a gas cooker, and the traditional fireplace, and even a wash basin and bath.

As usual we do our morning exercises alone. Reporters and television cameramen lie in wait for us. They particularly like our energetic knees bends.

The *Daily Mail* has an article under the heading: 'Russian Mountaineers Start The Day With Intensive Gymnastics, Introducing Into Their Drill Touches of Russian Folk Dancing, And Then They Bathe In the Icy Water Of The Mountain Torrent.'

There is entire self-help in the hut. The typical English breakfast, which tastes good, bacon and eggs, is cooked by the first man on duty, the volunteer John Hunt. Michael Borushko helps him. Apparently we're to the liking of the commander of the hut, Jack Nelson.

"I have never met any Russians before," he said to the reporters, "but these lads are wonderful. We British climbers were still stretching and yawning after breakfast, when we suddenly found that all the washing-up had been done by the Russians."

'Finally, what bastion is it that we are now supposed to be defending if we oppose the motion? The huts are mixed all round, whether Helyg goes that way or not is at the discretion of the Committee as the motion suggests, but what bastion is there that the people who do not want to admit women are now thinking that they are defending. It cannot even be the lavatories, because the lavatories at the Alpine Club are incomparably worse (laughter) than any of the huts managed by the Climbers' Club. Most of us in our homes if we do not actually live at Chatsworth do not in fact normally separate the female members of our families and make them use a quite different elsan (laughter). Let us not be in this extraordinary situation in which we shall have to be taught a lesson. Thank you. (Applause.)

Sir Jack Longland at the 1975 A.G.M. Women Membership Debate.

'An impressive group of hard men developed round Hugh. They climbed nearly all but the hardest climbs without ropes including an impressive corner called Flake Crack, which had a hard finish. The first custodian of the Climbers' Club hut, Helyg, in the Ogwen Valley had fallen fifty feet to his death from the finishing holds on to the unyielding sandstone boulders at the bottom. Later on it claimed another victim. The Helsby lads took perhaps 90 seconds to climb it and thought nothing of it. But I was then the custodian of Helyg and being superstitious never led the climb even though it was only graded Hard Severe.'

Trevor Jones, 1974 C.C.J.

'I have the happiest memories of Helyg, where I often stayed, especially before 1930. Then, I took up gliding; Morland and I built our own sailplane - 2,000 hours, in evenings and weekends; I did a 35-mile cross-country flight in it. After the war I returned to climbing, mostly with Kevin FitzGerald; but then we usually stayed at P.y.G. Mention of Kevin reminds me: I wonder how many have read his thriller, "Throne of Bayonets"? The story begins with a thinly-disguised description of P.y.G. and with Chris Briggs, and goes on to dramatic (and lethal) action on Lliwedd.'

Dr. H.L. Richardson, 1985.

'I was first introduced to the Idwal Slabs by A.B. Hargreaves, who sponsored my membership. From 1929 to 1939 I stayed at Helyg over 50 times.

I was introduced to Helsby by Colin Kirkus the day after a merry evening at a C.C. Northern Dinner in Liverpool. He routed me out at breakfast time. We cycled from Liverpool via Runcorn Transporter Bridge and back. At our 20th climb I failed through sheer exhaustion.

Bill Stallybrass.

'It has been well publicised that this is the 60th year of Helyg, but I would like also to remind you that it is the 10th year since we have had the pleasure of having lady members and enjoyed the benefits of their various contributions to the running of the club. I have been personally indebted to them on two particular occasions. There was one climb which particularly fascinated me, but I had been frightened of it for 50 years by the following description by G.D. Abraham: — 'The complete ascent should be left severely alone. Recent fatal accidents confirm the opinion that it is not a justifiable climb by reason of the peculiarly unreliable nature of the rock.....' It was at the 50th anniversary of Helyg that Marge led me up The Devil's Kitchen and I found out what a splendid expedition it is. Unfortunately my visions of a nice tete-a-tete picnic were dashed when Jack (Longland) and A.B. (Hargreaves) arrived to meet us at the top.

Ivan Waller, 1985 C.C.J.

'In conclusion I must mention the little things that the influence of Stuart Chantrell did for Helyg: the fir wood that John Watson planted and which now gives shelter from the east and north-east; the planting of daffs to make the springtime even more beautiful. There is no limit to what may be done by men of good will for the common good.'

Herbert Carr, 1985.

WANDERERS IN WALES

ROBERT CROOKALL

WE walk into Helyg late on a Friday night as though we had been there the week before — the water's still leaking from behind the sink, the fire will soon be filling the kitchen with smoke, the mattress covers are just that much dirtier than a year ago, and Tony Jones is almost certain to be there, the embodiment of the spirit of Helyg at its most rugged, secure and sincere - how lucky the Club and Helyg are to have him there.

What mental vignettes emerge as one looks back over eighteen years to that grim winter of 1963? Here are a few, adapted from diaries kept at the time.

Jan. 1963. Pen-y-Pass. Park the car. Never known such cold. Few people to be seen. Why not coffee in the hotel instead? We follow the Miners' Track. The ground is iron. A dislodged stone reverberates. Llyn Llydaw is frozen solid. No need to use the causeway. Path a sheet of ice. On to Glaslyn. Stop for food, sheltering in ruins of miner's cottage. Out of their mittens hands freeze in seconds. Dangerous to unzip. Whole mountain from here seems solid blue and green ice. We start cutting steps, but give up; we need all the daylight to return.

Jan. 1964. We are a large party. Bobby (doctor), Ray (education officer), Denys (bookshop proprietor), his two sons Jez and Bruce, my son David, Steve his friend, Barry (youth service). It is muggy and misty, with sloshy snow. Bobby insists on filming us slithering about. Aim - Snowdon via Cwm Glas and Clogwyn (we are at Ynys). Mist thickening. We have no idea where we are but push on, each keeping the man in front in sight. Reach a ridge. Are we east or north of Crib-y-ddysgl? We turn right; guess proves correct. By now we've had enough and seen nothing, so slither down the Pyg track. Tea at the hotel (as it was then). Never did tea taste so good.

Jan. 1965. Lie in sleeping bag listening to the gale. Hope Denys will brew up tea before conscience makes me do it. He does. Cold and clear we decide on Tryfan, via Heather Terrace because of the westerly gale. At Bwlch Tryfan we cannot cross the wall for the wind. Have to choose our moment and fight our way over. Tryfan seems impossible in this gale, so we follow the path to Llyn Bochlwyd.

Follow the stream down, the wind driving it back into our face. Exhausted by this time. Stagger back along the road, thumbing for lifts. Bloody motorists don't want hikers messing up their cars! Gale increasing. Thank God for Helyg's thick walls, and for tea.

Jan. 1966. A wash-out. Unceasing rain, sleet and wind all Saturday. We stay in, read, sleep eat, look at maps, talk, go to pub. Sunday the same but we must get our boots on once. Pack up, clean hut, go to Capel Curig. Follow Crafnant path for one hour until utterly soaked and frozen. Return to cars, mutter goodbyes, curse Wales, go home.

Jan. 1980. How nice to be back in Helyg. Weather perfect. Ground frozen hard. No wind. Sun with enough haze to add mystery to the landscape. For two days we explore the Crafnant region. The lake rivals Gwynant for peace and beauty and surroundings. Lovely heathery country to the north, rising to Creigiau Gleision above Llyn Cowlyd. Soft snow on heather and boulders makes progress slow and exhausting. We cut down through the plantation, discovering impressive falls, now hidden by trees from the valley. Hills encircling the lake to the west are warm, heathery, craggy, intriguing. Best views I've ever seen of the three main mountain groups. A great semi-circle with Hebog, Lliwedd, Snowdon, Crib Goch, the Glyders, the peak of Tryfan, the Carnedds, shining white above 1,500 feet in the afternoon sun. Grey, brown, purple below. A small patch of dark green, the copse sheltering Helyg.

1980 C.C.J.

SENIOR MEMBER

JOHN POOLE

I had the great good fortune to join the Club in 1920 on the introduction of one W.J. Williams, who had been an Original Member, and with whose son, the late Professor Gwyn Williams, I subsequently climbed on many occasions, at home, and abroad, including the Monch, the Jungfrau and the Eiger (by the Mitellegi Arete) also the Finsteraarhorn and many other peaks in the Oberland, the Valais, the Dolomites, etc. Joining the Club was a great milestone in my career as it opened the door through which I was introduced to many more companions. (Have you ever tried to open a door with a milestone?). Another milestone was a few years later when I married and found to my delight and relief that although she knew nothing about mountaineering until then, except what I had told her, my wife took to climbing with a great aptitude and has been my companion on a very large proportion of the climbing I have done since. I had gone to live in London shortly before my marriage and thus had the opportunity of making contact with more of my fellow members of the Club and I soon found myself on the Committee and soon after that for a couple of years as Honorary Secretary. I joined the Alpine Club in 1931, the same year as my wife became a member of the Ladies Alpine Club, and with the recent take-over bid by the A.C. of the L.A.C. she and I are now both members of the Alpine Club.

Two of my closest companions in those early days were Will McNaught and M.G. Bradley. I climbed with them (not in fact often with both at the same time) on innumerable occasions in Wales and also many times (especially McNaught) in the Alps. One or two reminiscences of them: I was once taking McNaught and a young woman friend of ours, Biddy Deed, up the Chasm Route on Glyder Fawr and as we approached the Vertical Vice McNaught said what a terrible situation he found himself in. When I asked why, he said "Well, Vice above and Miss Deed below!" In the Dauphine, after the Ecrins, trudging home along the Bon Pierre glacier, McNaught said it was getting Bon Pierre and Bon Pierre. In the Englehorner, while we were staying with Bradley at Rosenlaui, G.R. Speaker took me and my wife and the aforementioned Biddy Deed up the Rosenlauistock. Bradley did not join us but he knew the climb well and he told us that on the way down we should have to abseil over an overhang called the Luftschwingort and that we should suspend the rope from a piton already there which was 'almost certainly safe'. We found the piton but it wobbled ominously as we tested it and resisted all attempt to drive it further in with a piece of rock (we had no hammer). So we had to risk it and I was nominated to be last man down on the principle that we could not leave the responsibility to either of the girls and it could not be Speaker as he was a better route-finder than I was and if he got killed I should be unlikely to get the party safely off the mountain. I had never abseiled so cautiously in my life as I did on that occasion and when I finally touched down felt greatly relieved that my wife had avoided or at least postponed widowhood.

But it is on my earliest climbing days that I really wished to dwell, as, I suppose like other octogenarians, I take great delight in recalling incidents of my youth. I must find room to refer to the many occasions when I stayed in Helyg in its earliest days. I remember being there once with my brother Harry and we came across a young man named Kirkus who was on his own so Harry and I condescendingly took him up the Pinnacle Rib on Tryfan Central Buttress and ensured his safety by putting him between us on the rope. He did the climb well enough. I climbed often with Charles Marshall, Helyg's first custodian, and my brother Gerard was probably the last member of the Club to see him alive as he visited him in hospital in Chester after Charles's calamitous fall at Helsby.

I think it was from Helyg that I made the first of my innumerable ascents of the Grooved Arete, this time leading George Lister to whom I had been introduced by Herbert Carr (to whom I owe so much, and so does the Club as he practically resuscitated it from oblivion when it nearly expired in the aftermath of World War 1) on my first visit to the Alps. This was before they had published their classic book 'The Mountains of Snowdonia'. Lister had a daughter named Eira, whom I first knew as a school-girl, and when she was old enough I took her up the Grooved Arete, Many years later, when I had retired from my job and come to live in Anglesey, I met her again, she having now married and produced a son who was then a medical student, and I took him up the Grooved Arete. I think there cannot be many people who have led three generations of the same family (except perhaps their own family), up the Grooved Arete.

I have just mentioned my retirement from work and coming to live in Anglesey and this must provide me with the opportunity to conclude this rambling article. When I came here in 1959 I learned of the existence of the Mountaineering Club of North Wales and made haste to join it and before I knew where I was I found I had become President, in succession to Charles Evans. In next to no time I had made a host of new friends, many of whom were first class climbers, and quite a number of these were exceedingly kind to me and took me up routes which, in my old age, were beyond my capacity to lead. Thus the M.C.N.W. did for me in my declining years what the C.C. had done for me in my youth and I shall never cease to be grateful to both clubs for the help and friendship I have had from them. I went on climbing up to Hard Severe standard until I was 70, then unhappily contracted osteo-arthritis in my right wrist and had to give up rock climbing altogether. But I still went on with my mountain walking until a couple of years ago when hardening of the arteries and other inevitable concomitants of incipient senility gradually overtook me and I am now reduced to ambling about on the lower slopes. But my enthusiasm for the mountains remains undimmed. So does my gratitude to the Climbers' Club, which has contributed so much to my happiness.

1980 C.C.J.

BREAKFASTS AT HELYG

RENNIE BERE

Editors are strange people. Some wait for articles to arrive. Others worry potential contributors until they eventually give in. Others again complain that no-one ever sends them anything. Geoff Milburn is different. One wet afternoon about two years ago he arrived at my home (the nearest house to the Compass Point crag on the culm coast of north Cornwall) carrying a cardboard box full of paper — 'papers' he would probably prefer me to say. 'Had I known Ted Hicks?' I had and was able to help with material for the article which he and A.B. Hargreaves wrote for the 1978 C.C.J. and which most members have probably read. The ideal editor I thought. He encourages you to waffle about climbs done many years ago and then does all the real work himself. But I was mistaken. One more visit and several letters later, there comes a suggestion. 'Would you feel like writing a nostalgic sort of article for us?'

Where do I begin? The last time I wrote for the C.C.J. was about East Africa — at least thirty years ago — and before that there was a long walk with my wife in the Sikkim Himalayas. So perhaps it should be Compass Point as I spent many hours long ago looking hopefully but helplessly at the face which now provides most of the climbs. Once, probably in 1935, I escorted my father to the end of the ridge and climbed the nose ('North Ridge') on a top rope — the first lead of which I know was by David Pasteur in 1962. I also climbed the easy 'Troy' and its variation solo, so the late Keith Darbyshire did not make the first ascent in 1974 as the guide books suggest. For a few years before I went to Africa (in 1930) I spent as much time as I could in North Wales or the Lakes without ever becoming a particularly good rock climber. But I was extremely lucky in the people with whom I climbed.

After two visits to the Alps with my parents and a few guided expeditions, I went up to Cambridge in the Autumn of 1926, joined the C.U.M.C. and, on a meet at Wasdale, was taken up my first British rock climb by Jack Longland — Kern Knotts Chimney if I remember correctly. Shortly afterwards I met Ted Hicks. I was walking along a road on the outskirts of Cambridge when I saw someone comporting himself rather strangely on the trunk of a tree. I stopped to watch. "Excuse me", I said, "but what are you doing?" It was Ted Hicks trying to solve a climbing problem. We were both in our first year and soon became firm friends, climbing together as often as we could in Wales, the Lakes and on Cambridge roofs. My home was then in the Isle of Wight which meant that I could not get to the mountains as often as Ted could from Birkenhead. However, we were soon climbing 'severes' and occasional 'very severes' which few people did in those days. One result of this was that on C.U.M.C. meets (which Ted usually avoided as he did not like being told what to climb or who to climb with) I was often in demand as a second by those who wished to try themselves out leading the harder routes — I recollect particularly some good days on the face of Scafell Pinnacle with Peter Lloyd.

One summer Ted came to stay with us in the Isle of Wight. We did a few nameless scrambles on the chalk cliffs and achieved, probably for the first time, the long traverse round Culver Cliffs from Sandown Bay to Bembridge. Expecting to come off — there was an awkward hand-traverse which had precipitated me into the sea on an earlier attempt — we climbed naked with some clothes tied to our heads in a turban. Whether the trouble was indecent exposure or a rescue attempt I do not know but we were hailed by a boat-load of coastguards and rapidly made for the top of the cliff and safety. When the boat had moved away, we came down again and completed the traverse without further complications.

In June 1929 Ted and I were at Helyg with Charles Warren and Archie Spence. After a day's climbing Ted decided that he wanted to spend the night alone on the Heather Terrace and to walk there barefoot. Would we meet him next morning on the top of Tryfan bringing his boots with us and a pair of 'rubbers' in case we should feel like climbing anything interesting. Ted then left us. There was no-one else in the hut, and while we were breakfasting next morning a stranger arrived from Liverpool on a bicycle. As he did not seem to have any food with him, we reluctantly asked him to share our meal. With dead-pan face the stranger said "I usually just eat bread fried in vaseline". And that was my introduction to Colin Kirkus.

The rest of that day has become a detail of climbing history. Charles led us up one of the standard Tryfan ridges and insisted that Colin should rope up, though he did not really see the point; we soon realised why and that we had with us a climber of quite unusual quality. We found Ted sitting on a rock between Adam and Eve studying his sore feet, but from that moment Colin took over. He first introduced us to Belle Vue Bastion and then took us to Glyder Fach where there was 'something interesting' he wanted to try. The result was the first ascent of Lot's Groove (by Colin and Ted alone) and an enjoyable foursome on the Direct Route where, according to the old guide book, the final crack was 'like all Gaul, divided into three equal parts'. Not long afterwards, when I was staying with Ted at Birkenhead and attending a C.C. dinner at which General Bruce was the principal speaker, Colin introduced me to Helsby which gave me a startling new view of climbing.

The Piton Route, Holly Tree Wall. Ted Hicks wearing loose 'plus-fours' with a canvas seat, leads on a historic route.

Right: Hicks at The Crevasse, Scafell Pinnacle Face during an ascent of the Girdle Traverse. Note the 'Bowie knife' used for cutting slings off the rope to thread round chockstones.   *Photos: R. Bere*

During those years with Ted we paid a few visits to Wasdale and climbed most of the better-known routes in Wales — does anyone now climb the superb Avalanche or Paradise on Lliwedd? My own most vivid recollection, however, is of becoming firmly and alarmingly stuck in the Monolith Crack when taking what was intended to be a quick and easy way down from Gribin — a singularly unpleasant experience, particularly when two rude and mocking individuals are threatening all sorts of indignities from above. We also started looking around at various exciting possibilities many of which were eventually incorporated into that surge of new climbs for which Colin, Ted, A.B. Hargreaves and Menlove Edwards were to be so largely responsible. But by that time — after a memorable early spring visit with Charles Warren to a completely snow-bound Skye — I was on my way to Africa and a very different way of life.

After nearly three years and frequent debilitating attacks of malaria, which was very prevalent in northern Uganda before the days of modern prophylaxis, I came home on leave early in 1933 and made for Helyg as soon as I could. There I met Menlove Edwards for the first time. "Are you RMB who used to climb with FEH?", he asked me — we tended to be known by initials rather than by names in those days — if so would I like to climb with him. His deeds on mountains were well known to me, and I was told that he was even capable of climbing feet-first into the sleeping loft of the old Helyg; so perhaps I should have known better. But I accepted with alacrity and followed him up Devil's Dump and several repeat climbs which I much enjoyed. Later Menlove and A.B. Hargreaves, an old friend, asked me to join them on the second ascent of Colin's Great Slab route on Clogwyn d'ur Arddu. What happened was described by A.B.H. in his obituary of Menlove in the 1958 C.C.J.

'Menlove made no bones at all about that slippery little slab and the long green caterpillar but it was when I joined him at the top of it that I first saw an exhibition of his enormous strength. Our third man, weighing fully fifteen stone, just made a dash at the slippery slope and shot off into space at the end of 150 feet of line... Menlove lifted that chap with his hands until he was able to get hold of something and be pulled back on to the climb by the fourth man. We then sacked number three and proceeded.'

I was the villain of that incident and my only complaint about the account is that I certainly did not weigh fifteen stone, though I must have felt like a ton at the end of that line. However, I met them at the top, and we then made the third ascent of Curving Crack without mishap.

Also that spring (18 March 1933) came the opening of the 'new' Helyg and the 'Reformation Banquet' at Pen-y-Gwryd. There were thirty or so members present including the then President, Dr. Tom Longstaff; the guest of honour was L.S.

Amery, politician and former Colonial Secretary. It was an excellent party with witty speeches by both Amery and Longstaff, and a talk by the latter on expedition techniques mainly for the benefit of those who were about to set off for the Gangotri Himalayas with Marco Pallis — the 1933 Everest expedition was already in Tibet. The next morning Colin Kirkus, Menlove Edwards and I found ourselves cooking breakfast for the whole party: sausage, bacon, eggs and bread fried without the vaseline. Whenever we produced a presentable platter we reserved it as the presidential breakfast and put it in the oven until there was another good enough to take its place. Members emerged sleepily and sat around — all except Longstaff who stayed in his bunk apparently asleep. The scene was the familiar one of climbers lounging about in various stages of undress, digesting their overlarge breakfasts, talking, smoking, putting things into their rucksacks and taking them out again — doing almost anything, in fact, except putting their boots on.

Eventually there were signs of life from the presidential bunk. The cooks rushed forward with their offerings only to be swept aside as Longstaff swung straight into his boots, ate a couple of spoonfuls of pemmican from a tin and demanded to know who was ready to start out for Lliwedd. Nobody was. With his red hair and bristling red beard, Longstaff could play to perfection the part of a fierce little man, but his natural aggression was tempered by a great sense of humour. He told the three of us that he had watched us slaving away at the stove, wasting our time on a lot of good-for-nothing layabouts — 'wastrels' was the word he used I think. Then he told the rest of the company what he thought of them which wasn't much. "Now let this be a lesson to you", he ended. "Do your boiling overnight!" Good fun and a strangely expressed thought but I must admit to having been influenced ever since by that extremely sensible advice — and not only in relation to food and mountains. I wonder how many others still remember that occasion almost exactly fifty years ago. A.B.H. who was there, will certainly do so.

I often look back at those years, and at the three climbers who dominated them so far as I was concerned. Both Colin Kirkus and Menlove Edwards had better records than Ted Hicks, and these extended over a far longer period. But Ted always looked the better and safer climber on difficult rock, though one hesitates to measure climbing in terms of style. Having reached his peak, Ted stopped climbing. This was partly because of an accident from which he escaped more or less unhurt. I suspect also that temperament came into it. Ted had a very secure personality. He found fulfilment easily enough in many spheres and not only on hard rock. I doubt if he could have committed himself totally to climbing for any length of time at what then appeared to be the limit of the possible — particularly so in view of the hopelessly inadequate safety precautions for leaders in those days. Menlove, the most remarkable climber of the three, was a complete contrast, and his life became a total disaster. It was Colin who genuinely found himself on the mountains, only to be killed on active service during the war. But I digress from my brief.

On my next leave (1935) I joined a C.C./O.U.M.C. Alpine meet, based on Lognan beside the Argentiere glacier. David Cox and Robin Hodgkin were in the party, and I recollect particularly climbs on the Aiguille d' Argentiere, the Aiguille Verte and a traverse of the Grepon led by David. We bivouaced on the Nantillons glacier before the climb and slept on the Montenvers station platform after it. Rain dripped through the roof, and I cannot pretend that we had a very comfortable night; nor were we popular with the stationmaster when he found us there in the morning.

By this time, my English home had moved to Cornwall. David then lived at Yelverton on the edge of Dartmoor, and that September we joined forces for an attack on the Devil's Rock of the Dewerstone in which he had been interested for some time. A splendid day produced the climb which has become known as Climbers' Club Ordinary. I don't know why — nor does David.

What happens nowadays? I wander on to the Downs to see if there is any activity on Compass Point. There usually is when the tide is out and the weather fair, and I watch climbers overcome almost nonchalantly problems unimaginable to my generation. Once there was Pat Littlejohn and Keith Darbyshire, a few days before the latter's death when climbing in West Cornwall. Then came Pete Whillance making the first ascent of Dreadlock Holiday, a beautifully controlled lead on very small holds. Afterwards over a drink, we talked and looked at some of my old photographs from earlier days. Standards may have changed but we still used the same language. While I was writing this article, Ashley Greenwood (for many years a member of the C.C.) paid us a visit. Together we watched another fine lead, up and over a savage little overhang. What would Menlove or Colin have made of it, I wondered. With modern harness and a well placed piton they would probably have managed but I doubt if many others would have done so. Today so many more are climbing to these new standards. I am indeed lucky, after more than half a century, to be able to keep in touch with this tiny fraction of modern developments.

MY HELYG TEN YEARS

TREVOR JONES

For a decade I was warden of Helyg - from 1962 to 1972. I admit that at first I used the pretence of getting away to looking after Helyg every week-end to escape the responsibilities of shouldering the burden of looking after two small children.

"I'm sorry dear, I really would like to go and see your mother on Saturday, but the Helyg garage roof has some slates off it."

"Isn't it wonderful your gran is 80 on Sunday. I wish I could be there, but unfortunately the builder is coming from Bethesda to give us a quote for the septic tank."

"I really wish you could come this week-end now the kids have gone to your mother, but it's a men-only meet at Helyg."

"By the way, the pipes have burst at Helyg. I really don't want to, but I'm forced....."

There's a wonderful crop of daffodils at the front of the hut in the spring. I used to take a bunch home with me, often with ice crystals still glinting in the flowers, and they didn't thaw out till the car heater raised the temperature; that is when I was allowed to drive, which seems a long time ago now that the police in Llanberis are so vigilant.

We built a big pile of stinking mattresses one week-end by the rhododendrons. Dafydd Williams Isaf rushed over with a pack of yapping sheep dogs and asked me in his best sing-song North Wales accent, "Are you on fire?".

Another week-end there was a school party staying in the hut; it was a horrible mess. The teacher in charge asked me in an off-hand tone, "Are you a member?". I thought I'd have apoplexy..... I stuttered for a few seconds, then let him have the verbal blast.

It's a pleasant way to get into Helyg by climbing over the metal gate and walking over the soft carpet of pine needles crunching underfoot. The trees were planted by Brian McKenna - a big man who died on Cnicht. I was one of the rescue party that found him. My brother Stan was the first person of the rescue party to reach him. Stan was a professional cyclist and thought you had to run up mountains as if it were another version of the Tour de France in which he had been the 'lanterne rouge' - the last man.

Tom Peacock had a low-slung car which caught on the edge of the road as he was pulling out from the garage; while he was inspecting the problem another car crashed into it at high speed - fortunately no-one was seriously injured. That's the reason for the concrete ramp now leading down into the car-park.

After a long day on Craig yr Ysfa, I was walking down the A5 back to Helyg where there was a university club staying. As I got closer to the hut I noticed someone on the roof. With a shriek of rage and a clumsy, loping stride, which is all that is possible when carrying a heavy rucksack I rushed to remonstrate. I was quite close before I realised it was only the chimney-pot. On the Monday I went to the optician's.

The best times on the hill while staying at Helyg were when I stayed there with Ralph Jones before the Welsh Dinner. We went slowly up the hillside because by then it was carpeted with bilberries and eating one's way uphill slows the pace to an acceptable level before tackling the Lower Amphitheatre Wall. On one occasion we went to try a new route in the Cirque. Exhausted from the walk I put the rucksack down. Wretched thing that it was, it promptly decided to roll off the ledge and bounded down the hillside in ever-increasing arcs to rest far down on the valley floor. I looked at Ralph and to his credit he didn't laugh.

Ivan Waller leading the 1st ascent of Belle Vue Bastion.   *Photo: C.H.S.R. Palmer.*

A FEW DAYS AT HELYG

PETER HARDING

One day, well over fifty years ago, Alfred William Bridge was mulling over the possibility of a climbing holiday in Wales when an unexpected telegram arrived. It read, "MEET ME IN DERBY, STOP, EVENING DRESS, STOP, ROLLER SKATES, STOP, IVAN" (There was of course a date, a time and a place.). Always ready for adventure, Alf duly met Ivan at the appointed spot, appropriately attired and carrying the specific equipment. He soon found himself being ushered to a front seat in the Grand Theatre, at the first house of a variety show. However, long before it ended, he found himself, together with Ivan, quickly ushered out; a result of the latter's ribald comments and cat-calls to various performers.

After visiting a nearby fish and chip shop they meandered along eating an early supper from newspaper and Alf queried their seemingly incongruous dress. Ivan informed him that, later, they would be going to a rather posh dance, and with a couple of elegant young ladies too. At once expectant and impatient, but still somewhat bemused, Alf demanded, "Then what are we going to do with these bloody roller-skates?" "As soon as we've finished our chips we're going roller-skating", came the obvious reply.

Missing out any mundane details of pastimes such as roller-skating and ballroom dancing which were so popular in the thirties, suffice it to comment that the first did nothing to maintain Alf's sartorial smartness for although he had balanced in wet rubbers across Hadrian's Wall on Pillar's Girdle Traverse, A.W.B. had scant aptitude for remaining in equilibrium with wheels on his feet. As for the second pastime, this soon had his elegant lady longing to get Alf's feet off hers and hers off the dance floor because his dancing shoe placement was nowhere near as precise, or as delicate, as that of his plimsolls on Kinder Scout's Pavlova Wall. Whether this situation contributed or indeed led to a third, more intimate, pastime can only be surmised but it was in the early hours of next morning when Alf boarded a train back to Manchester.

He had thanked Ivan for a splendid night out and, suspecting some ulterior motive, asked what it was all about. Ivan had then explained about his entry for a motor race in Ireland and how, when doing a spot of practice in his Alvis Silver Eagle, his mechanic had unfortunately fallen out on a sharpish corner and broken a collar bone. Then came Ivan's carefully nurtured punch line, "I thought you might help me by sitting in for him" (In those days it was conventional in sports car racing

166

for one's 'mechanic' to be in the car beside the driver.).

Despite Alf's protestations that he was no motor mechanic and moreover had planned to go climbing, he did finally agree to accompany Ivan, in the Alvis, to Dublin's Phoenix Park racing circuit, for I.M.W. had played a trump card; on the way there of course, the team which had recently conquered Lean Man's Superdirect on Cromford's Black Rocks would certainly stop off and spend a few days at Helyg. In fact just to make sure, Ivan had made it an ace, "About time you became a member of the C.C.", he said.

Before A.W.B.'s train steamed out of Derby Midland Ivan had outlined some of the splendid benefits of the insurance policy he had already secured in the name of A.W. Bridge; loss of an eye, an arm, a leg; even life itself. The monetary sums were almost too good to miss! But, during his homeward journey Alf began to have serious reservations; for one thing he couldn't think of any rich, one-eyed, one-armed, peg-legged climbers who could lead V.S.s.

Less than two weeks later, in a racing Alvis fully equipped with all the latest gear: rope, rubbers, climbing boots, tent and sleeping bags, as well as a trusty friend, Ivan departed for Snowdonia. Alf had never dared tell his widowed mother that their family bread winner, namely himself, was going to take part in something dangerous such as motor racing. Climbing was different, it was after all what Alf, a steeplejack, did to earn his 'bread'. In fact he had just returned from Paris with a rather lucrative loaf, a contract to inspect the struts and girders of the Eifel Tower. His bold quotation successfully undercut all opposition by costing for only himself, a rope and a new pair of rubbers - when everyone else's bid involved large gangs of men with ladders and scaffolding! So Alf told his mum, with some truthfulness, he was off for a well-earned climbing holiday; he was going with Ivan Waller to spend a few days at Helyg. "Take care then Alfred", she chided, "and don't let your daredevil pal drive too quickly on those winding Welsh roads".

After a day or two's climbing around Ogwen, the leader of the Climbers' Club Motor Racing Section, together with its latest recruit, left Helyg at dawn to catch the morning boat from Holyhead. He drove in an uncharacterisically sedate manner, not out of any respect for the exhortation of Alf's mum, but to treat the Alvis with a gentleness which must surely increase its chances of a successful appearance at Phoenix Park. Passing the Milestone Buttress, Alf was just musing whether to suggest a quick stop and rapid attempt on the virginal grass of that prominent vee-groove when, with a sudden, staccato roar, a speeding motor-cycle hurtled by. Crouched over its tank, the rider ear 'oled his machine round that fast right-hander and disappeared up the straight towards Ogwen Cottage. It was plain to see he was out for a bit of a dice because, held to his head by his goggles, was one of those flat hats with the peak on the back instead of the front and the still, morning air carried that evocative smell of burnt Castrol 'R'. Quickly forgetting all good intentions, Ivan double de-clutched, changing down, then floored the go-faster pedal. The Alvis accelerated in hot pursuit as three carburettors gaped to feed the gulping demands of all 2,198 c.c.s of its six-cylinder motor (That tempting groove would now have to wait for the exploring team of guide-book writers, Wilfred Noyce and Menlove Edwards.).

There followed a two versus four wheel duel all the way down the Nant Francon to Bethesda... through Bangor... then on across Anglesey, although for much of this journey it is doubtful whether all, or indeed any, of those wheels were in actual contact with the ground. On reaching Holyhead, whilst Ivan supervised embarkation of his sizzling Silver Eagle, Alf chatted to the nutter on the nimble Norton who turned out to be Stanley Woods, leading T.T. rider of the day, returning to his native Dublin from some race on the Continent. And he reckoned it had been much less hairy than the one he'd just had!

That night, Ivan and Alf established their base camp near Castle Knock Lodge in Phoenix Park and next day set about stripping the Alvis, getting rid of mudguard and all other extraneous weight and windage. When the official practising for the race began Ivan found himself suspended from taking part in it because he had been scorching round the circuit before the specified practice period. Tim Birkin, perhaps the leading British motor-racing exponent of that time, had declared the secret of getting round Phoenix Park quickly was to take the fast bend of Zoo Corner flat out; so Ivan had been out on the track early, without his second man, to make sure he could do it. The leader of Clogwyn-y-Ddysgl's Fallen Block Crack and Tryfan's Belle Vue Bastion had an eye for a good line, whether it was up a crag or through a bend!

On the day of the race, cars on the grid, engines revving, Alf remembered how he came to be there and was well belayed to the Alvis's passenger seat - rubbers braced against the scuttle and ready for anything. He eyed the competition through a haze of smoke and glacier goggles. It was an impressive array; angry Alfas, rasping Rileys and burbling Bentleys. In his hand he held a matchbox which Ivan had given him. This contained one dozen matches, the same in number as laps of the four and a quarter mile circuit which they must complete during the race and Ivan had instructed for one match to be thrown away every time they passed the grandstand. Thus without any pit crew, they would always know how many laps remained. When the race got under way it was not without its fair share of thrills and spills; competitors spinning or making unscheduled excursions from the circuit as if it were de rigeur: Alf tightened his belay.

Approaching the sharp Mountjoye Corner at the end of the long straight, a troublesome Alfa which had been battling with them for most of the race suddenly

skidded sideways in front of the Alvis. It went broadside on, blocking the middle of
the track, leaving a gap at one side, bounded by the crowded spectators, and a
narrower opening on the other, between the Alfa's tail and a grassy bank. Without
hesitation Ivan pointed his Alvis at the narrow gap, steering through, grazing the
grass bank (Alf swore that after the race he discovered some clover, or a shamrock,
in his left ear!).

In those days English drivers were not all that popular with Irish motor race fans,
especially when the favourite to win was an Irishman - in an Alfa Romeo! But the
Irish crowd did appreciate Ivan's skill, and his gallantry, in going for that gap on the
opposite side and when the Alvis came round Mountjoye Corner on the following
lap they cheered and waved their programmes.

Above the engine roar Ivan shouted to Alf, "How-many-laps?" A.W.B. remained
silent, eyes riveted ahead, the matchbox crushed in his tightly clenched fingers, as it
had been since the very first lap. Although he was utterly without fear of
desperately difficult rock or difficult desperate men, (an archetypal Don Whillans),
Alf found himself well and truly gripped in the fast seat of a racing car. On the next
lap when they passed the grandstand everyone was standing grandly, waving
frantically and cheering loudly. Other cars were slowing; the race was over. Ivan
drove into the pits and, as the Alvis came to a halt, an excited crowd hoisted him
and Alf out, carrying them off, shoulder-high. They had won the Irish Motor
Club's Senior 50!

That night the écurie Climbers' Club team was wined and dined and local
dignitaries would not allow the race victors to stay in a tent, they had to sleep at
Castle Knock Lodge. In the morning Alf awoke thinking he must have been killed
in a motor-racing accident and admitted to Heaven by some strange act of God. He
lay on a great white bed in this huge white room, the ceiling of which was decorated
with pinkish cherubim, seraphim and other heavenly bodies. But his head hurt like
Hell and he could distinctly hear the ringing of its bells! In fact these symptoms
were quite unrelated, the after effects of too much alcohol and of a butler pressing
the room bell; while the former effect continued, the latter one stopped when the
butler entered carrying a small jug of water. With considerable relief, Alf took the
jug and a large swig of its contents. "Begorrah!" The mystified man-servant
regarded Alf with awe; he had simply brought the jug containing a sample of near
boiling bath water to see if it met with the approval of his master's guest. In another
room Ivan had spent a miserable night, his bed dreadfully damp and unaired.

Alfred William Bridge, one-time racing mechanic and member of the C.C.,
returned to Manchester without delay. There were steeples which needed a jack.
Ivan Mark Waller, one-time racing driver, likewise, stayed a few days in Dublin, his
stripped motor-car needed a re-build. When Alf arrived home his mum enquired if

he had enjoyed his few days at Helyg. "Good climbing Alfred?" she asked. "Yes mother", he replied, "I did some good climbs with Ivan." "Then I don't suppose you will have seen the newspaper", she said, handing it to him carefully so he couldn't miss seeing a large picture on the back page. It was one of himself and Ivan Waller being chaired, with laurels, to the winner's rostrum at Phoenix Park.

*   *   *   *   *

(This story is one which Alf Bridge told me on two or three occasions and about which a careful questioning of our honorary member, Ivan Waller has elicited a frank admission of guilt for his part in the affair — as well as a print of the photo concerned, together with a few details.

The Alvis Silver Eagle was a 1929 sports model in which he had covered some 100,000 miles, much of it on the Continent, before winning the Senior 50 race in 1932. Earlier that same year Ivan had driven it in the Monte Carlo Rally breaking the record for the 'Mont des Meiles' hill climb, only to find himself ultimately disqualified from the whole event for having arrived in Monaco 5 minutes too early so his hill climb record did not stand. In the following years Ivan lowered and shortened the chassis, replacing its original fabric-covered body with an aluminium one; in this form it did a further 50,000 miles before he sold it in 1937. Before then, Ivan drove up from Sussex (near Brighton) to North Wales, went round the Snowdon Horseshoe (on foot!), then drove back again — in under 24 hours.

Alf, having completed his Eifel Tower contract, continued with other notable climbs, mainly on rock!

I am indebted to Ivan, as I was to Alf, for so many things including the making, and the telling, of this story. P.R.J.H.)

1985 C.C.J.

The Winners (Alf Bridge 'mechanic' and Ivan Waller) of the Irish Motor Racing Club's 'Senior Fifty', 50 mile race in Phoenix Park, Dublin, 1932. Photo by courtesy of the Irish Times.

HELYG RHYMES

CLIMBING of old meant "hardy Scouting";
a rural misanthropic outing,
where each might move alone at will
upon some never-mentioned hill,
and rend the nails from hands and boots
on bastions barren of all "routes."

But times have changed. Young nature stoops
to amiable Gangs and Groups.
In companies our climbers roll—
roisterous-wise from Pole to Pole,
saluting with a braying "honk"
The Presidential car of ... (Mr. Donkin, of course).

They leave their Liverpool betimes:
at night they're back; with twenty climbs
scored on their knees—a score of scalps
torn from the pates of Cymrian alps.
Of yore, Cimmeriam darkness hid
the secrets of the Wal of Id,
and cloaked discreetly in a fog
face-wrinkles near the Wen of Og;
yet now they're turned, by leaps and hops,
to junior jaunts and Sunday "Pops,"
and every novice eats his grub
on "Faith," by dint of scrape and ... (rubber, of course).

Some flee bright air; and batlike flit
to hang, in clusters, on a ... (piton, of course).
Some beat their axes into rings,
carabines and char-a-banc-like things,
and rope on roundabouts and swings.

What Climbers' Eve but now belongs
to a "community" of songs?
Bees, rhythmically bombinant,
rules by their Chorus, or their ... (Chantrell, of course).
And still the forms of what-has-been
pass in their turn across the screen:
the age of gîtes, the age of tents,
the age of sleeping-bag-rag gents,
the age of gully, and of face,
the age of "grab," and (last) of grace,
the age of stunts, the age of speed,
and the—eternal youth of ... (W.R. Reade, of course).

Till HELYG burst upon our view,
ancient of build, of purpose new.
Swift in establishing its claims
as hostel for the King of Games,
it changed the stern Rule of the Club
to ways more suited to ... (its Public, of course).
A garden Paradise, men tell,
surrounds these porticoes of ... (Helyg, of course):
Piazzas, pergolas rise ranked
about its precincts sacrosanct.
Within the sensuous inner shrine,
on houri-divans there recline
suggestions of the form divine.
At morn, dim shapes of whiteness break
the cold repulse of stream and lake:
at night, it fills its sleepers' dreams
with Tryfan, under starlight gleams,
a Pillar of silver Fire, to show
the path our dream-ascents should go.

Again our old-world-order changes:
upon our obscurantist ranges
we need more LIGHT. Our Pagan fires
must teach their flames to dance on "wires":
that Virgin Age, with Foolish Lamps,
must flower into bulbs and "amps";

and Helyg-radiance flash or fail
at touching of one finger-nail.
Switch on! Switch off! The shepherd now
benighted upon Carnedd's brow,
shall mark that guiding blink, and thank
the flame-eyed Dragon of the ... (Nant Francon, of course).
A "shorter circuit" soon shall bring
Lliwedd as near as anything;
and "switches" lend propulsive shocks
to hurl us headlong up the rocks.

A few more years; and we shall see
no reason for return to Tea;
for climbers, plodding up the track,
no need for provender or sack.
We feel a void—We prod a button—
and there's all Helyg, with the hut on,
spread by the next well-gardened crack,
with toast all buttered on the rack,
and our kind Guardian's beaming face
to grace our meal—and say *his* "grace"!

For these, and for all coming mercies,
we've blessings, and no Balaam-curses
(for Balaam *rode, and* on an ass,
and turned back from an easy "pass").
We welcome Light! We welcome Space!—
and Garages about the place:
fires that dry us without smoke;
and stoves that need no Primus poke.
We look that home-like Helyg times
shall, soon, go with us *on* our climbs!—
Such Helygs are no Travellers' Tales,
nor the sole privilege of Snails,—
Jonah's went with him, in *his* ... (Wales, of course).

GEOFFREY WINTHROP YOUNG. 1937 C.C.J.

THE ASSAULT ON SLAB RECESS

KEVIN FITZGERALD

(AUTHOR'S NOTE.—Since 1949 I have read little, other than the collected works of Mummery, Whymper, Stephen, Winthrop Young, Smythe, Tilman, Shipton *et al.* Any resemblance in the following account of a difficult and extremely dangerous expedition, to the styles of these great ones must, however, be regarded as purely fortuitous.—K.F.)

THE idea came to us one evening at Pen-y-Gwryd. Great deeds had been performed during the day and now we were at peace, our singing done for the evening and our well-earned tankards brimming. "Let us one day," said Hilton Jones, "try to get up Slab Recess Route on the Gribin Facet."

I paled. "It beat Kirkus and Edwards," I said, thumbing rapidly through the Glyder Guide. "Look!" I pointed with a hand which shook a little, to the relevant passage: "Rope, if considered necessary, 80 feet." "You see the implication?" I said. "What point could there be in taking a rope to that awful crag."

Moulam chipped in. He had just run back in his bare feet from a dip in the icy—but oh so beautiful—waters of Glaslyn. "Where that cliff is not absolutely vertical," he said, "it overhangs. There are no holds."

"Do you mind going into the Alcove?" said Mr. Briggs to a party staggering from a "first day" muscle-opener on Cemetery Gate. "This Smoke Room is reserved for climbers." We relaxed as Hilton Jones outlined his plan.

"We must be fit," he began, "not only fit but ready for anything. We must train for two years, saying nothing to anyone in the Club or outside it." He began to sing:

In Pen-y-Pass there lived a lass
(With a rope and an axe and a tricouni nail),
Who sat with a Deacon consuming a Bass,
On the summit of Snowdon, Alas, oh alas,
For she had to come down to Llanberis by rail,
(With a rope and an axe and a tricouni nail),
And that is the end of my sorrowful tale,
Oh, that is the end of my tale.

How we laughed and stamped and roared as the song brought back memories of lonely nights in lonelier huts with the lightning playing round the seracs and the boulders flying off the roof. We went to bed sober, reflecting on the joys of fitness, on the Lovableness of the Unrelenting Mountain and the need for stout hearts in the morning.

Three months later training began in earnest. There was one exhilerating week-
end during which Moulam did the first pitch of Charity in boots, Hilton Jones
reconnoitred the lower slopes of Moel Siabod and FitzGerald gained the upper
reaches of the Pig Track, ultimately, after many hours of exhausting effort, winning
through to the Plateau of Bwlch Moch. Unhappily the weather broke for the
attempt on the Summit Ridge of Crib Goch; but that triumph was to come.

In the high summer of 1951 FitzGerald and Hilton Jones cut up the arête and,
more dead than alive, achieved the passage of the ridge itself. Towards the end of an
arduous descent they encountered a famous mountaineer sunning himself on a
gentle slope. It was H.R.C. Carr. He spoke to them. Too often in these moments
the *obiter dicta* of great men are misheard or forgotten. But not on this occasion.
"Carr's Remarks," as it has come to be known in climbing circles, from South
Audley Street to the top of the Namche La, was committed at once to the paper
round a packed lunch by the writer of this article. "You look tired, FitzGerald,"
Carr said.

It was shortly after this that Alan Hargreaves was told of The Plan and
pronounced in favour of it. When shown the guide, he waved it away. There is still
some doubt as to the words spoken while he waved. Some aver that he said: "I can't
read mountaineering books." Others that he merely stated his inability to read. Of
his next sentence there is no doubt. "The cliff will go," he said, "I've seen it."

Hargreaves put forward a vigorous programme of training walks. Under his aegis
the Miners Track was explored from end to end. A long look was taken at Tryfan,
including a day spend in searching for the mice, said by early explorers to frequent
the mountain. None was observed. Later the summit was gained by a strong
party—except FitzGerald who collapsed from mountain sickness when a mere 1,500
feet of easy scrambling from his goal.

That night there was a green sunset, and great snakes wormed out of their
fastnesses on the Cliffs of Llewyd as all nature stood hushed while the Spirit of the
Mountain brooded over Capel Curig. "Cor ad cor loquitur," murmured
Hargreaves, as he set off on the lonely walk to Helyg. He was deeply moved. We
were all moved. Even Longland who had walked over from King's Lynn to collect a
forgotten pipe was moved. It was a moving experience.

The Great Day drew nearer. In Seymour Street, the clang of hammers told of
special nailings and the forging of pitons. In Pontypool, chemists watched anxiously
as 80 feet of nylon rope began—but oh! so slowly, so very slowly—to take shape.
Nothing was to be left to chance. One thought was in every breast, The Summit. If
fear gnawed sometimes there was that tag of Browning's to sustain us or
recollections of the grim day—so long, so very long ago, "O Postume,
postume"—when FitzGerald was roped off Milestone Buttress.

The Great Day dawned. Outside Pen-y-Gwryd, a long line of cars packed with enthusiasts awaited the emergence of the party. Alas, that Moulam could not be with us. He was tied to a desk in the hotel sitting-room, trying to map a route up Snowdon which entailed the minimum of severe climbing. His place was taken by Mervyn Hughes who had prepared over the two years' training period, in the passionate hope of a place in the assault party, by taking part in expeditions to Switzerland, the Atlas Mountains and the Sierra Nevadas. How good it was to see this young mountaineer, his face alight with expectation, his rucksack bulging with drink, as he leaned on an ice axe for the preliminary photography. A man from Llanberis began to offer synthetic cream ices. Someone raised a cheer and we were off.

The long journey to the cliff was much as other journeys of similar difficulty. Hospitality was offered, but alas, could not be accepted, by the inhabitants of a beautiful chalet perched, all shimmering green, on the grassy slopes of an unnamed peak. We plodded on in silence.

And so at last to Ogwen on the great bend in the Holyhead road. From a nearby hostelry greetings were shouted, to be returned by us in the quiet tones which the seriousness of our mission and our love for the peace of the great wild places enjoined upon us. There at Ogwen we heard the rattle of tea cups for the last time on our journey. "Come," said Hilton Jones, "it is time." We plunged up the hill into a wilderness of boulders.

At last the cliff. With shaking hands and with our thoughts unspoken we took off our boots and donned rubbers. FitzGerald hastily wrote a last message of cheer and goodwill and placed it reverently in a sardine tin which some earlier traveller, averting his gaze doubtless from the grim basion of the cliff, had paused there to open.

We roped up. Who should have the honour of leading? Solemnly Hilton Jones produced a coin and flung it skywards. "Heads," cried Mervyn. FitzGerald stooped to the coin and inspected it as it lay. "It would appear to be a salmon," he remarked, pocketing the Irish florin. Without hesitation Mervyn led up the cliff. At 15 feet he reported a narrow ledge and we heard him driving pitons. With difficulty FitzGerald gained his side. Soon the party was up and pacing anxiously about the stance while the next lead was worked out move by move. Far above a great tree thrust outwards from a cleft. Could this be avoided; was there a simpler way? We paused for photographs. The tension was extreme. Nerves were frayed. Buzzards wheeled slowly in the air around us. From somewhere came the plaintive cry of the stonechat. A small ball of clay hummed past us on its descent into the void.

Above us (after resting for an hour or so) Mervyn struggled with the cliff as inch by inch FitzGerald, enveloped in belays, paid out the rope. By midday, exhaustion and hunger on every face, we had gained a stance below the tree. The passage of this obstacle appeared from 10 feet below to be impossible. The tree overhung. "I'm going up," said Mervyn, and flung himself at the wall. For 20 anxious minutes he clawed his way and at last we were rewarded by his cry of triumph. We little knew then the appalling consequence of his action. By this time we were a full 60 feet on the crag, and FitzGerald was beginning to fail. At last he was hauled to the tree only to find that the rope had been taken—for him—the wrong side of it. His cries of distress, as like a fly in a web he cast this way and that, were heard, it is said, by fishermen ankle deep in the cool waters of Llyn Ogwen. A green sunset—a phenomenon hitherto unobserved at 2-30 p.m.—began to manifest itself. From far away came the deep booming of a gong calling the Midland Association of Mountaineers to prayer. FitzGerald clung to the tree.

There are occasions in the life of every true mountaineer when he is afraid. Fear this time dogged our every step. The tree at last surmounted we were confronted by the crux. This involved nothing less than a step of nearly two feet on to a projection no bigger than a small desk. For the hands there was nothing, nothing at all, other than a ledge nearly four feet above the projection and barely two feet in depth. Failure stared us in the face.

Hilton Jones said something in Welsh, to which FitzGerald replied in Irish. Hughes said nothing, in Spanish. We were resolved. We would not admit defeat. We would press on. We pressed on.

If one had a gift for writing, which one has not, one would extol the delicate move of Hughes as he made his step, the blundering rush of FitzGerald across the chasm, the calm precision of Hilton Jones. But at long last we were safely across. As we gained the stance a green moon swam gently into the sky, her rays mingling with the deeper green of the departing sun. Clearly there would be a green dawn a bit later on. We struggled upwards.

About half-past seven the last stance was reached. It was small (a mere projection) but it sufficed. We lay down while Hilton Jones fitted together the collapsible divan he had carried in his sack. He pointed a minatory finger. "Rest," he said to FitzGerald.

By nine o'clock we were ready for the last dash. A desperate effort, a scramble among knife-edged blades of grass touched by the evening frost and we were up. Slab Recess Route had been conquered.

For a while we lay there tasting the sweets of victory and regretting that none of us smoked pipes so that we might afterwards describe the pleasure of this exercise on mountain tops. Then FitzGerald sat up. "I've left my boots down there," he said.

"Pity," said Hilton Jones, "I'll just run back for them." And he did.

C.C.J. 1954

ALONE

C.W.F. NOYCE

WAR has one mighty disadvantage. It is seldom that friends can fix days together, and the climber rushes to Helyg or Wastwater alone, to snatch what he can. War has led me to solitary climbing; and reflections on it which are often truisms, but come with fresh force to one who has himself indulged in the vice.

Of course, all the old arguments still hold. Of course, there is more risk of perishing from a broken leg, for instance, through not being able to get help. There is (possibly) more danger of falling off simple things, or coming to grief on the stray loose hold. But from the purely practical point of view, I doubt if there is much in it, provided you are careful to lower the standard suitably. A man who climbs Grooved Arête alone is no more likely to come to grief than the same man if he were to climb the Central Gully on Lliwedd leading on a rope. But if he climbed the Holly Tree Wall alone he would run more risk than if he climbed the same climb with a companion. Therefore provided you are cautious, and if it helps you belay with rope slings, and choose the climbs, you have as good a chance as another—sometimes better, because the heightened nervous tension of loneliness induces self-mistrust, and does away with false reliance on belays (often bad) and other people.

If you are cautious ... But as with other climbing, the temptation in good weather may be severe, and I have found myself reflecting in the Devil's Kitchen with a heavy sack or wedged into the Curving Crack on Clogwyn du'r Arddu, on pretty problems of life and death. And I am a coward, I die many times beforehand, nor does it help me to know that I and others have often before "willed more mischief than we durst," and are likely to do so again.

> "If in the breathless night I, too,
> Shiver now, 'tis nothing new."

Yet I know quite well when I am astray, as I have been on rocks and once in the icy gullies of Y Wyddfa. Yet just equally, a man with a companion might attempt a harder place, and be in much the same plight; his fate in the Kitchen, for instance, would probably be the same. And alone, there is no feeling that one could yield, and swing on the belay. The thing must be done, somehow.

The pleasures of lone climbing have been advertised many times; but they, too, come with fresh force. Last February I was alone in icy stillness, in Wales, so frozen that you had to chip many steps to the foot of Lliwedd cliff, so dry that your hands

179

hardly got cold up Horned Crag. The gullies of Snowdon, and rambling on the Moelwyns and Hebogs, and to Cwm Silin, made me think afresh that you do get a heightened feeling for the beauty of objects, as objects, when alone; at times pausing simply to breathe the air, and whisper: "This can't be real." Because there is so little to come between you and the picture. You make your pace, and in Wales or Cumberland it matters little whether it be fast or slow. No hurrying to keep up, trying not to show, like Dante, that you are breathless.

> "Leva mi allor, mostrandomi formito
> Meglio di lena che non lo sentia."

> "I got up then, showing myself outwardly
> better furnished with breath than I felt."

Stop and take a photograph when you please; do up your bootlace when you please; and, not fretting, enjoy the hills more, because more directly free. There is less worry, on rocks, with "ropes and things" (heretic!); no shouting across a high wind, or intolerable "strangling in a string," waiting for a turn with hands that grow colder and rocks that look bleaker the longer you survey another's struggles. Therefore the rock structure itself can be appreciated, because you rest where you like, not necessarily at the top or bottom of a pitch, but as things are seen and felt best. Or you can just go to sleep, as I slept once, halfway down Amphitheatre Buttress, in delicious sun.

Granting that the standard is lowered, and that the climber is cautious, even new rocks are within range. Chockstone Edge, at Buttermere, and the Garden Path on Drws Neoddodd were for me exciting discoveries; because I knew them just within my power, and that I could retreat. Another point. Herford's dictum that one should be able to descend anything one can ascend is pretty sound, especially for one who is alone. But for most the old routes are good enough, or, at any rate, a line somewhere near them. Central Rib, on Idwal Slabs, is such a one—a memorial to faith and friction. Friction is conspicuous by absence, faith there is because there must be; but determination is undermined by the whiteness of Hope and Charity scratches, seen aslant from either eye. Alone, one is tempted to wander from the Via Media. And why not, if alone?

Solitary climbing is a thing of mood; but perhaps not so much as is climbing in company, because the single person is a more constant quantity than one who is shifted and swung every second by his reactions to the party. It is curious how this custom of companionsip remains, even when there is no companion. With me, it takes the form of a dialogue between two halves of me, one competent and the other incompetent, the incompetent an unwieldy novice who does all that he should not, as I inevitably catch myself doing when alone, uses his knees, drops the sack, sits on the ice-axe, etc. Very often a running commentary goes on, the better half trying to bully his colleague into some sort of efficiency, and this most vocally in the so-called easy places, at the foot of Lliwedd East Buttress especially, or on Scottish heather scrambles. But the relative constancy of these two characters does give a certain stability to lone climbing; as if you were going out daily with a tried, if clumsy companion. And mood varies mainly with the weather, fitness, the will to do. Once Belle Vue Bastion "went" in 10 minutes—or again, complete ignominy has been my portion on Craig yr Aderyn.

Climbing alone could become too pleasant a habit. It is idleness, really, to escape the harness of a companion, just as it is the companionship which is the real joy of mountaineering, the link and the light. No one can enjoy mountains unless he can enjoy them with another; and solitary climbing is exasperating by its incommunicability; always, if it is good, I want to share the experience, or to perpetuate it somehow. Hence babbling in journals, or the ecstatic postcard home ... "Had another glorious day yesterday." The individual is too limited to get the best by himself. But because too much beer is very bad for you, it does not follow that a little beer is slightly bad. And if solitary climbing, too, can be indulged in moderately, and just occasionally, the climber may catch glimpses among the hills, which he would miss in company.

MEETING MENLOVE AND OTHER WORTHIES

C.H.P. VERRINDER

The first cause of my meeting with Menlove was a shortage of water in the Dee. To elongate a short story, in April '33 with wife and two friends we had a week in Glencoe. After long bashes up one Buchaille we tried the Chancellor ridge, the Aonach Eagach. The first mistake was to eat all the food at midday: the second was to exuberantly climb along the ridge till nearly nightfall. No easy way off could be found, so we bedded down in the heather and were lightly snowed on. Next morning we decided the easiest way was up to the ridge and over the top. I had my first lead up a frozen waterfall — in hob-nailed shoes! We finally got our first meal for 30 hours at 6 p.m.

Meanwhile my wife and my friends were regaled with stories of climbers who had fallen into gullies and were then pounded by falling stones till they were unrecognisable.

A small S.M.C. party looked for us on the Glencoe side, but we had gone O.T.T. in every sense. After that we took up canoeing! Thus in August '38 with a young brother we did the Wye as training for the Dee, but alas there was not enough water in the Dee, so we went fell-walking round the hostels of Snowdonia. In one hostel I met a climber who enthused about the Idwal Slabs, so when we arrived at Idwal Cottage (in the dark) our next day's plan was 'to look at' the slabs. There was an inviting groove up the centre, which I soloed. I didn't know that one had to scramble a further 200 feet to an easy way off, so I nearly descended a V.S. as a way off a Moderate. I was hooked at the age of thirty, when many climbers pack it in and hang up their P.A.s and vibrams.

So in April '39 I was back in Ogwen with a borrowed rope (Beale's hemp with the red thread) and old ski boots nailed with clinkers - which soon began to rotate and had to be rotated back again before the harder moves. I hung about near the foot of climbs and thumbed a lift upwards. People were generous: a climbing pair would often take on a novice with a rope.

I was lucky to meet some memorable characters. Happy Hughes gave me Hope and Home Climb; he was reputed to carry a book of Latin verse in his back pocket. Joe Gianelli took us to, and up, the Chasm route; he was the author of several good pictures of the Slabs, which were on sale as postcards at Mervyn's by Ogwen Falls. A legend was Dickie Morsley who had a passion for the Kitchen. (I met old Mrs Jones of Ogwen Cottage, who warned me against the Slabs: it was her coal hatchet that helped Owen Glynne Jones up the Kitchen in ice and snow.) It was rumoured that so many joined on Dickie's rope up the Kitchen that he was on the train back from Bangor to Liverpool before the last man on 'his' extended rope reached those steps like wet toffee near the final pitch. Menlove described it as 'Scenery for a murder'. Dickie apparently had a favourite game, of seeing how many parties he could climb through on 'Gash' on a Bank Holiday. There were stories of the great and exuberant Colin Kirkus who, tired of the conventional descent down the Slabs Ordinary, did it upside down, head first.

In April '40 I had ten days in the Lakes, joined the 'Fell and Rock' and thus became a kindred clubman, and Helyg and Glan Dena were available to me. I was a full-time teacher and a part-time fireman on duty every sixth night, but by doing two or three nights together I could get away for a fortnight's climbing. Hoping to save money I cycled from Dorset to North Wales; sadly I got so hungry that eating cancelled the fares saved. The chief encounters on this '41 trip were Harold Goodger and his son Kingsley, who introduced me to many fine climbs, such as the Direct on Glyder Fach, Zig-Zag, Hawk's Nest Buttress and the Great Gully on

Craig yr Ysfa. We explored Craig Cwrwgl, Creigiau Gleision, and their waved slabs, in memory taller than Idwal's. Harold Goodger encouraged me to lead: Chasm Chimney was the first, followed by the Chasm itself, up which I later led many of my novices. I was given Lazarus, Holly Tree Wall and Flake Crack — once thought to be the hardest climb in Wales! So with a variety of Diffs and V. Diffs under my waist rope (before the days of harnesses) I began to lead school parties. One more, only one, memory: Idwal hostel only allowed three nights then one had to move e.g. to Llanberis, or Capel Youth Hostel. Arriving too late at the farm Ty Gwyn down the valley we spent an itchy night in new hay: the menu next day was Monolith Crack and Zig-Zag, never to be forgotten! At Helyg I met Kretschmer, Barford, Bechervaise and Waller. I remember that Ivan Waller, with friend, fell asleep in the hot sun at the foot of the Slabs whilst I was climbing: half-way up I was sad to see sheep next to Waller eating my carefully saved sandwiches. In '43 with the Goodgers and two or so novices - a party of six - we did the Great Gully but arrived at the complex top cave in the dark. Some of our party were extracted by semi-prussik loops on the rope. We very cautiously crept back to Helyg, avoiding lyns, and had a chicken supper at 2 a.m. (Harold Goodger came with us to the Austrian Alps, and also cruising. On one trip in Germany we met F.E. Hicks, once the faithful second to Kirkus, who had taken up sailing in middle-age, I believe hehad six or eight Atlantic crossing under his safety harness.)

I think it was April '44 when I was at Helyg with a school party, one of whom thought climbing Tennis Shoe was too easy to be exciting. We came in one evening to find another occupant of Helyg: he had enormous shoulders..... could it be...? A glance at the log book showed small neat initials 'J.M.E.'. So it was He, of the Very Strict Standards, who described the Milestone as 'Moderate: some of the little variations such as the Super Direct are difficult'!! We regarded Edwards and Kirkus respectively as the Classic and Romantic guide-book writers, and usually equated an Edwards 'Diff' as a Kirkus 'V. Diff' (except for Zig-Zag).

Menlove in 'How I Climb' said he took out a tin of sardines, a peg, and a length of line and when exploring a new cliff if he got stuck inserted his peg (with what?), ate his sardines, and then descended on his line. That April he was exploring a small cliff near the glacier-worn rocks of Cwm Tryfan. There was no evidence of sardines, pegs, or line. Menlove's climbing jacket was an old cowbrown Harris (very porous) held together by safety pins. Breakfast and supper were unsweetened porridge washed down by unsweetened cocoa. Coming from a small boarding school however, our rations were relatively luxurious.

Menlove was very interested in what we had done each day and when we came back from Amphitheatre Buttress he enthused about the 'longest layback in Wales', now climbed and known as Mur y Niwl, I think. Sadly he didn't offer to lead us. Being loath to waste the bash up the Heather Terrace we usually did two of the

Tryfan routes, a trifle exhausting for some of our novices, if satisfying for others.
One day one of our climbers was very tired and Menlove ordered a day in the bunk
and said he would look after him. (This lad was J. Brook-Little, now Norroy and
Ulster King at Arms.).

We had to leave Helyg before Menlove and we had a large pot of stew which I
tried to give him. He insisted on paying two half-crowns, then real money. (Full
board at the Youth Hostel was less than that a day.) So when we left I put the two
half-crowns under the pan of stew with a note which read 'The balance here is
delicate', which J.M.E. MIGHT have written of some route. There was a rhyme
which may be unknown to some C.C. members:

>'Edwards differed from Noyce,
>About the Vertical Voyce:
>Noyce thought it a mild severe,
>Said Edwards "Nowhere near".'

Does anyone ever go to the 'Direct' and 'Hawk's Nest' and 'Needle's Eye' these
days?

Some wartime humour is remembered. Me: "Got a good belay?" My leader, up
above, "Yes, could hold an Italian battleship from here". That became a cliche.
With the Goodgers a song evolved, with chorus, 'If the juggy hand holds come off
in your hand, remember there's a whoreson war on'!

To skip to April '51. I had three novices and some spare rope when we were about
to attack 'Hope', or possibly my favourite bastard route, Chari-Hope-Faith, ending
on the catwalk, the best of all slab-worlds. I saw a well-built youth, about 16, (not
yet bearded like the pard) looking envious. I knew the look. It was my own of a
dozen years earlier. "Would you like to tag on?" I asked. "Yes, please". His name
was Chris. he ran up the slabs to join us, "Have you anywhere to stay?" "Well,
no." "Come and join us at the Climbers' Club Hut at Helyg." "I'd love to."

So we took this young climber and introduced him to Helyg. It turned out that his
Prep. school had been evacuated to Bettws and he had been fascinated by the Welsh
hills (sensible fellow) and he had done a little climbing at Harrison's Rocks. Next
day we went to Sub-Cneifion Arete, that elephant's trunk with a few rugosities that
I thought I could lead. On the first pitch 'it wasn't going too well' (i.e. I wasn't) so I
passed the rope to Chris, putting him at the sharp end. He semi-ran up that pitch. I
could have done the second one, but damn it, you've got to be fair, so Chris
completed the climb. For several days he was our chief leader: he was a natural
climber. He enjoyed Helyg but at first he was mildly surprised to see one of my
sixth form pupils bring me a mug of tea and a slice of bread and jam in my bunk;
but he accepted it as part of life as lived at Helyg. When I came to fill in the log I
had to put his name. Have you guessed it? It was Bonington. I believe he has since

continued his climbing career.

Later in the summer of '51, I met another fine young climber in the Val Gardena, in the Dolomites, who took me on several climbs in the Sella region. He was Toni Demetz. I believe some C.C. members brought him to Helyg in '52, and showed him the Munich, Lot's Wife etc. up which he romped. Sadly he was killed by lightning on the Langkofel when aged only twenty. I have ski'd quite a bit in that region with Kingsley Goodger, and this year, '85, I have again taken pictures of my favourite peak, the Fünffingerspitze, on whose thumb I got lost in '51, when trying it guideless. Scarpetti do not mark the trade routes as did clinkers and tricouni on the rocks of Ogwen and the Pass. This year I was delighted to meet a cousin of Toni Demetz: there is a hut named after him on the Langkofel. I remember him taking me up the classic Schmidt Kamin, but can't quite find where it is.

One more friend of my climbing days I must mention, and that is Trevor Peck. We met in Cornwall (where else?) in the fifties and he came to Ynys in '56 to help me with a school party. He said I was to introduce him to North Wales, but he had a week or two with Scotty Dwyer, so he knew more climbs than I did. He gave us the Gambit, Crackstone Rib, Wrinkle, a repeat of Grooved Arete and best of all the Kirkus Route in Cwm Silyn. In those days Trevor walked to the climb in Tricounis, then changed to rubbers, which were dried when necessary, by two strips of towelling carried in his waist loop. Ten years later he helped with a school meet in Cornwall, then in P.A.s. A great character and a climbing millionaire; making half a million pairs of Pex Sox a week was not enough for him. He just had to make climbing gear, AND indulge his love of puns. His climbing axe was named Terrordactyl. I still have some of his nuts, labelled 'Crackers' ("Perhaps I am" said he, "but so are many climbers — thank God!") He lived on weak tea laced with honey, green peas and bits of chicken. When he and a pupil discovered they were both Bee Keepers the lad (with two hives) asked Trevor how many hives he had. He pondered and then answered quietly "I think about 170". If asked how many new climbs he had done he would have said "One or two, perhaps more". Trevor started climbing by an unusual method. He fixed a top rope, went to the bottom of the route, put the rope through two or three karabiners on his waist line, then in his own words 'abseiled upwards'. Try it if you are solo: it works.

Harold Goodger, a C.C. member from 1926, had climbed with Alf Bridge and seen Kirkus in action: he thought that Trevor Peck was the best he'd seen. He once, with Peter Biven, dragged me up a thing called 'The Little Whizzer' in Llanberis Pass. Does it still exist? Little Brown Jug will certainly survive.

Peter Newman, of Cwm Glas, was years ago one of my novices: generously he kept me climbing till nearly 70 and undoubtedly one of the best routes that we did together was Main Wall.

THE HELYG CUSTODIANS

1926-1928	Charles W. Marshall
1928-1957	E. Stuart Chantrell
1957-1962	Tony J.J. Moulam
1962-1972	C. Trevor Jones
1972-1973	Johnnie R. Lees
1973-	Tony S.G. Jones

CHARLES WILLIAM MARSHALL

On March 3, 1928, the Club suffered a very great loss by the death of one of its most esteemed and energetic members — Charles William Marshall.

During the preceding months he had several times visited Helsby (Cheshire) with the object of compiling notes on the various rock climbs for publication in a book to be issued by the Wayfarers' Club. His last visit was made on Sunday, February 26, and this was to have been the final survey to complete his data.

While attempting a new climb, he found himself in difficulties. Despite all the efforts of his companion, he lost his hold and fell to the base of the cliff, sustaining the injuries from which he died six days later in Chester Infirmary.

Marshall was born and educated in Birkenhead, and on leaving school began those successes at sport for which he will be so long remembered. Joining the Birkenhead Park Cricket Club in 1899, he very soon became a regular member of the 1st XI, in which he played until 1914. In addition to his natural ability in the field he was an extremely sound batsman, at his best in an emergency. During the winter months he devoted himself to hockey, his success with the Oxton Club earning for him the distinction of being chosen for his county and later for his country. The latter honour was conferred on him on nine occasions, and he is said to have been one of the finest full backs who has ever played for England.

It was in 1912, when on holiday in the Lake District, that he met S.W. Herford, and under his leadership made his first real climb. Possessed of a fine physique and excellent stamina, it was at once seen that he was to be a climber of the first rank. Before the end of the next year he led a number of difficult climbs, including Gimmer A and Gimmer B.

Photograph by E. M. Wood
C. W. MARSHALL AND ROBERTSON LAMB ON THE HORNED CRAG, LLIWEDD, 1927

On the outbreak of war in 1914, Marshall joined as a private the 17th Battn. King's Liverpool Regiment, and earned a fine military record. He served with distinction in England, France and Russia, rising to the rank of captain. While in France he was awarded the Military Cross.

He was only demobilised in 1920, and returned to take up the position he held before the war with the Sea Insurance Company in Liverpool.

Renewing his association with the Birkenhead Park Cricket Club, he played consistently in the 1st XI until his retirement from the game in 1924, having captained the team with great success for his last three seasons.

It was not until Easter of 1925 that Marshall again turned to serious climbing, and was overjoyed to find his powers unimpaired by the passage of years. He joined the Climbers' Club early in 1926, and, at the request of the Committee, accepted the position of Hon. Custodian of 'Helyg.' No Committee ever made a wiser appointment. Of his work in this connection it is impossible to speak too highly. He threw himself enthusiastically into the task of making the cottage the success it has become. He himself in his speech at the Northern dinner in 1927 referred to 'Helyg' as 'the jewel in the crown of the Climbers' Club,' a description with which few will disagree.

In June of last year he visited Skye with a party which included the late Robertson Lamb. While there, he led, among other difficult climbs, 3rd Pinnacle, Sgurr-nan-gillean, Cioch direct and Slab-Notch, Sron-na-Ciche. Among his many fine climbing feats in Wales may be mentioned his ascents in boots of the Tennis-shoe on the Idwal Slabs. Marshall's slab on the Milestone Buttress is, of course, well known. He also led for the first time a short slab at the top of the Super-direct above the cave and greatly improved that climb. His last climb in Wales was the ascent of the Devil's Kitchen in October of last year.

Charles Marshall was a man of great strength of will and a charming personality. Gifted with a keen sense of humour, he was a most excellent companion on an expedition. By the Clubs which he served so faithfully all his life and by his manyfriends, he will be sadly missed.

E.S. Chantrell.

E. STUART CHANTRELL

Stuart Chantrell's special contribution to the Climbers' Club started when he was appointed Hon. Custodian of Helyg after the tragic death of its first custodian, Charles Marshall. Helyg had been acquired in 1925 — a great event for the Club — and Marshall was an ideal first custodian, a very good rock climber, and a bit of a

Stuart Chantrell.

I'm **Helyg**'s Hon. Custodian,
A busy Mop-and-Bucket **Man**,
Jeystising every hut-defiling sinner.
Meanwhile do not forget the date,
  — SATURDAY — MARCH — 28 —
Bring guests and all support the—NORTHERN DINNER.

(*Drawing by C. H. F.*)

martinet (he made all the young climbers swim in the Llugwy before breakfast!). When Marshall was killed in a climbing accident at Helsby in 1927, Stuart was chosen to succeed him. He had good connections in cricket and rugger — promising sources of recruits for the Club — and this would stand him in good stead. Stuart, who had been a great friend of the Marshalls, doubtless accepted the custodianship, in part, out of respect for his friend. Thus he began, in his own quiet way, the long stint of thirty years during which all that Marshall's fine beginnings at Helyg had promised came to fruition.

There followed a period of great development in climbing, especially by Liverpool members such as Menlove Edwards, Kirkus and A.B. Hargreaves. Liverpool now became an important centre for the Club as, with Stuart as Chairman of the Northern Committee (on which he served from 1930 to 1951) and in this responsible role, he 'oversaw' another great event for the Club, the extension of Helyg. This ambitious undertaking, turning a small, rough and ready one-room building — the present kitchen, often flooded to several inches in spring — into a fine well-built and well-equipped hut with its large bunk-room, the entrance hall and its sea-going bath, etc., entailed for Stuart, and many others, a great expenditure of time and effort.

Stuart was always introducing young men to climbing and the Climbers' Club, believing strongly in the worth of both. He got on well with young climbers and would tolerate even those who seemed at first out of place, speaking up for them when others were reluctant to welcome such people. And these young climbers submitted willingly to Stuart's gentler but still definite discipline: bunks unfailingly tidied and pots and crockery washed before going out, lats. cleaned out when necessary and the contents buried! He also brought Brian McKenna into the Club, that skilled and jovial horticulturist from Anglesey, who did so much to 'landscape' Helyg — the fine copse, the magnificent rhododendrons and much else. He was a close friend of C.H. French — the dinner-jacketed cartoonist and catcher of fish in the Llugwy (and rats!) for breakfast. Those who knew Stuart all through those many years attest to his steadfast loyalty to the Club and his great influence on its character.

Many climbers such as David Watson and Bill Ward wrote in to testify to Stuart's service to the Club. Bill commented:

'I never climbed with Stuart and never recall seeing him climb, he was too absorbed in Helyg housekeeping and training young members to keep the place tidy. He reprimanded offenders in no uncertain way and this sometimes made him unpopular!'

He was a Morgan enthusiast (always keeping them in perfect condition) and a good raconteur. He would arrive at Helyg late Saturday afternoon, invariably with a

Above: Helyg in 1933.
Below: The Custodians, E.S. Chantrell and B. McKenna.

yarn about some escapade in mist, fog, or snow when crossing the Denbighshire moors, carrying a carton of rations, which invariably included lamb chops. He would groan and complain about the mess and untidiness and set about organising cleanliness and order. When this was done his happy moments came — as could be seen by the twinkle in his eyes while frying his chops and sucking his pipe in a tidy kitchen. He always slept in the loft, hence the label 'Reserviertplatz fur der Hutternwart' which some affable C.C. member had filched from a DOAV hut and nailed on the door (is it still there?).

I suppose I got to know him best during the first two or three years of the War, especially during air raid times, when I would arrive from the South of Wales on a motorbike and he in his Morgan from Liverpool. Both glad to get away from the turmoil to the peace and quiet of Helyg. To have a good sleep without fire-watching, sirens and the drone of planes was a complete rest cure. Stuart always slept in the loft with the fanlight fully open, while I slept in the dormitory. One morning Stuart greeted me in a state of despair, "The bloody planes were over here last night; I had to get out and shut the fanlight".

M.R. Loewy writes (a la Times obituaries!):

'Stuart had four loves: Cricket, the Climbers' Club, the Air Training Corps — during the War, and Animal Welfare. They were all represented at his funeral; a strong contingent from the Birkenhead Cricket Club — Stuart was scorer for 62 years! He also revived the club after the war; Birkenhead Park would have died without him. Some of his climbing friends were there, the R.A.F., and the ladies of the local Animal Welfare Society — for Stuart had been that rare phenomenon in the Society, a man and very active in its interests'.

Many C.C. members will have affectionate memories of Stuart in his beloved Helyg; Stuart endlessly busy tidying up, cleaning, doing repairs; Stuart sitting contentedly by the fire with his pipe when the rest of us got back to the hut. For Stuart would be at Helyg every week-end, despite the long journey from Wallasey. In winter we would drive down on Saturday afternoon (of course we worked on Saturdays then), in summer in the evening, after cricket. On the return journey the back of the Morgan was piled high with used pillow-cases; these must have puzzled the laundry greatly. Here was an apparently respectable suburban house, with the usual kind of laundry list, but always with anything up to 50 pillow-cases! What could be going on there? In fact 39 Cliff Road was a model of decorum; a bachelor household consisting of Stuart and Maurice Eggleshaw (once an active member of the then C.C. Northern Committee), who jointly owned this spacious house, and two or three other C.C. members, and Porgy the cat.

Stuart was very precise in all he did — our household account, the Helyg records, and I am sure, in his scoring and in his job at the Harrison Line shipping office in

Liverpool. He was also instant in all he did. As soon as he came home from the office he would go out and trim the hedge, cut the lawn, paint the window-frames, and any necessary chore. In the lunch-hour each day he would drive through the tunnel to Birkenhead and work on the cricket ground, fork the pitch, feed the club cats, have his sandwiches, and then drive back to the office. But although apparently 'always at it', there was no fuss or rush about Stuart and when he had done, in the same quiet manner he would sit in one of the great 'elephantine' armchairs at 39, smoke his pipe, with Porgy on his lap, and listen to music. He had one of the best radiograms of the day and a fine collection of records.

Stuart was a friend of Menlove Edwards, and a very fine true friend. When Menlove's depression became deep and dangerous Stuart several times went to his aid and helped him back to living. He was also guide, counsellor and friend to more than a few young men, in his business, in the Cricket Club and in the C.C., continuing in that role over a great span of years, long after they were no longer 'young men'.

Finally a happy and amusing incident associated with climbing and cricket. A few years after the war Stuart came to the Alps with me — the Silvretta, the Engadine, a glimpse of Italy and the Ticino. He had some idyllic moments. As we were going up to the Silvretta hut from Schruns — the 'back way' up the modest and quite deserted valley behind the main ridge, in glorious weather, Stuart stopped more than once to look around and declare that this was the best day he had ever had in the mountains. When we got to Lugano, however, it rained ceaselessly. Towards evening of the second day Stuart was thoroughly down in the dumps. Suddenly he said, musingly: "If I caught the train tonight" — it was all train then — "I could be in Manchester tomorrow evening." And then with relish: "I'd be in time for the Test!" And so it was. At once Stuart was full of beans again; back to the hotel to pack, check the train times, a cheerful last dinner, and he was off to good old England and the Test.

1984 C.C.J.

Photograph by E. M. Wood

C. W. MARSHALL ON PARADISE, LLIWEDD, 1927.

Photo: Douglas Milner.

Geoffrey Winthrop Young.

C. Myles Mathews.

RESURRECTED OBITUARIES

C. MYLES MATHEWS

C. Myles Mathews was the son of C.E. Mathews of Birmingham, the famous mountaineer and President of the Alpine Club. He died after a severe but short illness on November 24, 1928.

Myles Mathews was educated first at Edgbaston Preparatory School, and subsequently at Uppingham. At Uppingham he was captain of his house. In 1898 he went up, an Exhibitioner, to King's College, Cambridge. He took a First Class in Part 1 of the Natural Science Tripos, and a Second Class in Part II, his position in the latter being affected by the amount of time given in his final year to swimming and to rowing in his college boat. He was Captain of the University Swimming Club for two years, and a half blue.

On leaving the University he became articled to his father's firm, Mathews, James and Crossking, Solicitors of Birmingham. After he eventually took his Law Final he followed a distinguished career.

As a boy C.M.M. spent nearly all his holidays at his father's cottage, Caer Saer, near Machynlleth, and this early association with the scenery and hills of Wales he always delighted to renew.

His first signature in the visitors' book at the Pen-y-Gwryd appears to have been in 1900, but there can be little doubt that he must have been there before that time with his father. He first visited the Alps at the age of thirteen, when he accompanied his father to the summit of Mont Blanc. He climbed Mont Blanc three times between the ages of thirteen and twenty-one.

He became a member of the Alpine Club in 1899 and was an original member of the Climbers' Club and served on the Committee from 1906 to 1909, and again when he resigned the Presidency. He became a Secretary of the Club in 1908, an office which he filled with devotion and energy until he was made President in 1925. He was President from 1925 to 1928.

During his period of office as Secretary, the Climbers' Club increased its membership and its activities despite the difficulties during the War period, and during his presidency the membership grew larger than it had ever been before.

There were times when C.M.M. seemed to surpass even his father as an after-dinner speaker and perhaps the most notable of these was the occasion of his last

speech from the Presidential Chair of the Climbers' Club dinner during the winter
of 1927-8, when he and Winthrop Young vied with each other in extempore
rhymes. Mathews's lines are as follows:

> You tell me you're promised a climber,
>   My careful Committee next week.
> I hope you'll make even sublimer
>   The Qualifications you seek.
> Alas, if he seems like a Rambler,
>   A Rocker and Feller, or, oh,
> Not a walker but rather an ambler,
>   My own Geoffrey Winthrop say "No!"
>
> If he loosens the stones from his stances,
>   If he tangles his feet in the rope,
> If on Girdles or Garters he dances,
>   If he boggles on Faith or on Hope,
> If he snores in his bunk in the Cottage,
>   If his pace is too fast or too slow,
> If he's aged and near his dotage,
>   My own Geoffrey Winthrop say "No!"
>
> If in Cornwall he dives in the ocean,
>   From a Traverse that Andrews once did,
> If he says that he hasn't a notion,
>   Where on earth the Club library's hid,
> If he comes off his pitch on your luncheon,
>   If he wants a fresh foothold and so
> Seeks your head his tricounis to scrunch on,
>   My own Geoffrey Winthrop say "No!"
>
> If his climbs are described in the papers.
>   If his photograph peers from the press,
> If he cuts on the Slab any capers,
>   If his route finding's often a guess,
> If he thinks the Black Cleft is too easy,
>   If he says that the Kitchen will go,
> If he's fresh when his leader is wheezy,
>   My own Geoffrey Winthrop say "No!"
>
> If his sub isn't paid till November,
>   If he knows a new way to Cwm Glas,

He need not become a new member,
  Don't let such a candidate pass,
Take him on to the hillside that mellows,
  Try him out upon rock and on snow,
If he isn't the best of good fellows,
  My own Geoffrey Winthrop say "No!"

From In Memoriam, 1929 C.C.J. by S.B. Donkin.

WILLIAM ERNEST CORLETT

By the death of W.E. Corlett last June, at the age of 94, the Club lost one of the Original Members. He joined in 1898, already having been climbing in North Wales for more than ten years. The records show that, with his regular companion M.K. Smith, he led the first ascent of the Nor' Nor' Gully on Tryfan in 1891. He continued to climb until the outbreak of World War I in 1914.

It was in 1926, at a Northern Dinner in Liverpool, that W.E.C. made his offer to build a garage at Helyg. Gregory, in Caernarvon, quoted a figure of £250 but, due to bad weather conditions which held up work for days at a time, wages alone totalled £600. Those who knew him well were not surprised to learn that Corlett had insisted on paying the full cost. This was typical of his generosity to many clubs — particularly Rugby and Cricket — though he was always anxious to avoid any publicity. On one occasion he was heard to say that having thoroughly enjoyed his own youth, he took pleasure in helping young men to enjoy theirs.

Corlett had many interests, though these came second to his business life as a solicitor and, for many years, Chairman of Higsons Brewery. He gave no thought to retiring, and up to a week or two before his death he was at his office every morning by 9.30. Most of his contemporaries had retired 30 years before.

An enthusiast since the early days of motoring, he had owned three Mercedes, the first — 90 h.p. — previously belonging to Prince Henry of Prussia and the winner of some important races. It was in the last of these cars that we once took General Bruce to Helyg following a Northern Dinner.

His beautiful steam-yacht 'Helig' (the name a coincidence) has for years been an object of interest to visitors to Conway where he kept it. For his annual holiday it took him to Scotland to stay at his house at Loch Moidart.

In 1946 Corlett suffered a great loss when his younger son was most tragically drowned in a yachting accident at Hoylake. The modern life-boat at New Brighton was given by the family in his memory and named Norman B. Corlett. It has already been responsible for the saving of many lives.

E.S. CHANTRELL.

REV. J.E. GROSVENOR

Few men can have had a more full and varied life than Ernest Grosvenor, and one of his few regrets was that he did not begin to climb until he was about 38. He joined the C.C. in 1925, served on the Committee in 1944 and was elected a Vice-President in 1945. He was for many years a member of the Alpine Club and at one time President of the Midland Association of Mountaineers.

After leaving Harrow he joined the family carpet manufacturing firm in Kidderminster, and was its Chairman from 1923 to 1946 when he retired from business. During this period he entered the public life of Kidderminster and was Mayor in 1926. He was a Magistrate for Worcestershire for 25 years and High Sheriff in 1939, in which year he was made M.B.E. for political and public services.

During the 1914-18 war he served with the Worcestershire Regiment in France and Flanders, and was promoted to the rank of Major in 1917 and commanded the 181 Brigade Machine Gun Company in Palestine. On his retirement from business, at the age of 60, he was not prepared to be inactive. He began his theological studies and two years later was ordained. He served as Curate in his local parish until shortly before his death at the age of 75.

Grosvenor never had any ambition to be a climbing 'tiger', but he nevertheless enjoyed many visits to the Swiss and French Alps, climbing with or without guides. He had also climbed in the Dolomites and Corsica.

When over 60 years of age he did the Dent Blanche from Arolla. He climbed a lot in North Wales and was a very sound leader on routes up to V.D. or mild Severe standards. He usually stayed at Helyg, and his first visit was memorable. I well remember the sight of his tall figure in the door of the old cottage, holding in his arms a 4½ gallon barrel of Joule's Ale, his favourite beverage. When he brought in his case of food it was found that his butler had packed a variety of delicacies but no bread, butter, sugar, etc.!

From the first Grosvenor was completely happy with the Helyg life of those days, and proved to be a most amusing and entertaining companion. The novel experience of cooking his own meals and helping with hut chores appealed to him immensely. He also liked the evening parties at Cobden's Hotel.

Only once did I see any sign of ill-humour. I was representing the C.C. at the M.A.M. Dinner in Birmingham, Grosvenor being President at the time. I was invited to stay at his house with L.S. Amery and General Bruce. There was a most entertaining conversation between the three old Harrovians till the early hours of the morning. Next day Bruce demanded to be taken to the Malvern Hills which he had never seen. Except during a stop for refreshment he slept soundly throughout the trip. His host was not amused.

When his daughter, Mary, was still at school, Grosvenor introduced her to the mountains and I was usually asked to act as second. We had many happy days on Snowdon and Tryfan. Later on she was to develop into a very sound leader and became a prominent member of the Pinnacle Club, a matter of considerable pride to her father. He will be remembered by his many friends in the Club and greatly missed.

STUART CHANTRELL.

G.L. DENSHAM

Many people knew George Densham in only one or two of his many guises — cricketer, climber, car driver, philosopher, photographer, or, from the naval point of view, as an extremely competent and enquiring engineer and a popular and original naval officer. I was privileged to know him in most.

As a climber and hut companion I first met him in 1936 when he joined a party of brash undergraduates at Brackenclose. I don't think we knew him as more than George for the first week, but, from the first, his naval sense of orderliness and his complete lack of fuss and wry twist of humour made him a delightful hut companion; and so he remained all his life.

As a motorist before the war he owned an almost legendary Riley tourer, somewhat doctored internally, in which he would arrive in London from Plymouth (rarely more than five hours on the road) with that same lack of fuss, and would load up for a weekend at Helyg or a mass attack on Harrison's Rocks using his parent's home as a base camp (his parents' generous hospitality without reference to numbers or warning was proverbial). As a driver he was always courteous, could be extremely rapid and enjoyed rather ordinary-looking cars with unordinary machinery under the bonnet.

As a naval officer he passed through Keyham in probably its vintage years and exploited to the full its nearness to the moors, the workshop and the cricket field. In 1941 he found himself based at Gibraltar as the Engineer Officer H.M.S. Foresight working the Malta run. He was unconventional yet never flamboyant, respected and held in great affection by his engine-room staff. Overworked yes, but harassed and impatient never. As ship's store officer he had access to rope, and when I arrived, the nucleus of a climbers' club had already started. The naval padre Father Howard, a Dutch submariner, George and myself spent many unconventional afternoons on the steep South-east Face of the Rock, and certainly on one occasion the final pitch ended at a gun emplacement with the gun as a final belay. Later we both moved to the north Russian run and had walks and climbs together in Russia and Iceland and even sighted Spitzbergen. It was after an afternoon in the mountains around Seidesfjord that he sailed for the convoy in which his destroyer was torpedoed, and it was his efforts that were largely responsible for its timely arrival in port still, but only just, afloat. The strain had told on him and the award of the D.S.C. seemed to him poor reward for an appointment ashore on indefinite sick leave. Few people knew that the self-administered cure, against medical advice, was a week at Helyg and days spent walking, mostly done on the wet Welsh hills. On one occasion our leaves coincided and we spent a wonderful week in deep snow walking from Cockermouth to Langdale, and I began to know him as a philosopher. He owed much to the mountains and I sense that the service he gave to the club in his later years was his thank-you to the Good Lord who provided the mountains that cured his soul.

I hope others may write of his ability as a climber in the post-war period. I think he modestly thought of himself as a reliable second, but a glance at the hut books would suggest that this is an understatement.

As a man he will always be remembered for his untold courtesy and thought for others, for his patience and preparedness to listen and for the firmness of his opinions if opinions were honestly required. He was a devoted son and a wise and generous uncle.

I remember discussing with him what he pictured by the phrase "life after death" as we sat eating lunch in the snow and spring sun on Glaramara. We reached no conclusions but the gist of one phrase stuck. "I don't believe the evil men who think only of themselves live long after they have died." If the converse is true, as I believe it is, then in this unorthodox Christian sense George is with us for a long time to come.

E.W.K. WALTON.

T.G. LONGSTAFF

Dr. Tom Longstaff, who died in 1964, was the last surviving pre-1945 President of the Club. But long before he ever joined the Club* he had made his name in the mountaineering world, with his incomparable record of mountain exploration, to which he was able to devote a major part of his long and active life. His travels covered the Alps, the Himalaya, the Caucasus, the Rockies, the Arctic; the story of them is given in his engrossing book *This My Voyage*. The highlights were perhaps his Himalayan exploits, which included the ascent of Trisul (for many years the highest peak in the world to have certainly been climbed) and the exploration of the Nanda Devi area, the discovery of the Siachen Glacier and the Teram Kangri group, his journey in Tibet and attempt on Gurla Mandhata, and the 1922 Everest expedition. In the Caucasus he made a number of fine first ascents of peaks. He served capacities in the Alpine Club and the Royal Geographical Society, being President of the former and Honorary Secretary of the latter (which awarded him its Gill Memorial Award and its Founder's Medal).

He was elected an Honorary Member of this Club in 1932, and was President from 1933 to 1935, serving on the Committee from 1936 to 1939. During his Presidency the Club was an active one, though perhaps the fierce fire of the renaissance from 1928 on had diminished to a steady blaze. The chief event of his term of office was the rebuilding of Helyg, in which he took a close personal interest.

In latter years he retired to live in a remote corner of Wester Ross, where despite the remoteness he was sought out by the younger active climbers, and encouraged their visits and their activities. He had a vivid, light-hearted yet tenacious personality, and was an extremely hard goer on the hills. In old age some part of the fire of his youth yet remained, and caused anxiety to his family, who feared he would exert himself in excess of his capacity. We give our sympathy in their loss.

J.N.

---

* He was first elected to the Club in 1902, but fell by the wayside at about the time of the first world war, and rejoined only in 1932 as an honorary member.

COLIN FLETCHER KIRKUS

Club Member 1928-1942

Pilot-Officer C.F. Kirkus, who was a navigator and bomb aimer, was reported missing after a raid on Bremen in September, 1942, and is now 'presumed killed.' This was about his twenty-fifth 'Op,' which included the first 1,000 machine raid on Cologne. He was proud of the fact that he had never failed to find the target or to cox his machine back to base, despite on one occasion 'a few splinters in the face.' As one of the first Pathfinders I think he must have been very efficient, and he certainly was very interested. He also had to avenge his elder brother who was lost in the first important British Air attack of the war, on Kiel in September 1939.

I first met C.F.K. at Helyg in September 1928 when he would be about 18 and I, 24. I had been climbing a little over a year and had begun to lead a bit but he already had considerable experience of rock climbing, mostly solo, and even had new routes to his credit on Moelwyn and Craig Cwm Ffynnon Lloer. The

Climbers' Club people seemed to think that he was a bit mad and our introduction was on that basis — possibly they thought I was too — anyway we were promptly dubbed 'The Suicide Club' because our first climb together was the Holly Tree Wall in nails on a nice wet day. I certainly think we would have been 'disapproved of' by Charles Marshall who, for some time, had been kindly but dominating mentor to the young climbers who were beginning to use Helyg, and whose fine career had come so tragically to an end a few months before. However, not only did we survive this rash expedition but founded thereon a partnership which was to flourish.

All through the winter of 1928-29 we tore our fingers to pieces at Helsby or in Wales or the Lake District, whenever we had the time and money available — which meant that it was mostly Helsby — so that by Easter 1929, we understood each other very well. We then did, in addition to a number of climbs of Holly Tree Wall standard, an ascent of the Direct Route on Glyder Fach, by Gibson's Chimney, which, as far as we could find out, had not been done for very many years. That was quite an event, and not only from our own point of view, because it might be said to have confirmed the revival of Welsh climbing which had been set going (at a very much higher level, of course) by Pigott and Longland on Clogwyn du'r Arddu in 1927-28.

A few weeks later we had a fortnight together in the Lake District during which we did quite a number of 'very severes,' including what was probably the third ascent of Esk Buttress and such things as Eliminate B, the North West on Pillar, the Pinnacle Face climbs, and Botterill's Slab. I think Colin really found himself as a climber during this holiday, and although impressed with what was then the much higher standard of climbing in the Lake District as compared with Wales, he obviously began to feel that in due course he would be able to tackle anything. It will be appreciated that at that time very few people indeed were leading 'very severes' — round about half a dozen.

The next stage of Colin's development was a spell of about three weeks at Helyg during which he was lucky to fall in with F.E. Hicks who, as a member of the C.U.M.C., had quite a lot of experience. When he arrived there Colin had been climbing alone for some time, and Hicks, who was by no means unenterprising, was rather staggered by what this rather queer looking lad had done — up and down the Tryfan buttresses for instance and over most of Lliwedd. I believe that Hicks' party was a bit chary about taking him along with them on their first day, and they might well have been because Colin lured them on to the Glyder Fach and there pointed out Lot's Groove as something he thought he would like to try. They obliged with a rope from above and in due course, to their astonishment he led it, only Hicks being able to follow. The next day he led the shorter but even more difficult Central

Colin Kirkus.

Route on the Terrace Wall of Tryfan, up which no one was able even to follow.

Of course these were more or less stunt climbs and were not evidence of judgement, but on the 29th of June 1929, Colin led the second ascent of Longland's climb on the West Buttress of Clogwyn du'r Arddu which most certainly required judgement. This took about 4½ hours and we had to shift tons of turf, soil and loose rock. Colin was maturing quickly. Later that year with Hicks and myself he did the eighth ascent of Scafell Central Buttress and the fifth ascent of the Gimmer Crack.

Next year (that was 1930) there was no stopping him, although it began badly with an accident on the Great Central Route, Easter Gully, Dow Crag when, because of over confidence and poor condition, he came off whilst leading, getting away fortunately with very little damage to himself. On the 15th June, with Macphee, he made his classic Great Slab Route up the centre of the West Buttress of Clogwyn du'r Arddu and this, I think, is the climb on which his fame will mainly rest. To take out 130 feet of line on to this entirely virgin face up a steep, loose and grassy wall, tremendously exposed, with no knowledge of what difficulties lay in the 600 odd feet above, was surely mountaineering courage of the highest order. And it must have required the utmost skill and route-finding ability, as well as courage, to finish that climb. Despite the many more-difficult shorter routes that have been done "unseen" I think this expedition will stand out in the history of British rock-climbing as a most important event.

Later he made the fourth ascent of Pigott's Climb on the East Buttress of Clogwyn du'r Arddu and completed his Direct route up the nose of Dinas Mot, an almost perfect climb and one of the most beautiful.

The following year we fell in with Linnell and Bridge, and under the stimulus of each other's climbing, Kirkus and Linnell during 1931-33 reached an incredible level of performance only equalled, perhaps, by Menlove Edwards. This was truly a 'golden age' in rock climbing and during it Clogwyn du'r Arddu and the East Buttress of Scafell were practically worked out; the first by Kirkus with the Chimney, and the Terrace, Pedestal, Curving and Birthday Cracks, and by Linnell with his Narrow Slab, the other by Linnell and A.T. Hargreaves; but it was Colin who had made the first breach in the East Buttress by doing Mickledore Grooves, which was a veritable "tour de force" involving a final run out of 140 feet of rope during a period of over one hour. It should be noted that, like most of his other major first ascents, this superb climb was led by him without previous exploration on a rope from above. He also opened up Craig Ogof in Cwm Silin and the great Pinnacle Wall of Craig-yr-Ysfa. This was a wonderful period and during it I think it was generally recognised that he was the leading climber of the day — first among very few equals.

In the summer of 1933 he went on an expedition with Pallis, Hicks, Warren and others, to the Gangotri district of the Himalayas, and there proved, I believe, that he was not merely a 'rock gymnast' but a first-rate mountaineer. Many people whose judgement is entitled to respect thought that he would have been a success on Everest, and there is no doubt that Colin himself was disappointed that he was not chosen, though he never showed it unduly. I must, however, leave it to others to appraise his qualities on the bigger mountains. All I can say is that on British hills he was practically as good (if not better) on snow and ice as he was on rock.

At Easter, 1934, there was the terrible accident on Ben Nevis when Linnell was killed and Kirkus was seriously injured, barely escaping with his life and showing incredible powers of endurance in doing so. After that he was never quite the same and the nature of his interest in climbing seemed to change. For quite a long time he did not climb at all but gradually he came back to it, preferring, however, to do ordinary courses, only occasionally going for the difficult things. He frequently took novices and oldish people up standard climbs, laying himself out to make things safe and enjoyable for them. He was care, skill and confidence embodied and there must be many who owe to him a sound introduction to climbing. During this period he undertook the production of the Club's guide to Glyder Fach; in the course of the work pioneering a considerable number of new routes. Incidentally, this concise guide is generally considered to be a masterpiece of clarity, well conceived for use by the ordinary climber.

So much for the historical record of Kirkus's rock climbing career, during which he made something like 40 first ascents, including some of the most formidable climbs that have ever been done in this country, as well as many second and other early ascents of important routes. There is probably no British rock climb that could not have been done safely by him, and, in fact, he must have ascended most of the Welsh and Lake District climbs as well as many of the Scottish routes, including the Chasm of Buchaille Etive.

It remains to attempt an assessment and appreciation of his climbing. He was practically always first class as a leader, being confident, solid and safe whatever the conditions. He was not merely a 'gymnast' although, as his record shows, he was a brilliant technician. There was nothing showy about his climbing, in fact he liked to take things slowly, and was occasionally awkward and ungainly in his movements. He was not temperamental and never got rattled under even the most difficult circumstances. His principal physical characteristic was his extraordinary endurance and insensibility when having to sustain himself on small awkwardly shaped holds for a long time and for a long distance. One never saw him flapping about, kicking with his feet, or hauling himself up by main force. Everything seemed to go according to plan, up or down. He was always very careful and ingenious in the handling of the rope and the arrangement of belays, but so far as I know he never descended to the use of pitons except by way of a joke. It did not seem to matter to him what he had on his feet or whether he had anything on them at all. Cold and wet did not seem to affect him as much as it did other people. He was a wonderful route finder on rocks and some of his climbs bear the hallmark of genius in that respect, notably Mickledore Grooves, Dinas Mot Direct, Lot's Wife and the Great Slab Route. Unlike many expert leaders he was also a very good second; that is he was content to follow someone less good without showing impatience or tactlessly making little of pitches which his leader had found difficult. He always tried hard to make things easy for his followers according to their ability and many and ingenious were his methods of getting weak climbers up difficult places. His confidence in himself was such that except on the hardest climbs it did not seem to matter much to him whom he had got following; anybody would do to hold the rope if they would follow his instructions; he even put up with grumbling and defeatism.

As a man he was a delightful companion on the hills, full of fun and interest in the things about him. He was kindliness itself and also most unassuming about his climbing, yet never carrying his modesty so far as to appear to be fishing for adulation. To those who did not know him well he may have appeared dull, but this was not so — he was a simple soul, not much interested in the complicated ways of modern life, finding his escape and true expression in his mountaineering. In a better-ordered world he would have been able to become an explorer or something of that sort, where his rare talents could have been used to the full, but in fact he was a clerk in the office of an Insurance Co., where, though he worked hard and with some success, he was rather out of his element. In the R.A.F. he seemed to have found himself properly and if he had survived I think he would have become a man famous in other ways.

He died doing his duty for his country and he leaves a great name in the fine sport of mountaineering, with very many friends to mourn his passing.

A.B. HARGREAVES.

JOHN MENLOVE EDWARDS

J.M. Edwards, honorary member of the Club, died on 2nd February, 1958, at the age of 48.

Whether on the Helyg boulder or in a rowing-boat or climbing in clinker nails on rubber 'very severes,' Menlove Edwards was a man who performed the sort of feats

MENLOVE EDWARDS   *C. W. F. Noyce*

that become legendary. Judged, however, by the simple yardstick of the number and standard of his new climbs, his record is sufficiently remarkable, for hardly any other leader can have had such an output of first ascents, sustained over more than 20 years. Nor was it merely that he made many new routes; his climbs, like his mountain writing, had an intensely individual quality. Perhaps few of his routes, anyhow up to the outbreak of war, had quite the classic touch of some of Colin Kirkus's, yet they reflected an equally bold mental approach; for the steep, loose, wet and vegetated rock on which he so often climbed was then regarded as hardly fit for climbing at all. A great number of his ascents remained unrepeated for years, until it began to be realised what an extraordinary repertoire of new climbs — even of new cliffs — had been opened up, and that this type of climbing could be done for pleasure by more ordinary leaders. A glance at the list of first ascents on Clogwyn y Geifr, or on any of the Three Cliffs, will show how completely Menlove was a pioneer; and even on Lliwedd, where by 1938 Central Gully seemed to be the only remaining problem, his genius for the less obvious paths produced a dozen new routes in the course of a single month.

Guidebook writing, to which he turned in the middle 'thirties, was his other outstanding service to Welsh rock climbing, and three of the first *C.C.* guides are his, written alone or in collaboration. To these he was later to add the first guide to Clogwyn Du'r Arddu. His guidebooks show the same individuality of approach that is evident in his climbing; accepting the conventions of the modern requirement, they nevertheless manage to convey something much more than technical information. *Lliwedd* was a masterpiece in this respect, and although it is arguable that the subjective treatment makes this a difficult guidebook for the ordinary user, it is very doubtful whether so complex a crag could have been better dealt with in any other way; certainly only Menlove could have written it as it is. Most of his climbing time for seven years must have been devoted to guidebook work, and the debt which the Club owes him is immense.

The articles which he contributed to the *C.C.J.* will be remembered, especially 'Scenery for a Murder' *(C.C.J. 1939),* which is perhaps the most brilliant piece of imaginative writing the *Journal* has ever published.

Yet although Menlove's personality stamped itself on everything that he did, the bare record of his achievement in these different fields leaves out of account an essential side of him. It is the side which is associated with Helyg in its brightest period and with the climbing companionships of those years, of which he himself wrote: "Then, the day far spent, at the top, flinging time away, we would eat and, as mortals should who have stormed Olympus, we laughed, and laughed until we could not laugh." These are the associations that will remain, for those who knew him, along with the wider recognition of his great place in the history of the Club.

A.D.M. Cox.

A boy of 17, I was staying at Helyg over an Easter meet. On the Friday evening, while the others descended to Capel, I stayed in. The only other person in the hut was a man in tattered coat and seaman's jersey, a man with powerful looking shoulders and a strange face, handsome in its way. The hair was auburn, almost woolly; the jaw firm and jutting, so far as to force a hollow below the full lips; the face smooth, rather childlike but for the eyes, which were those of a man who has seen a good deal.

"Let's have tea," the stranger, whom I knew to be one of my 'heroes', said. And we got talking.

So it started. Next day Menlove suggested climbing, and we went to the Three Cliffs. "Going to dig in your back garden?" somebody grinned. At that time the Three Cliffs were considered dangerously loose and full of vertical vegetation. We got a lift round to Pen y Pass. "I really go there because I like to walk downhill to my cliff," Menlove said. He never spoke with any pleasure of walking uphill for its own sake, or of the hills themselves with affection, though "Good old Tryfan" might slip out, almost apologetically, at times. It was obvious, that first day, that something else was in the air. Each of the three routes that we did was a struggle, each demanded the power to wrestle in an uncomfortable position. Several times Menlove seemed defeated, whether by rock or grass, but hung on, clinkers scrabbling, while he hitched the rope over a minute projection. Several times those enormously powerful arms got him up. I learned a lot that day.

There is no space to do justice to Menlove's major contribution to rock-climbing, nor even to give much of a picture of him as a climber. He was an originator in the way in which he developed new cliffs ("because other people don't go there," he said), often on variable rock, and in his use of safety devices which have now become commonplace. Long before karabiners were used he fell off Eliminate on Helsby, where others had been killed. But he managed to protect himself with a sling, and this art he found most useful on his hunting grounds round the Devil's Kitchen, on Craig Rhaiadr and the Three Cliffs.

To climb with Menlove gave the impression of strength rather than of lightness (Colin Kirkus's quality). The whole was a wrestling match, and specially so in the clinkers he usually insisted on wearing. In 1935 he struggled for nearly an hour, in clinkers, to repeat his feat of climbing Flake Crack on C.B. unaided. When that failed, he waited placidly for my nailed boot on his head. It was this leaning towards effort which made him the first (and only?) man to row solo across the Minch to the Outer Hebrides and back. Or he would take a canoe to the Isle of Man over a Whit weekend. And yet Western Slabs on Dinas Mot and Bow-Shaped on Clogwyn Du'r Arddu showed that he could be delicate too, when he wished. It was a question of mood, and, as he said himself, on some days he would fail to get up Hope. As a second he gave a feeling of confidence and strength that was not illusory. Under his eye I was made to lead climbs I had not dreamed of, but to profit even more from the experience of his mature and affectionate loyalty than from that of leading.

With people, with writing, it was the same story. "My over great intensity with people is not v. good for them either," he wrote once, "except that it's necessary with patients to be absolutely following every least mental shift" — and that made him a brilliant psychologist. In writing there was the same sense of convulsion, the same conquest of obstacles as much in himself as in the material. Nothing came easily, but what came was worth waiting for. The Climbers' Club owes him three full guides (since my own part was entirely subordinate) and the Clogwyn Du'r Arddu interim offprint. These set a new standard. They took the climber to the rock face, not just to the line up it which somebody had traced, and described that face in remarkable prose. One may quarrel with the underestimations but not with the descriptions, and his talent for this type of writing comes out more vividly in the few short stories. These, with fragments of tortured and yet wonderful verse, are all that he has left. Being a psychologist, and Menlove, he was one of the few who could come near to putting on paper the states of mind of the climber.

The years after 1939 have been years of tragic waste. Menlove received absolute exemption as a conscientious objector, but he never recovered from the shock of war and the suspicion that his fellows were engaged in a madness which in a real sense threatened him personally. If the war had not come, he would have fulfilled himself in the psychological work he set out to write. As it was, nearly 20 years of frustration are now succeeded by a death which should never have been. We mourn one of the great personalities of climbing, and a man who might have been many things besides.

WILFRID NOYCE.

BRIAN McKENNA

Brian joined the Club in 1929, but it was not till March of the next year that he ventured to stay in Helyg. He feared a mass of Rules and Regulations with a Custodian who would order him about. In his army life in both wars he hated the restrictions and the routine, but he found the kind of life we enjoyed at Helyg what he liked and soon he became a regular visitor.

During the ten years prior to the outbreak of war in 1939 there was a strong section of the Club from the Liverpool district, and it was unusual not to find half a dozen of them in Helyg at week-ends. These were, of course, the years when rock-

Left: Raymond Greene.
Right: Brian McKenna.

climbing in North Wales was developing so rapidly, led by Colin Kirkus and Menlove Edwards. Brian very quickly made many friends, his unfailing good humour being quite infectious, and he was invariably the leader in any kind of 'rag'. The only occasion when I saw the least sign of temper was when he and Menlove playfully began a wrestling match in the bedroom and each was astonished to find the other equally strong. It seemed, for a few minutes, that things might become serious, and I had to calm them down. Needless to say, both of them were bitterly ashamed of themselves.

Brian's strength was very evident in his climbing. Without professing to be a 'tiger', he was a very sound leader on climbs of V. Diff. standard and always ready to help and encourage beginners or those in difficulty. Much as he loved the Welsh mountains he always longed for the Cuillin of Skye, to which for some years he and I organized a party. Such wild country particularly appealed to him, though he was a true countryman and happy to be on lesser hills, particularly when well-wooded. Trees he loved, and it was a matter of regret that he had never gone in for forestry. Instead, he earned his living as a landscape gardener, his speciality being the making of rock-gardens and growing the plants for them. At his home in Anglesey he has left a perfect example of this art, the object of constant admiration of the summer visitors. He greatly enriched the natural beauty of Helyg with the trees and shrubs he planted, and which never ceased to be his constant care.

His work for the Club was not confined to Helyg and it is not generally known that we owe to him the finding of Cwm Glas Mawr and the original Ynys Ettws.

E.S. Chantrell, 1960 C.C.J.

RAYMOND GREENE

World War I nearly put an end to the Climbers' Club. In the years just after it membership fell to an all-time low. Active members were resigning right and left, and there were few new recruits. Raymond Greene and I were amongst those few, and we were both surprised to find ourselves on the Committee barely a year after joining. (Raymond had less reason than I to be surprised as he had been recently appointed Hon. Ed. and was already working on the 1923 Journal.) Mallory had just become President, and at his first Committee meeting he enquired about the state of the Club. The Secretary, Myles Mathews, had to admit that it was practically on its death bed. Mallory then proposed that a Sub-Committee be set up to recommend measures to bring it back to life. S.A. Marples, then V.P., was to head this body, and Raymond and I were to be its other members.

The sub-committee, which Raymond so very irreverently dubbed 'The demoribundisation sub-committee', met and deliberated, but it soon became apparent that what was needed was not measures but a man. Raymond suggested Herbert Carr for the job. Without delay Herbert was inducted into the Club and given a free hand. It is now matter of history that he brought the club back to life by his almost unaided efforts. Raymond helped to some extent by bringing out some lively 'Club Bulletins' — an outward and visible sign that the Club was not so moribund after all.

The sub-committee as such may not have done much for the Club, but for me it brought the inestimable benefit of a life-long friendship with Raymond Greene.

He was the eldest of the three Greene brothers. When he died of heart failure in December 1982 (aged 81), his obituaries in both Times and Telegraph asserted that all three brothers were alike, and went on to list some disagreeable traits which (in the obituarist's opinion) they had in common. I do not know to what extent Sir Hugh and Graham Greene felt maligned by these aspersions, but from my own intimate knowledge of Raymond, extending over 60 years, I can say categorically that not one of them was true of him. He was in fact the kindliest of men, warm-hearted, generous and with a fine sense of humour — in short, an ideal companion on the hills or off them.

In one respect he resembled his brothers; they were all well over six feet tall. Also they went to the same school, Berkhamstead, where their father was Headmaster. Raymond went on to Pembroke College, Oxford, where he studied medicine. After graduating in 1927 he did a number of Resident jobs at Westminster Hospital before embarking on private practice in London and Oxford. After the War he became consultant physician to several London Hospitals, and began to specialise in endocrinology. In time he became a leading authority in this branch of medicine, and his writings on the Thyroid Gland are now acclaimed as the most authoritative works on the subject. He spent the last twenty years of his life as a Harley Street consultant in his speciality.

Apart from his medical work and mountaineering, one of Raymond's main interests lay in Zoology, and he was for six years Vice-President of the Zoological Society of London. In an article on him in the Journal of Zoology the Society's President, Lord Zuckerman, pays high tribute both to the value of his scientific work and to his warm approachable nature.

In his childhood Raymond was introduced to the Lake District by his father, a keen mountain walker, and his long legs took him over every mountain of note in the District. Then a lantern lecture at his school by Ashley Abraham inspired the urge to climb rocks, and Abraham himself found for him companions for his earliest climbs.

'... He introduced me to a lone climber called Binns who took me up the Napes Needle. The obsession was born.

The next year Abraham introduced me to Weeks, with whom I did the Needle again and other climbs of moderate difficulty. I fell in with Holland and Speaker, great rock climbers in their day. I especially remember the day when the three of us polished off in one day all the climbs then known on the Napes. We did not stop for lunch and it was only as I ran rejoicing back to Langdale that I knew I was hungry.'

As a student Raymond explored the 'crags' of Oxford with other O.U.M.C. friends:

'There was then no Cambridge mountaineering club and we always invited climbers from "the other place" to join us. Once I had a "return match" in Cambridge, the most terrifying weekend of my life. We did all the standard climbs on the colleges and finally Elliot Wallis, Gilbert Adair and I attempted King's Chapel. We failed high up at an overhang, but a fortnight later I had a card from the other two. They had succeeded. By stretching out the left arm, they had succeeded in holding a lightning conductor between finger and thumb, thus keeping their balance as they surmounted the drip course that had defeated us.'

Prior to qualifying Raymond spent some time in Edinburgh where he was accustomed to visiting Salisbury Crags every Sunday morning:

'Here I nearly ended my climbing days. My friend "Bunny" Mansell, a novice, was stuck out of my sight above me. Stepping back carelessly to see what had halted him, I fell over the edge of my stance and landed on my back some twenty feet below, happily in a small patch of bog. In doing so I pulled off Bunny who joined me rather painfully in my bog. Both were unharmed...'

While at Oxford, he helped Herbert Carr revive the O.U.M.C., and was introduced to the Alps through a meet of that club. When I first met him he had already made a name for himself as an alpinist. But it was a chance meeting with Frank Smythe when both were soloing on Gimmer that opened the door for him to the scene where he felt most in his element — the Himalayas. He was with Smythe's 1931 expedition to Kamet, the first 25,000-foot peak ever to be climbed. The ascent was made in two parties, Raymond leading the second. Around the 23,000-foot mark he succumbed to the altitude effect and sent the other two members of his party ahead while he rested in the snow. After a short nap he felt fresh again, and had the unusual experience of reaching the summit alone.

'Some 300 feet above me was a white ridge in full sunshine. I thought if I could get thus far I would be able to see the top and relieve what was beginning to be a gnawing anxiety for their safety. The way became excessively steep, and the snow dangerous, a shifting powder a few inches deep on hard ice. Once the surface slipped, probably only a few inches but enough to alarm me. Here a serious slip would have meant a fall of some 7,000 feet down the eastern precipice. I felt quite confident about stopping myself, but the others were less experienced and my anxiety grew. I gave a shout and heard a cheerful and unintelligible noise above. Almost at the same moment I saw their tracks. I cut across to them and upwards again towards the ridge I had picked as my look-out.

Then suddenly my head rose above the ridge and my eyes, expecting a further snowfield and yet another ridge, saw for one moment nothing. Then casting them down, I saw a sea of white cloud stretching without interruption to the purple horizon. A few yards to my right lay the summit...'

After Kamet, Smythe's team went on to explore the almost completely unknown Badrinath range, and conquered numerous peaks and passes of over 20,000 feet. Later in life Raymond looked back on this time as the happiest he had ever spent.

Two years later he was back in the Himalayas as chief medical officer to the 1933 Everest expedition. Here he contributed a great deal more than his medical skill, and the venture would not have achieved the limited success it did if he had not been there to back up the leader, Hugh Ruttledge, and even to take charge himself when the occasion called for it. Retreating from the mountain led to a delightful incident:

'Of the day when Jack Longland and I, stark naked, raced our ponies across a great green plain and, forgetting our state, into a village of which the inhabitants had never seen a white man, least of all a nude one.'

Other useful contributions Raymond made to mountaineering were his researches into high altitude respiration and his invention of the 'Greene Sack' for carrying down victims of climbing accidents. This latter device was to prove invaluable in commando raids during the war. One of Raymond's own wartime activities was commando training in rock climbing.

But rock climbing for its own sake had no strong appeal for Raymond. Once he had savoured the more varied pleasures and thrills of greater mountaineering in the Alps and Himalays he came to look upon our home crags as no more than the best available substitute. Not that he didn't fully enjoy the substitute. We had some wonderful days together in Wales and Lakeland. But he had no ambition to pioneer new rock climbs, or even to raise his personal standard, which was about the same as my own. His tremendous reach gave him the advantage on some routes, but for the kind of delicate balance climbing which was all the vogue during our years together a shorter man may benefit from his lack of inches (witness A.B.'s exploits in a later era!). But one could not have asked for a more congenial companion on the rocks.

Raymond was essentially an adventurous character. When he wasn't seeking adventure (as, in his younger days, he usually was) it seemed to come to him unbidden. This will surely be agreed by all who have read his enthralling book of autobiographical fragments published in 1974 under the title 'Moments of Being'. I was privileged to hear many of these stories from his own mouth just after the events had occurred, and from my memory of his narratives I could justly chide him for playing them down in the book rather than over-dramatising. For example, the whole of the Aleister Crowley story as he told it to me was far more dramatic and thrilling than it sounds in print.

'During the war I was attached to the Emergency Hospital at Aylesbury. Someone asked me to tell the Crowley Saga, which I did, including the incident of Frederick Gambier MacBean. "Why," asked the very attractive anaesthetist, "didn't you put a curse on him? You must have learnt a few good curses at the Abbey."

"It never occurred to me," I replied, "but I will do it now." I made up a long and resounding curse, partly out of the nonsensical rituals of the Crowley sect and partly from my own imagination. Two days later I found the anaesthetist staring with troubled eyes at the front page of The Times spread out on the table. Frederick Gambier MacBean was dead.'

Raymond also writes of the episode when he and his sister Molly were descending New West on Pillar with C.F. Holland coming last. When Molly fell off on the traverse, her rope to Holland ran out freely, and though Raymond held her from the far end of the traverse, she had a long pendulum swing and sustained quite a battering. It seems that Holland, whose motto on the rocks was never 'Safety First', was actually climbing down the chimney instead of attending to the rope. This is how Raymond tells it in the book. What he does not tell is that a fourth member of the party witnessed the incident from the screes below. This was a suitor for Molly's hand who had been wooing her for an unconscionably long time without screwing up the courage to propose. But, after seeing his inamorata in such peril, he popped the question on the spot and they lived happily ever after. This seemed to round off the story nicely when I heard it from Raymond.

Senior members who may recall the unhappy Giveen affair in the 1920s will be interested to learn from this book that Giveen made a serious attempt to murder Raymond for no better reason, it seems, than that Raymond had blocked his admission to membership of our Club. He actually shot in the back (though not fatally) a tall man whom he mistook for Raymond. Then, discovering his error, he killed himself with the other barrel.

In his heyday Raymond must have been, like Leslie Stephen, 'Fleetest of foot of all the Alpine brotherhood'. He resembled Stephen also in that, after he married and his two children were born, he kept his adventurous spirit sternly in check and settled down to be a good family man and a respectable Harley Street consultant. It must have cost him a great effort to give up difficult mountaineering, but he found some consolation in dashing off to the hills whenever he had a day or two to spare and indulging in long solitary walks. It caused him great distress when even this mild consolation was denied to him by physical disability.

Maurice Guinness, 1983 C.C.J.

GILBERT F. PEAKER
1927-1984

With the death of Gilbert Peaker at the age of 80 the Club has lost one of its oldest members — one of a select group of climbers who joined the Club in the 1920s. A Yorkshireman by birth Peaker studied celestial astronomy at Cambridge prior to taking up Cartography within the Civil Service, a calling which took him abroad to work in Nigeria for some time. On his return he taught Mathematics at King's College, London, and also in Leicester. Not only did he become an academic in the field of Education, but he was also very active in the hills for many years and he was a frequent visitor at Helyg — mainly in the late 20s and 30s. There are many memories of him:

'I can only remember meeting Gilbert Peaker three times. He had an entirely unsought after reputation as something of an iron man, and all three of my recollections of him are consistent with this image. I was with an undergraduate party in the Alps, probably in 1935, about to go down from the Montenvers to Chamonix. The weather had broken completely; and we were surprised when a snow-covered figure walked in, trying to find a companion willing to attempt some fairly serious climb from the Argentiere glacier in the early hours of the following morning. No-one volunteered, and Gilbert went out into the snow disappointed.

Two or three years later, we did a climb together on Lliwedd. I was staying at Helyg, and (as on the previous occasion) he had looked in the previous evening, to ask if anyone was available for a climb the next day. I cannot remember what route we did, but what does stick in my memory is that, whereas I drove round from Helyg and left my car at Pen-y-Pass, Peaker walked all the way back again.'

'Peaker and I climbed together from Helyg many times. He was remarkably tough and impervious to bad conditions. There was some story about his exhausting some boys by over-climbing them — probably apocryphal. He and I put in a lot of climbing during the day — we were both keen on climbing down as much as up. I remember traversing Tryfan with him from north to south by going up the first climb and down the next and so on, and I think we did the same on Lliwedd. He was an interesting and amusing companion....'

'My first lead on British rock was the Amphitheatre Buttress on Craig yr Ysfa. My two supporters were Gilbert Peaker and Eric Shipton. I wonder if anyone has had two such competent mountaineers behind him on his first lead.'

Within the Club, Peaker served on the Committee in 1937 and was also a member of the Northern Committee between 1937 and 1940, but some of the best stories come from visits to the huts:

'Two endearing habits in huts are worth recording. On occasions he would snore continuously for a time and finally awaken himself by a particularly violent outburst. At this point he would leap out of bed and shake all fellow inmates and accuse them of snoring! At breakfast he would often ask to put his bacon in the pan with the batch being cooked. After cooking he would extract with mathematical precision, the exact number of square inches of bacon he had put in. No-one dared tell him that bacon shrinks when fried!'

'...His energy on the other hand did not extend to catering or cooking and he was quite content to leave that side entirely to his companion, whose reward for his labour was sallies such as: "This breakfast is fit for a king" — (pause for surprised acknowledgement) — "two days after the revolution. Now pass me the tobacco!" '

Apart from his natural humour and intellectual drive Gilbert clearly had great physical strength, which manifested itself on many occasions.

'Climbs were punctuated by his expounding some philosophical or mathematical point, usually when one's whole attention was focussed on working out the next move.'

'During the autumn and winter of 1938-39 Peaker and I spent four weekends together at the Robertson Lamb Hut in Langdale and one at Helyg. He was a man of tremendous energy and was reputed to be the heaviest man to have run a Marathon in standard time (It was said at the time that he just failed to make the Olympic Team for the Marathon.). Days on the hills with a man of such stamina were an unforgettable experience. He would cram as many climbs as possible into a day, whatever the weather....Despite the passage of 44 years, the eight days which we spent on the hills together have left an indelible impression of an enthusiastic, stimulating and witty companion.'

Although Peaker is not well known for first ascents on British rock he did however team up with Menlove Edwards at one stage and seconded him on the first ascents of both Bracketside Spout, a Severe on Lliwedd, and the far more famous Slape on Clogwyn y Grochan. At the time of the Harding Pass guide Slape was regarded as a very exposed and strenuous Hard VS — in fact one of the hardest routes in the area prior to the Brown and Whillans era. It must have been quite a traumatic and memorable event watching Edwards work his way up the 'short wall' without modern protection to safeguard the pitch.

During the Second World War Peaker was attached to the Treasury and had some responsibility for the working of the rationing scheme, then at the end of the war he became an HMI in 1945. This led to an interest in 'declining standards of national intelligence' in 1948. Having developed skills as a statistician he carried out research for the Newsom and Plowden reports some years later.

In 1948 Peaker organised and directed the first (and only) Ministry of Education Training Course for Mountaineering. This was advertised to be an extension of a Ministry Course on Organised Camping in Langdale. In the event Clifford Bingham was the sole member of the Camping Course selected to go forward to the Mountaineering Course. The other recruits were all either members of the C.C. or the Alpine Club! Bingham found himself roped up with Jack Longland and A.B. Hargreaves for the first session. As the first course of its kind it attracted press coverage and also had reporter/photographer cover from the Times, Picture Post and Illustrated London News.

'Peaker had no mercy. The non-climbing reporters were dragged to Napes Needle for photos of the whole group, a few other Longland specials behind the Needle and then a quick jog over to Pillar to complete the day.'

Despite Peaker's considerable strength he was involved in several accidents, including one rather serious incident in the 50s.

'...also on Lliwedd it was the day of the C.C. Welsh dinner in the late autumn. This was the occasion on which the 'Matchstick' a 15-foot spike of rock weighing many tons which, although not part of the mountain, had stood the strain of parties climbing over it for 60 years, slowly keeled outwards and disappeared with an immense crash down the cliff. We were climbing in two ropes of three, and I was very glad not to be on the first rope, which was actually using the Matchstick as a belay. Naturally, they all went with it. However, the party was miraculously preserved when the Matchstick dug itself into a wide bilberry terrace some 25 feet below. Peaker was one of the three who survived; he was obviously hurt, but refused to wait for a rescue party. His injury was later found to be a broken pelvis, and it must have required extraordinary determination on his part to complete the climb and walk all the way back to the road from the top

of Lliwedd. He must have been in his middle or late fifties at the time.'
Clifford Bingham in fact ended up in hospital just after Peaker:

'My next encounter was when I moved into the bed recently occupied by Peaker
in the Bangor Hospital after his fall on Lliwedd. As he was allowed out I was
admitted having slipped on the ice at the summit of Glyder Fach and landed in
Cwm Tryfan.'

'Two memories persist — one of his habit of breaking into a trot over the
Carneddau summits after a hard day's climbing and secondly his casual attitude
to belays. I always assumed I was free climbing (soloing) when he was leading.'

'After he was crippled in the accident, he managed to get about with the aid of
two sticks, and would descend a hillside at some speed leaping from rock to rock,
with great agility.'

With such an outstanding character as Peaker it is hard to sum up his life as an
active member of the Club, but perhaps the following comment is most apt:

'I always enjoyed meeting Gilbert Peaker in the hills. It was relaxing yet
challenging both physically and intellectually. There was always an element of
surprise around the corner, coupled with a boyish enthusiasm for just being
there. His death is a sad loss both to the Club and to mountaineering in general.'
Compiled with extracts from:

Clifford Bingham, Bill Stallybrass, David Cox,
Charles Marriott, and A.B. Hargreaves, 1984 C.C.J.

CUTHBERT H. FRENCH
1930-1984

C.H. French joined the Club in 1930 and remained a member until his death
earlier this year at the age of 90. In the 1930s he was one of the real characters to be
found at Helyg, often reeling in trout for breakfast, and was often observed smoking
a cigar while pursuing his hobby of observing others — which accounted for the
uncanny likeness of all his sketches to the unwitting victims. His sketch of Stuart
Chantrell is appropriately included in this journal.

Reminiscing in the 1984 C.C.J. Stuart Chantrell added a touch of flavour with a
sketch of 'the lads' at play:

'C.H. French's skill in making sketches for the Club Guides has helped to make
them successful, and we could do well with more of his caricatures than the few that
adorn the walls of the Helyg Kitchen. It was not so easy to appreciate French's
introduction of fireworks into the Cottage, and a fitting retribution awaited him

PRESIDENT

VICE-PRESIDENT

COLIN KIRKUS

THE LEADER

when he was forced to satisfy the demands of nature closeted with a large and explosive "Rip-Rap". I could hardly sympathise, having suffered a previous experience of a Roman Candle being fired under my bed and a "Sprinkler" inserted in my cigar'.

From 1933-1940 and again from 1946-1951 French was a member of the Northern Committee and during the earlier period he put in a great deal of hard work to draw the crag diagrams for several of the C.C. guides. Starting in 1937 he did the diagrams for both the Tryfan and the Glyder Fach guides. Later, In 1939, he produced a whole-crag diagram for the Lliwedd guide, then a year after, he illustrated the revised Cwm Idwal guide for Menlove Edwards — altogether an impressive tally. Ask any of 'the old brigade' of the Club, and they will remember not the guide diagrams but the brilliance of his caricatures of such eminent figures as Solly, Ruttledge and General Bruce.

During the war he served as a Lieutenant in the Pioneer Corps and it was said that he had served with distinction in the First World War. In fact, he played the part to perfection, being short, dapper, neat, meticulous and looking every inch an army Officer.

Although he is not well-known for his ascents on rock his near-perfect technique made it a joy to watch him climb. He was unambitious and kept well within his capabilities, although he did accompany Menlove Edwards on the first ascents of three rather vegetated routes on Clogwyn y Geifr: Dump Crack; the smooth and delicate VS, North Slabs; and Devil's Dive, which in 1948 was described as:

'It must have taken some daring to launch up the centre of this steep cliff. A serious undertaking, both in position and execution. The initial steep vegetation is part of the strong character of this route...'

Dispensable rock and remarkable plant life were the attributes of these routes and it needed a man of character to follow in the steps of Menlove. French was such a man.

1984 C.C.J.

Portfolio of photographs taken at the Helyg Diamond Jubilee celebrations in June 1985.

1. Noel Odell toasting the event.   Photo: Ian Smith.

2. Herbert Carr (nearly 89) in June 1985 at the Helyg Diamond Jubilee Celebrations.
                                                                       Photo: Ian Smith.

3. The Helyg Custodian, Tony Jones with the plaque of Herbert Carr.   *Photo: Ian Smith.*

4. Tony Jones receives the plaque from Herbert Carr while Trevor Jones and Ivan Waller look on.
                                                                       Photo: Ian Smith.

5. Tony Jones (Custodian) looking on as A.B. Hargreaves greets Herbert Carr.   *Photo: Ian Smith.*

6. Chris Bonington and Noel Odell, Everesters 61 years apart.   *Photo: Ian Smith.*

7. The Climbing Party: L. to R., Malcolm Cameron, Hugh Banner, Trevor Jones, Derek Walker, Ivan Waller, Mike Ball, Chris Bonington and Claude Davies.   *Photo: Ian Smith.*

8. A historic gathering at Helyg, June 1985.   *Photo: Ian Smith.*

9. The Presidents: Derek Walker, J. Emlyn Jones, Trevor Jones, Mike Westmacott, David Cox, Harry Sales, Tony Moulam, A.B. Hargreaves and Herbert Carr (seated).   *Photo: Ian Smith.*

10. The Custodians: Johnnie Lees, Trevor Jones and Tony Moulam with Herbert Carr.   *Photo: Ian Smith.*

11. Derek Walker (President) speaking at the dinner (A.B. Hargreaves and Noel Odell are on his left).
                                                                       Photo: Ian Smith.

12. The signed menu.   *Photo: Ian Smith.*

13. Geoff Milburn (Editor), Herbert Carr (Helyg pioneer) and Derek Walker (President) relaxing in the lounge of the Pen-y-Gwryd hotel.   *Photo: Ian Smith.*

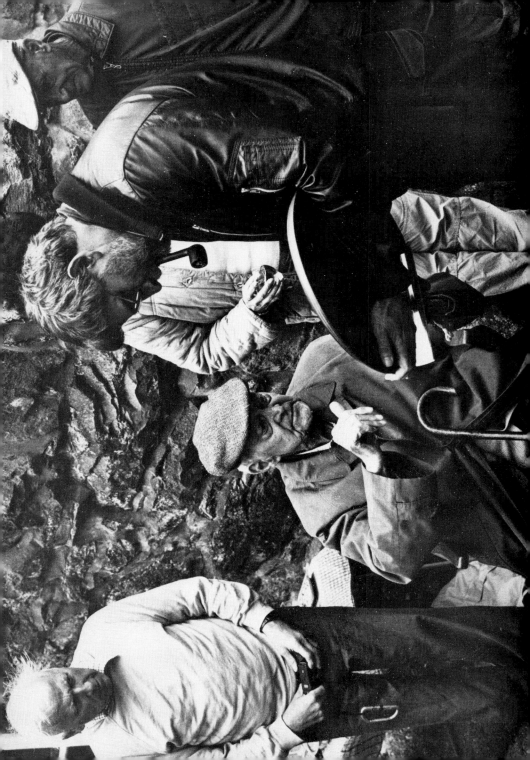

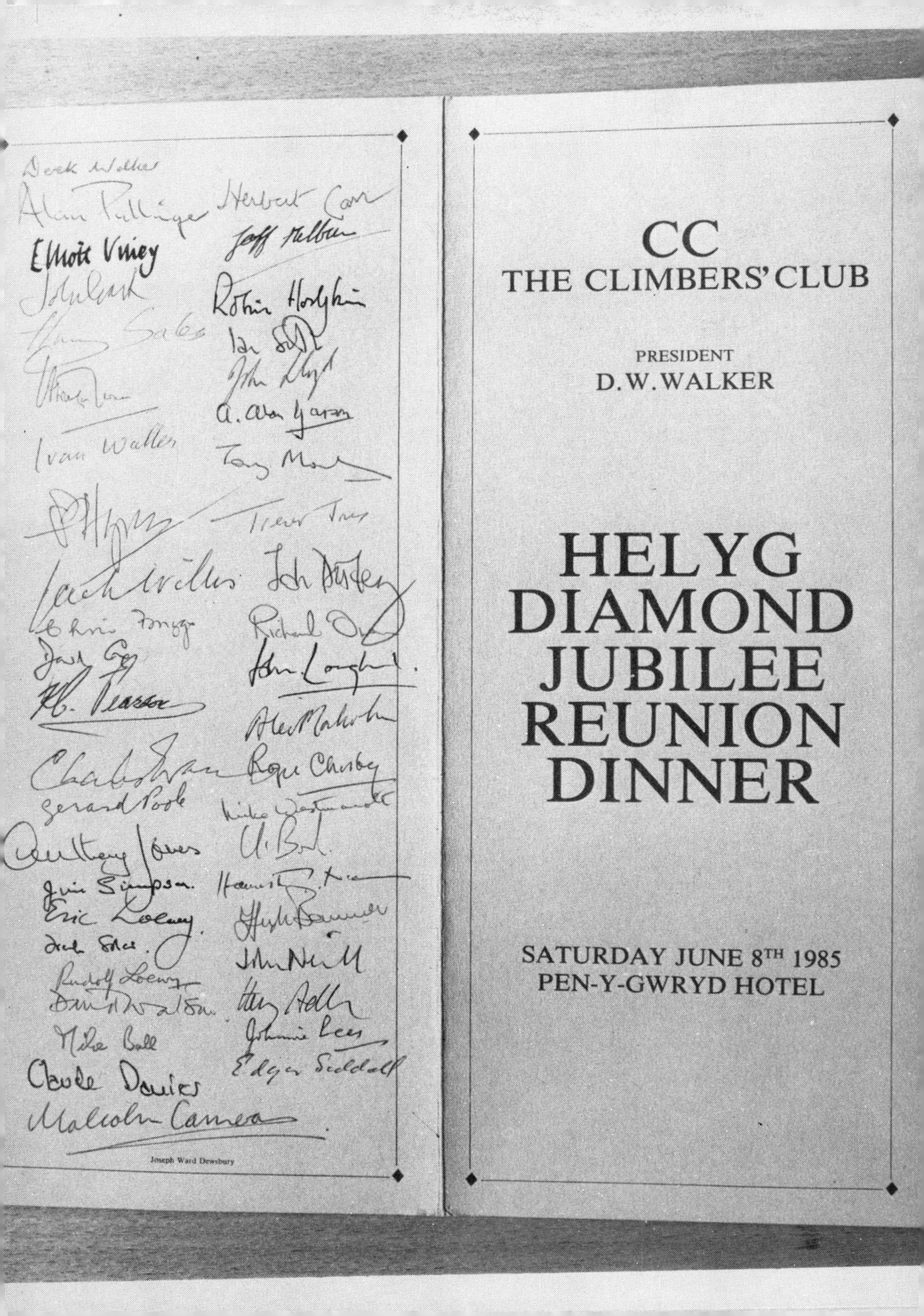

(Left page — autographs/signatures, largely illegible)

Derek Walker
Alan Pullinger   Herbert Carr
Elliott Viney   Geoff Milburn
John Last   Robin Hodgkin
Harry Sales   Ian Self
...   John Lloyd
...   A. Alan Yates
Ivan Waller   Tony Moulam
J. H. ...   Trevor Jones
Jack Willis   John Disley
Chris Briggs   Richard ...
Dave Cox   John Longland
R.B. Pearson
                 Alex Malcolm
Charles Evans   Roger Chorley
Gerard Peel   Mike Westmacott
Anthony Jones   Al Bond
Jim Simpson   Hamish Nicol
Eric ...   Hugh Banner
Jack Soper   John Neill
Rudolf Loewy   Henry Adler
David Walton   Johnnie Lees
Mike Ball   Edgar Siddall
Cecile Davies
Malcolm Carrea

Joseph Ward Dewsbury

CC
THE CLIMBERS' CLUB

PRESIDENT
D. W. WALKER

HELYG
DIAMOND
JUBILEE
REUNION
DINNER

SATURDAY JUNE 8TH 1985
PEN-Y-GWRYD HOTEL

HELYG - THE DIAMOND

GEOFF MILBURN

'Here's Triple Health!... Let the toast Peak-and-Pass!
Raise Helyg, Gentlemen!... And drain your whole Cwm Glas!'

Herbert Carr's toast rang out boldly across the dining room of the Pen-y-Gwryd, quoting Geoffrey Winthrop Young's words of long ago, to celebrate a unique landmark in the history of our club. The date was June 8th, 1985, and gathered in the one room were a few of the small select surviving group of climbers of a bygone era, as well as a formidable array of Presidents, Vice-Presidents and Honorary Members of the Climbers' Club. The distinguished members included: Noel Odell, A.B. Hargreaves, Ivan Waller, Herbert Carr (with his daughter and son-in-law) and many others - it is not likely that such a group will ever meet again and include in its ranks survivors of that golden age in climbing.

At the end of his speech Herbert Carr finished with a few apt lines which are well worth quoting:

'Look forward 50 years - and fifty more.
There'll still be Helyg with its ever-open door.
Bacon will still be fried there and a kettle sings.
Surely, they'll laugh at us
Old, far-off forgotten things!
Well - not to worry - when I'm dead and gone
I rather think that Helyg will live on!

The event was not merely to celebrate the 60th anniversary of Helyg, rather it was a moving occasion of great nostalgia to acknowledge the birth of 'modern' rock-climbing in Wales which triggered off a sequence of subsequent events including a notable phase in the development of the Fell and Rock Climbing Club and the acquisition of its several Lakeland huts. Helyg was not merely a hut — it was an island in the centre of a vast ocean from which waves spread out far and wide to influence the whole future of British climbing. It was from Helyg that Kirkus and Edwards operated and set out to make their great ascents on Cloggy, in the Pass, at Ogwen and on Craig-yr-Ysfa.

The Diamond Jubilee had started well on the Saturday when Ivan Waller, a fit and sprightly 78 year old youngster (who had cycled up from Bettws-y-Coed the previous day), followed the President up Belle Vue Bastion to repeat a route he had pioneered 58 years earlier in 1927. The party in fact only just got to Terrace Wall as Chris Bonington, back from his recent success on Everest, had somehow led the party slightly off route on the way up(!) which resulted in a lengthy traverse across gullies, ribs and vegetation to reach the Terrace. It was suggested that perhaps Chris was not feeling at home owing to the lack of snow. In fact Chris had returned to settle an old score. At the age of 17 he had fallen off Scars and concussed had hitched home. This time he had returned armed with sticky boots, chalk, friends etc. to redress the balance. Also on the face were Harry Sales, Rudolf Loewy, Trevor Jones, Hugh Banner and McNaught Davies. Ian Smith our 'official' photographer for the meet joined the Walker-Waller rope to capture a scoop which should be revealed in this publication if he remembered to load his camera.

Later in the afternoon a large crowd gathered at Helyg for the President's speech and to welcome Herbert Carr back to Helyg to thank him for his enthusiasm 60 years earlier. The crowd mingled enthusiastically as old friends bumped into each other and champagne (Buvet Ladubay Brut - NOT a cheap substitute!) flowed free. Herbert Carr presented a carved plaque to the warden and two rhododendrons were planted to mark the event. Although there was total silence for the speeches, as soon as a camera was produced for the photos chaos reigned supreme and the masses seemed to move away from the lens as fast as they were urged towards it. Nevertheless various Presidents, Hut Wardens and the like were urged and cajouled to line up to be shot in turn(!). Messrs Moulam and Jones even performed for the crowd on the Helyg boulder, and then just as the crowds began to depart a car slid to a halt beside the double white line and who should emerge but Hamish Nicol and Peter Newman fresh from a successful Scottish tour complete with a celebratory bottle of the hard stuff.

Once the champagne had been drained to the last drop the crowd departed leaving the occupants of the hut to gear up for the evening. Scruffs were exchanged for snappy suits and the warden descended from the sanctuary in the loft resplendent in kilt with sporran and dirk at the ready.

The pre-dinner mêlée made circulating almost impossible. Against the bar the Editor congratulated himself on having remained traditional to the last by his round of the Horseshoe earlier in the day while other less ethical types had resorted to ropes and the like on steeper rock — even though Hugh Banner had abandoned his lifeline on Tryfan. It was realised with some degree of hilarity that to emulate Ivan Waller's achievement Hugh Banner would have to make an ascent of Troach in the year 2,017. Perhaps some future Editor will note this prediction!

Before sitting down to dinner the ensemble had to run a gauntlet of paperwork to sign various manuscripts, locked books and the like, but eventually after the Grace we tucked into a rather fine pâté prior to Helyg Soup (which some wag hoped was

not brewed from the remains of the infamous Helyg Rat!). The local roast duckling, complete with apple sauce, new potatoes, peas and carrots soon disappeared but people began to flag through the apple pie and cream and only a few survivors kept on to the delights of an ample cheeseboard prior to the coffee.

It was well after 9.30 p.m. before the various toasts began and when Herbert Carr got up to speak on Helyg 1925, for those present with a sense of history, there was an awareness of those who have gone before but who have already died: Siegfried Herford, George Mallory, George Sansom, Fred Pigott, Ted Hicks, C.F. Holland, Raymond Greene and the like. In addition there were those who for personal reasons were not able to be with us: Jack Longland, Bill Stallybrass, Rennie Bere, John Poole, John Hunt, Dr. H.L. Richardson, Peter Bicknell and Maurice Guinness.

But it was Herbert Carr who stole the limelight with his powerful and evocative speech - and who better than the man who found Helyg for us so long ago. Not to be outdone A.B. (Hargreaves) stamped his own personality on the proceedings to make it quite clear to all present that the whole development of climbing revolved round Helyg — of course, where else. And it is for this reason that we are stepping out in faith to celebrate the Jubilee with a book that will underline the importance of Helyg for posterity. (The derogatory remarks in the bar the night before, "A horrible spot, Helyg, I never did like it", were just a pole apart. But then I don't like television computer programmes - they just haven't got a sense of history!)

Derek Walker, a President who has done the Club proud since he took office, finished off the evening with a polished speech to reflect the healthy state of the Club in 1985. Prior to his speech, Derek had presented Herbert Carr with a Jacobean Goblet engraved with:

H.R.C. CARR
HELYG DIAMOND JUBILEE
1925 - 1985

On the other side of the goblet was an engraving of Helyg and Tryfan which was taken from the photo in the 1926 Bulletin.

The one hiccup during the dinner was an impromptu game called 'passing the menu'. Eight 'official' menus went round to be signed by all present (for archives, absent friends etc.) as well as a variety of unofficial menus from members with an eye to collecting a unique souvenir of the occasion. A few of the lists are complete and some have even been signed twice owing to the fact that various clockwise and anti-clockwise combinations were tried to circulate the menus. Playing musical chairs during the meal couldn't have caused much more chaos. Of such sterling character is our Club well-enriched. It was a fitting build-up to a long session in the bar afterwards.

Now the Editor must make it quite plain that having sampled the beer and the wine to great effect he was not aware of the lateness of the hour when he arrived back at Helyg just before 3 a.m. It cannot be denied however that having brewed up he was about to embark on a lengthy discussion of a philosophical nature when the stentorian voice of our assiduous Hut Warden floated down from 'on high' in noble tradition (even to be applied on such a historic night/morning) to command the Editor to desist — or words to that effect. Suitably chastened the Editor (who was sleeping in his estate car to guard all the valuable photos which had been brought to him) grabbed his coffee and departed closing the door quietly behind him. Unfortunately, outside, the heavens had opened to such an extent that Herbert should perhaps have planted rice instead of rhododendrons. The door was locked! The Editor had no alternative but to follow his steaming mug of coffee up the steps. At the time following the white line down the centre of the A5 seemed a good idea — until the rain finally got through the Editor's best suit to sober him up enough to retreat to the shelter of a 'wretched hovel', which turned out to be the Garage. In the absence of the Hut Warden sleep came swiftly.

By morning Helyg was still, its occupants dead to the world, but in time life began anew. Sausages burnt to perfection in the pan seemed to highlight the night before and all its splendour. Even Tony was in a good mood and fought off the righteous members who were dutifully queuing up to pay their Hut Fees. Back at the P-y-G a leisurely breakfast was in full swing with waitresses busily ferrying delicacies to those who had been noble enough to give up their places at Helyg. In their warm rooms they had missed the dawn at Helyg where chattering magpies had flitted about in the wood: pale green larches, darker pines, white flowered hawthorns with the petals fading sadly, the willow's catkins nearly done (yes Helyg is not called 'The Willows' for nothing), and best of all the russet-coloured bracken stems providing a perfect contrast to the dazzling hue of the bluebells and the opening rhododendron flowers. There is no doubt in my mind that Helyg really is 'the jewel in the crown' of the Climbers' Club.

At the P-y-G a few parties were braving the elements, clearly inspired by the night before. Hodgkin and party appeared to be heading off for the mist and rain of Lliwedd, while a few gathered to bid Herbert Carr farewell. Herbert Carr was there when Helyg was 'discovered' for the Club and it is only fitting that this chapter in the Club's history should end with Herbert. On behalf of the whole Club, spread across the world, the toast is "Helyg, Maurice Guinness and Herbert Carr — we wish them all good health and a long life".

Overleaf: Derek Walker belaying Ivan Waller (Helyg in the background).   *Photo: Ian Smith.*

THE IMPORTANCE OF HELYG - SOME EXTRACTS

A.B. HARGREAVES

The decision to purchase Helyg turned out to be the most important decision ever made since the club began.

The setting up of Helyg had great effect, almost immediately on the club itself and started a Golden Age in the development of climbing in Wales.

The great virtue of Helyg was that it became a meeting ground where the young climbers could congregate, and operate from, instead of staying at hotels and guest houses, where they could not easily get together.

Another virtue of Helyg was that it was within walking distance of most of the main crags which was very important in those days, because few of the young climbers had cars.

*   *   *   *   *

My first visit to Helyg was in May 1927, as a very new member of the Wayfarers Club who were having a meet at Tal-y-Braich, then happily in the occupation of the Rucksack Club. In the centre of this meet, we thought we would go across the road and have a look at this place, Helyg.... I immediately decided that this was the place for me in the future, so I put in an application for membership of the club. That Wayfarers meet was the occasion of my first climb in Wales, when I had the privilege of being initiated by Roberston Lamb — an experience I have never forgotten. He took me up the Idwal Slab and then Holly Tree Wall in one run out, and then to the top of the Glyder by the Central Arete.

*   *   *   *   *

Now one thing led to another, from the setting up of Helyg. The Wayfarers, having appreciated the success of Helyg, decided to set up a hut of their own in the Lake District. This project was greatly helped by a gift from Robertson Lamb of the princely sum of £500 towards the acquisition of a suitable property. And in due course, after a long story of searching, acquiring and setting up, we got R.L.H., which was the first climbing hut in the Lake District.

*   *   *   *   *

In 1931 I left Liverpool to live in Lancashire, north of the sands, and very soon became Hon. Treasurer of the Fell and Rock Climbing Club. Now at that time, the Fell and Rock did not climb in Wales. They thought there was nothing worth doing there! So, naturally I decided to set about educating them, by putting an article into their 1933 journal to tell them about Wales and the wonderful climbs which had lately been done there.

Following that, under my persuasion, some of the leading climbers in the Fell and Rock came to Wales with me, which meant Helyg..... there was my namesake A.T. Hargreaves and Geoff Barker, and Bill Clegg. They quickly appreciated Helyg and we came back with an idea which was that the Fell and Rock ought to have a hut in the Lake District.

Helyg had little accommodation, the most primitive of equipment, and was often very damp and cold, though gradually Stuart Chantrell got conditions improved.

I remember a grim occasion there after a long, very cold and wet November day in the Great Gully on Craig-yr-Ysfa, when we did not get to the top until it was pitch black and there had been so much pulley hauley work in the top cave that we could not undo the knots in the rope, so I decided that we could remain roped until we got down to the valley. My reasoning also being, that we did not want to risk a repetition of the tragic disaster which befell a C.C. party a few years before, who in similar conditions got separated on their way down from the Bwlch and two of them died on the way. However, when we got to Helyg, still roped, there was nobody there with a fire going that we had hoped for. When we opened the door, and shone a torch, there was a spring rising under the firegrate, with a flow of about three or four inches of water towards the door. In those days there was no electric light.....

From a speech at the 1985 Jubilee Dinner.

Overleaf: When you are 78, stretching for a hold can be hard work. Photo: *Ian Smith.*

PRESIDENTIAL SPEECH AT THE HELYG JUBILEE DINNER AT THE P-y-G

DEREK WALKER

Gentlemen,

I must thank Herbert and A.B. for their magnificent speeches this evening.

Many of you have not been in close touch with the Club in recent years and it is only right that I should say a few words about the C.C. today.

Gentlemen, I think the club is in good shape. Our membership is now over 700 strong — a record number of 47 new members joined last year, and so far over 20 have been elected this year at two Committee meetings. Among these new members are not only many leading young rock-climbers but also some mature, experienced mountaineers, and we remain a club to which good committed climbers wish to belong — and we have not experienced the difficulty over recruitment felt by many of the other older established clubs — largely, I think, because we do try to project a youthful, forward-looking image — despite what you may see around you this evening. Everyone in the Climbers' Club is young — whatever his age — aren't you Noel, Herbert, A.B.?

As Herbert said in the 1926 Journal:

'The more climbers the Club gets the greater its capacity for service and the more important its position in the Climbing World.'

— and this still rings true today.

The kind of membership is, of course, different from your day in the 20s and 30s and even further away from that envisaged by the first esteemed President, C.E. Matthews who said at the first Annual Dinner in 1898:

'Climbing is a sport that from some mysterious cause appeals mainly to the cultivated intellect. 'Arry or 'Arriet would never climb a hill.'

We have indeed had our 'Arrys, one renowned in the legal profession though I can't disclose his speciality, our own distinguished ex-President who will live in our memories as the President who allowed women into Helyg, and who nearly severed relations with the Fell and Rock by his showdown in the Ladies' Loos at Rawhead.

And although we have no 'Arriets, we do have our Jills, our Geraldines, our Sallys and Daphnes. The Club has not only survived — that great row (over women membership) which caused such a schism in the late 60s and early 70s — it has

250

positively benefited from the wise decision taken in Hamish's presidency in 1975.

There has been no take over by the fair sex, Helyg has not been split asunder, there have been no chintz curtains, no influx of Fell and Rock type hutters. Rather we have seen a steady trickle of dedicated lady climbers — 23 in 10 years, and several of them such as Jill Lawrence and Geraldine Taylor climbing at the very highest levels, leading routes such as the Right Wall of Cenotaph Corner, which I don't think any of us here has done — yet!

And in the 80s, because of the ladies, our Club is friendlier, and healthier — the company at the dinners is prettier and the discos are decidedly livelier.

And what other changes? We now, of course, have six huts and I must say that at times, being the Climbers' Club who want to climb, we do feel over-stretched having to manage these properties in remote areas. It is a burden for the Custodians and for the Chairman of the Huts Committee, but we are fortunate that we do have at the moment such an able and caring Chairman as Henry Adler who has approached the job with such vigour in the past year — but we must give him our support and help.

Similarly we have been fortunate in having a dedicated Publications Committee, who, under the inspired leadership of Bob Moulton (our latest Hon. Mem.) and Alex Jones, have produced no fewer than 13 new guide-books in Bob's 10 year spell as Guide-Book Editor — a remarkable record. And we have a Journal Editor who is here tonight, Geoff Milburn, who has produced seven journals of a high standard in the last seven years — and is about to beat A.W. Andrew's record of 1904-11 this year.

As well, of course, this year Geoff is producing the Helyg book to celebrate this reunion, a venture which I am sure you will want to support, containing as it does the writings and humour of the Golden Age of Helyg climbing.

What else? On a 'National' front we have 'taken over' the B.M.C. in a grand slam at their A.G.M. in April when John Neill became President with George Band, Chris Bonington and Al Rouse as Vice-Presidents. I was asked to toast the B.M.C. at their dinner later, and after asking Dennis Gray to make the 'supreme sacrifice' and join the C.C. himself, I presented him with a large poster which read: 'C.C. RULES O.K.'.

And of our relations with other clubs - they are at an amazing 'high' level and I discussed matters of moment at the Blencathra Summit exactly a year ago with President Ironfield of the Fell and Rock and President Slessor of the S.M.C.

But what of the climbing - because climbing and having fun is what the C.C. is really all about. Well, climbing in the mid-eighties has reached unprecedented high standards; there are dozens, perhaps hundreds of young people climbing extraordinary pieces of vertical or overhanging rock.

We are well represented in the Club and on the Committee with climbers such as Peter Gomersall and Phil Davidson, operating at the highest levels. But the great thing about the C.C. is that it is not only the youngsters but the older members too who are actively enjoying their climbing. We have seen the perfect example today with Ivan doing the Bastion at 78, 58 years since his first ascent - and to mention a few others: Jim Simpson at 72 leading climbs in Cornwall; Mike Westmacott leading our newest lady member up hard climbs in Yosemite in his retirement year; Hughie and Trevor leading routes as hard as they have ever done; Mike Ball leading Tower Ridge on his 60th birthday and hoping to repeat it on his 70th; Hamish leading a group of 'mature' members up Paldor in the Himalayas.

And perhaps a special mention of one who could be called our most enthusiastic member. He was one of the C.C.'s leading and bravest rock-climbers in the 50s. Thirty years later you will have seen from the Channel 4 films that he still climbs as keenly as ever. He led his first E3 last year. He was ice-climbing in the Lakes the day before he left for the Himalayas - and then at the age of 50 he has just climbed Everest. Our heartiest congratulations, Chris.

And it is appropriate that here in the Pen-y-Gwryd tonight we have several other men of Everest - Noel Odell, who exactly 61 years ago today, saw Mallory and Irvine disappear at 28,000 ft.; and Charles Evans, Mike Westmacott and Don Whillans.

And it is so appropriate that we are in the Pen-y-Gwryd to celebrate this great reunion - the home of the Climbers' Club at the very beginning of its existence, and where Chris Briggs has made us welcome over so many years. So thank you Chris and Jane for the splendid dinner and hospitality this evening - and thank you ALL for coming to make this so magnificent and memorable an occasion. I should like you to rise and drink a toast to our club - THE CLIMBERS' CLUB.

Rudolf Loewy on Tryfan.   *Photo: Ian Smith.*

LIST OF SUBSCRIBERS

The Editor wishes to acknowledge the generous subscriptions made by those listed below towards the publication of this book.

0 Climbers' Club Archive	50 B. Martindale	100 Ken Milburn (N.M.)
1 Geoff Milburn	51 B. Martindale	101 N.A. Lyle
2 Derek Walker	52 Roy Small	102 Dr. J.L. Hart
3 H.R.C. Carr	53 Rod Hewing	103 Anthony Walker
4 M.W. Guinness	54 R. Handley	104 V.N. Stevenson
5 Ivan Waller	55 C.B. FitzHugh	105 John Innerdale
6 A.B. Hargreaves	56 C.E. Davies	106 John Innerdale
7 Sir Jack Longland	57 A. Carsten	107 J.R. Atherton
8 Dave Gregory	58 E.A. Wrangham	108 K.F. Edwardson
9 Ian Smith	59 G.W.S. Pigott	109 D.T. Roscoe
10 R.A. Hodgkin	60 Dr. David Hopkins	110 Frank Fitzgerald
11 D.J. Watson	61 J.F. Jones	111 Dr. E.A. Marshall
12 Rennie Bere	62 Graham Exley	112 Mark Kemball
13 Ken Wilson	63 N.M. Blackett	113 Malcolm J. Cameron
14 Nat Allen	64 C. Vigano	114 Pat Vaughan
15 Mike Browell	65 David Rhodes	115 E. Loewy
16 Dr. A.S.G. Jones	66 Graham Hoey	116 Vincent Birtles
17 A.D.M. Cox	67 A.G.L. Williams	117 J.P. Everett
18 A.N. Husbands	68 Roger Salisbury	118 Rev. Peter Norton
19 Chris Jackson	69 Alison J. Hargreaves	119 Murray Hodgson
20 H.R.C. Carr	70 Alison J. Hargreaves	120 R.B. Huddy
21 H.R.C. Carr	71 J.G. Rawlinson	121 W.L. Hannah
22 H.R.C. Carr	72 Lord Chorley	122 Sonny Lee
23 H.R.C. Carr	73 Rev. F.L. Jenkins	123 Chris Calow
24 H.R.C. Carr	74 B.G. Molyneux	124 Christine Walker
25 Bob Moulton	75 J.S. Milledge	125 G.M. Lee
26 Alex Jones	76 Bill Wintrip	126 Dr. J.D. Barrett
27 Bill Stallybrass	77 John Harwood	127 J.R. Mellor
28 M.R. Loewy	78 Dr. G. Jones	128 J.E. Ashburner
29 C. Verrinder	79 P.J. Drinkwater	129 J.C. Gravelling
30 Harry Sales	80 F.M. Hill	130 Dr. H.L. Richardson
31 David D.V. Fenton	81 Mrs. K. McElligott	131 J.S. Mercer
32 John Poole	82 Clifford Bingham	132 K.C. Pearson
33 S.J. Hawkins	83 Brian Cooper	133 R.H. Carter
34 Derek Walker	84 C.R. Simpson	134 R.H. Nieto
35 Derek Walker	85 George Band	135 P.H. Hill
36 Peter Hodgkiss (N.M.)	86 Martin Wragg	136 Richard Hargreaves
37 Dr. J. Braven	87 Mrs. Betty Cubby	137 Richard Hargreaves
38 D.G. Fagan	88 W.J. Cartwright	138 Paul Nunn
39 Colin Matthews	89 M.G. Hardy	139 D.M. Holdroyd
40 Roger B. Higgins	90 Lord Hunt	140 Frank Palmer
41 Tom Chatterley	91 Paddy Feely	141 Frank Palmer
42 J.M. Ball	92 J. Debenham	142 S.L. Thomas
43 Major David Ruttledge	93 T.A.H. Peacock	143 M.H. Westmacott
44 A.J. Edwards	94 Sir Anthony Rawlinson	144 John A. Mallinson
45 Frank Davies	95 D.N. Young	145 Sir Alan Pullinger
46 Ian Smith	96 Daphne Pritchard	146 R.F. Cope
47 J.H. Adler	97 A.D. Malcolm	147 David Murray-Rust (N.M.)
48 J.H. Adler	98 P.F. Holmes	148 Sir Kenneth Berrill
49 J.H. Adler	99 G.A.M. Robertson	149 Prof. J.N. Buxton

150 David Wall
151 C.J.S. Bonington
152 J.B. Allen
153 F.H. Jacob
154 Robert E. Crookall
155 T.W. Young
156 Alan Poxon (N.M.)
157 Elliott Viney
158 T.D. Leggett
159 C.B. Briggs
160 F.R. Brooke
161 Jack Baines (N.M.)
162 Maurice Guinness
163 Joe Brown
164 H.G. Nicholson
165 A.M. Dowler
166 D.I. Ibbotson
167 F.B. Horsman
168 J.R. Twigg
169 Louis Sancha
170 Peter Harding
171 Paul Stewart
172 R. Goodier
173 E.S. Williams
174 C.J. Gilbert
175 Godfrey W.V. Boulton
176 Richard Owen
177 Trevor Jones
178 A.J.J. Moulam
179 Don Whillans
180 William Russell
181 Alan Blackshaw
182 Edgar Siddall
183 Alan Garson
184 John Dickinson (N.M.)
185 R.H. Cooke
186 R.H. Cooke
187 Michael Vyvyan
188 D.P. Carter
189 Dennis Bateman
190 Keith J. Sharples
191 Charles Armour
192 H.R.C. Carr
193 H.R.C. Carr
194 Dr. Robin Barley
195 Robert Enwright
196 R.E. Kendall
197 P.M. Lewis
198 H.N. Fairfield
199 Ken Vickers
200 Ken Vickers
201 Ken Vickers
202 Ken Vickers
203 Ken Vickers
204 Ken Vickers

205 Ken Vickers
206 Ken Vickers
207 Ken Vickers
208 Ken Vickers
209 Grant Jarvis (N.M.)
210 H.R.C. Carr
211 H.R.C. Carr
212 Dave Baskeyfield (N.M.)
213 R.M. Biden
214 D.C. Unwin
215 Dave Thomas
216 Dave Matthews
217 Peter D. Barnitt
218 G.S. Roberts
219 W. Keith Marples
220 R.J.G. Reynolds
221 Roger C. Putnam
222 S.W. Town
223 Lord Chorley
224 R. Bloor
225 T.E. Fletcher
226 Derek Walker
227 Bryan Phillips
228 J.D. Derry
229 Nigel Peacock
230 P.E. Burt
231 Dr. M.J.E. Gann
232 Gerard Poole
233 G.M. Owen
234 Jancis M. Allison
235 Colin Abbott
236 Dr. H.L. Richardson
237 Richard McElligott
238 D.R. Parker
239 Stanley L. Thomas
240 John N. Slee-Smith
241 Frank Fitzgerald
242 John N. Buxton
243 A. Wildman
244 Mike Yates
245 B.H. Kemball-Cook
246 Diana McIlreavy
247 Bob Pettigrew
248 John Tyson
249 B.M. Crowther (N.M.)
250 Alan Milburn (N.M.)
251 Elaine Milburn (N.M.)
252 Peter Stone
253 Mike Ball
254 P.G. Hollinrake (N.M.)
255 M. Buck Ravenscroft
256 Mrs S. Paterson
257 G.W. Templeman (N.M.)
258 David Wall
259 Rev. Donald Monks (N.M.)

260 Dennis Hoare (N.M.)
261 Eric Byrom (N.M.) (In Memory)
262 P.B. Marks (N.M.)
263 John Buzzard (In Memory)
264 Ed Grindley (N.M.)
265 G. Roberts (N.M.)
266 J. Masters (N.M.)
267 Geoff Birtles (Ex. M.)
268 N. Clayton (N.M.)
269 C. Faulds (N.M.)
270 Sir A. Pullinger
271 Tony Shaw (N.M.)
272 Les Peel (N.M.)
273 F. Paul French (N.M.)
274 Ronnie Wathen
275 Dave Hope
276 Les Ainsworth
277 Paul Williams

Overleaf: Sunset over Llanberis Pass.　　　　　　　　　　　*Photo: Ian Smith.*